WAR MEMOIRS OF
DAVID LLOYD GEORGE

1918

WAR MEMOIRS

of

DAVID
LLOYD
GEORGE

★ ★ ★ ★ ★ ★

1918

WITH ILLUSTRATIONS

LITTLE, BROWN, AND COMPANY

BOSTON 1937

PREFACE

With this volume I finish my recollections of the War. They have taken the best part of my time for five years. The writing of books is a new business for me. When a man starts a new craft in his seventieth year he does not expect to gain that proficiency in the art which would enable him to become anything better than an amateur. It is as such I shall be ranked — it is as such I crave to be judged. I have sought to narrate facts as I remember them. I have given my impressions of events and personalities exactly as I found them at the time. Facts and impressions alike I have checked by a close examination and study of all available evidence, oral and written. I have revised impressions wherever I have found irrefutable proof that my memory was at fault, or that I was not in full possession of the facts when I formed those impressions. I have couched my narrative in such language as I can command to express my thoughts.

The only merit I claim for these volumes is that apart from the Official Histories of the War, they are the most carefully and richly documented account of the great Armageddon. Official Histories deal in great detail with the battles fought; I have only undertaken to give an account of the struggle as I saw it from the standpoint of a Minister of the Crown. I was the only Minister in any country who had some share throughout the whole of the War in its direction. During the last two years I had much the largest share in the Ministerial direction of the resources of the British Empire. No other Minister in any of the belligerent countries held an

official position from the 1st of August, 1914, to the 11th of
November, 1918. King Albert, King George, the Kaiser and
Poincaré were the only rulers who saw it through from the
beginning to the end. Of these Poincaré alone has given us
an elaborate and detailed account of his contact with events
during the War. For that reason his Diaries contain material
of great value for the historian of the future. But he confines
his story almost entirely to entries made by himself in his
Diary whilst the War was in progress. There is no attempt
at confirming and illuminating his version of events by quotations from contemporary documents. It is the necessity for
examining, collating and summarising an enormous collection
of written material which has been responsible for the drud-
gery and labour of my last five years. To write a facile narrative drawn from vivid memories would not have taken me
one-tenth of the time which these volumes have occupied.

The mass of papers accumulated by my secretaries during
the period of the War and the subsequent peace negotiations
filled me with dismay when I first entertained the thought
of writing my War Memoirs. When I was engaged in an active political career as leader of a party I had neither the
spare time nor the spare energy to undertake the gigantic
toil of rummaging through this mountain of printed, type-
written or written memoranda, minutes, notes or letters —
selecting those that mattered and choosing the passages that
could be compressed and summarised and those that had to
be given textually.

A serious illness, which disabled me for months in 1931,
happily gave me the opportunity I had many times sought
in vain to retire from the front line in politics. It is a mistake to imagine that when leading politicians say they have
a hankering for a tranquil life, they are shamming modesty.
The desire for periods of quiet and repose comes with increasing force with the advance of years. And although old

habits and aptitudes of work and conflict cling to your arm every time you take up a pen to write the letter of final retirement, it only means that you feel, in withdrawing from the struggle for causes in which you believe, that you are a shirker and it is your duty to go on fighting to the end. There is perhaps another reason. Men who have contracted the habit of hard work dread a life of idleness whilst their physical reserves are unexhausted. Providence decided the issue for me when I became a serious casualty and was thus carried out of action for months. That was when I started preparing for my book. I then got so interested in the work as well as the subject that I went on, and here I have finished. Had anyone told me five years ago that I, who was accustomed to commit my thoughts to speech or action, should ever have written six volumes containing a million words on any subject, I should have derided such a possibility. And certainly had I been informed that the public would have steadily maintained its interest in the contents of these volumes, I should have been doubly surprised. As this book has an autobiographical aspect perhaps I may be forgiven for noting these intimate personal musings.

I take this opportunity of thanking the Press of all parties for the generosity of the treatment they have meted out to my efforts. Reviewers have on the whole been kind and considerate. I am profoundly grateful for their indulgence towards a novice. It has been my first experience of the attentions of this important and intimidating profession. They are no exception to any other avocation in the fact that they can be divided into several classes. There are the conscientious and the skimmers — those who read what they review and those who review what they clearly have never read. There are the tolerant and the captious. There are a few — very few — who having formed preconceived opinions and repeatedly expressed them, only seek out passages that seem to confirm their established prejudices and ignore the rest. It is embarrassing for men who have for years expressed pontifical judgments, on military, diplomatic or political questions, to find that there are unanswerable documents of whose existence they were not aware, and which prove that the conclusions they had come to and had always so dogmatically expressed were entirely inconsistent with the facts. There are few who have the courage or uprightness to admit that they were misinformed. They therefore take refuge in the somewhat cowardly expedient of ignoring the evidence thrust upon them and reiterating with acidulated emphasis the allegations they had made in total ignorance of the truth. Refutation does not reconcile them, it simply incenses and exasperates them to a more infuriated exercise of their sting.

In the main the latter type concentrate on two criticisms. The first is based on the allegation that the War Cabinet could have achieved an honourable peace in 1917. This allegation has been completely exposed by a wealth of documentary proof which shows that at no stage of the War before their defeat in the autumn of 1918 were the Germans prepared to concede terms which would not have actually rewarded them for plunging the world into this horrible war. Any fair-minded perusal of the documents — German as well as British — which I have published, would have induced a change of opinion on the part of honest critics. Herein I have been disappointed. Men whose political bias is entrenched in misconception only dig deeper when their parapets are demolished.

Then there is the type of critic who with cockatoo persistency and irrelevancy repeats the cry that I condemn every General, Admiral, and statesman who took any part in the War, and that I consider myself alone as being above criticism. Had they really read these volumes, they would undoubtedly find much censure of two or three generals and one or two statesmen, but praise lavished on many statesmen, generals, and Admirals, and especially unstinted admiration given to the millions of officers and men who fought and endured to the end on land and sea and in the air and whose valour and sacrifice won the War. I might enumerate some of the military and naval chiefs and a few of the politicians whom I have sought out for laudation. On the British side there are Kitchener, Plumer, Allenby, Maude, Jeudwine, Cowans, Lawrence, Monash and Currie; amongst the Admirals, Henderson, Roger Keyes and Richmond. Amongst the French Generals, I have expressed my admiration of Foch, Castelnau, Mangin and Gallieni. From the Americans I have singled out General Bliss and Admiral Sims. That is not a mean array of high-class Generals and Admirals for any war. But I decline to join in the clangour of cymbals for the inefficient. As to statesmen, I have gladly recognised the service rendered by Bonar Law, Milner, Balfour, Smuts, Botha, Borden, Hughes, Geddes, Maclay, Arthur Henderson, Barnes, Clemenceau and many others. Without the help such men rendered, victory would have been unattainable. The war was won by the incredible valour and endurance of the men who braved — actually and physically — death in every element for the honour of their native land. But they would not have been given a chance to win had it not been for the skill of men who worked behind and outside the region of horror where the soldier, the sailor (of all services) and the aviator discharged their perilous duties.

In living over once again year by year the four years of the World War I find a deepening and intensification of reflections produced in my mind by a daily contact with the happenings of War.

The first is my amazement that there should be millions of men who could go through such horrifying experiences without a complete shattering of nerves and brain. Multitudes of young men in many lands endured it for years and have survived without any obvious impairment of either. I constantly meet survivors of the War who for years endured the terrifying sensations of modern warfare, haunted day by day and night by night by the menace of death in its ghastliest and most agonising aspect. Psychologically and spiritually it must have had repercussions which are not easy to trace. But physiologically they seem to be as calm, as steady of nerve and as full of the joy of life as the men who never passed through those scorching fires. This courage possessed by so many ordinary men has always been to me incomprehensible. It is immeasurably great. In training, in discipline, in equipment and efficiency there were marked distinctions between one belligerent nation and another. There was no difference in the high courage of the common man whatever his country of origin. What makes war so terrifying is that it is waged by men. No human effort brings forth so clearly and impressively the strongest qualities of mankind as a whole. But war is a prodigal and stupid waste of these virile attributes. Evoked, stimulated and organised by and for some beneficent movement which is productive not of ruin and death but of something which gives life and gives it abundantly to the children of men, it would transfigure the world.

And that brings me to another impression engraven on my mind by the events of the War. As a tribunal for ascertaining the rights and the wrongs of a dispute, war is crude, uncertain and costly. It is true that the World War ended, as I still believe, in a victory for Right. But it was won not on the merits of the case, but on a balance of resources and of blunders. The reserves of man power, of material and of money at the command of the victorious Powers were overwhelmingly greater than those possessed by the vanquished.

They were thus better able to maintain a prolonged struggle. Both sides blundered badly, but the mistakes committed by the Central Powers were more fatal, inasmuch as they did not possess the necessary resources to recover from the effects of their errors of judgment.

As I have pointed out in the text of this book, in 1915 the Allies committed the grave strategical error of concentrating their strength on a tremendous offensive against the German ramparts in France, and thus allowed the Central Powers with a few divisions to conquer the Balkans. But this mistake was more than counterbalanced by the incredible blunder committed by the German Staff in the spring and summer of 1916, when they hurled their best legions against Verdun in a vain effort to capture it. The Allied mistake prolonged the War. The German mistake lost them the War.

In the spring of 1916, if Falkenhayn, instead of wasting irrecoverable opportunity and time over Verdun, had taken Conrad's advice and attacked Italy and had adopted Hoffmann's proposal to finish off Russia, the issue of the war would have been different. Caporetto and Brest-Litovsk in 1916, instead of 1917 and 1918, when our army was not fully trained, with no America in the War and no starvation in Germany or Austria, would have forced the Western Powers to accept an unfavourable peace. The great offensive of March, 1918, came too late to save the Central Powers. By November, 1917, France and Britain were strong enough to rescue Italy from the consequences of her crushing defeat. And by the late spring of 1918 American reinforcements were pouring in to strengthen the Allied front just as the reserves of the Central Powers were exhausted. Judgment which is dependent on such contingencies is too precarious. Chance is the supreme judge in war and not Right. There are other judges on the bench, but Chance presides.

If Germany had been led by Bismarck and Moltke instead

of by von Bethmann-Hollweg and Falkenhayn, the event of the great struggle between a military autocracy and democracy would in all human probability have been different. The blunders of Germany saved us from the consequences of our own. But let all who trust justice to the arbitrament of war bear in mind that the issue may depend less on the righteousness of the cause than on the cunning and craft of the contestants. It is the teaching of history, and this war enforces the lesson. And the cost is prohibitive. It cripples all the litigants. The death of ten millions and the mutilation of another twenty millions amongst the best young men of a generation is a terrible bill of costs to pay in a suit for determining the responsibility and penalty for the murder of two persons, however exalted their rank. When you add to that £50,000,000,000 expended in slaughter and devastation, the complete dislocation of the international trade of the world, unemployment on a scale unparalleled in history, the overthrow of free institutions over the greater part of Europe, and the exasperation and perpetuation of international feuds which threaten to plunge the world into an even greater catastrophe, one must come to the conclusion that war is much too costly and barbarous a method of settling quarrels amongst the nations of the earth.

D. LLOYD GEORGE.

Bron-y-de,
Churt.
October, 1936.

CONTENTS

ILLUSTRATIONS

CHAPTER I

BEAUVAIS AND THE CAMPAIGN OF THE NORTH

1. THE BEAUVAIS CONFERENCE

Arrangement inadequate — Foch dissatisfied with Doullens agreement — War Cabinet opposes his appointment to Supreme Command — Cheerfulness of Fifth Army — Conference at Beauvais — Foch states his views — Foch thinking of an offensive — My speech to the conference — Haig and Wilson fall into line — The new agreement — Abbeville Conference — My promise to Foch — Long struggle to achieve unity of command — Set-back over Nivelle offensive — Pétain's limitations — Haig inacceptable — Foch under a cloud — A picnic on Clemenceau's lunch — Somme attack ends: German achievements — A brilliant failure — British forces ill-placed — Local superiority of Germans — Magnificent fight of Fifth Army — German tributes to its quality — No collapse of British or French — Offensive does not succeed — Renewed attacks.

THE Doullens Resolution did not work as satisfactorily as we had hoped. General Foch might flit from one Headquarters to another, and suggest and propose and urge in his peremptory and vehement way one plan after another, but it was for Pétain and Haig to decide and with their Staffs to work out the details and give their own orders in their own way and their own time. These two Generals were quite happy to share the responsibility with Foch, but they were not ready to part with any of their authority. The greatest defect of the Doullens agreement was that it did not equip Foch with the necessary authority gradually to build up the Inter-Allied Reserve which was essential to any great scheme of counter-offensive. Haig and Pétain had gone a long way but even in this moment of despair they were not ready to accept the Versailles decision as to an independent General Reserve commanded by Foch.

Reports came to the Cabinet that the Doullens arrangement was not working smoothly. Serious misunderstandings had arisen which were likely to affect prejudicially the conduct of the campaign. There was no one on the spot with any authority to settle these differences. Foch could not coordinate, because he was not in a position to command. That this was Foch's view is made clear by him in his Memoirs: —

"Now to plan this offensive action, to inspire and direct it, to ensure its being carried out by the Commanders-in-Chief, and also to arrive at an equitable distribution of forces, the powers conferred upon me by the Doullens Agreement were plainly inadequate. They were insufficient to cover even the present defensive operations; they would necessarily be all the more inadequate when, in the not far distant future, it became my duty to decide upon the strategic employment of the Allied Armies, renewed and strengthened by the coöperation of the Americans; to determine, according to circumstances, the point against which these forces should be applied; to distribute the offensive and defensive tasks, and possibly to effect exchanges between the French and Italian Fronts.

"The simple rôle of *coördinator* was not sufficient for the larger programme which would certainly have to be undertaken shortly. It gave far too little play to the *initiative* of the officer who filled it, if he was to react rapidly and forcibly to contingencies brought about by a defensive battle, or to organise and launch important offensive operations. The rôle should be changed into one of *direction*. If the Inter-Allied organ created at Doullens by an effort of mutual confidence was to produce all that was expected of it, its powers must at once be widened, and the strategic direction of the War on the Western Front entrusted to it. Its authority over the Allied Commanders-in-Chief should be affirmed, and this authority extended to include all the troops in line from the North Sea to the Adriatic.

"A few days' experience had been sufficient to expose the inadequacy of the Doullens Agreement. The present as well as the future interests of the Coalition required that it be amended without delay." [1]

[1] Foch: "Memoirs" (Translation, pp. 313 and 314).

It was decided that another meeting with Clemenceau and the Generals should be arranged to straighten out this unsatisfactory position. I knew there was only one practical solution and that was to appoint Foch to the Supreme Command of both armies, but at the meeting of the War Cabinet held to discuss the subject of my proposed visit I found that the majority were opposed to any such idea. Wilson, who was present, was thoroughly hostile to it. He said that Foch probably did not require any powers beyond those already accorded to him. This statement I subsequently found to be completely inaccurate. When I met Foch he was in despair at his impotence to direct the battle as he desired it to be fought. The Cabinet resolved that "the decisions must be left to my discretion after I had an opportunity of discussing the matter with Sir Douglas Haig." The meeting which finally led to the establishment of real unity of command was held at the Hôtel de Ville, Beauvais, on April 3rd, 1918. On my way to Beauvais, Wilson and I called at Haig's Headquarters. Haig and his Chief of Staff, Lawrence, then accompanied us to Beauvais. I drove part of the way with the Commander-in-Chief and the rest with his C.G.S. I thus was able to gather their views as to the progress of the battle. I found neither of them forthcoming on the subject of increasing Foch's powers. They saw no need for it. They were convinced that things were getting on quite well. When I reported to them the successful arrangements we had concluded for the shipping of American troops to France I expected not gratitude but some sense of relief over the good news. On the contrary they were both cool and sniffy about it. They gave me the impression that they did not think much of American help in 1918. It was only so much more trouble for G.H.Q. if they were incorporated in our divisions and when it was done it would be more a source of weakness than of strength! They thought of these masses that would soon be pouring into France as if they were an untrained rabble.

Not far from Beauvais I drove through the remnants of some of the broken battalions of the Fifth Army who were resting in villages behind the line. I have never observed a more cheerful crowd of men. There was no trace of dejection or despair. They accosted the delegation with smiling faces. It was not my picture of a defeated army.

When I came to the Hôtel de Ville I found Clemenceau, Foch, Pétain, Pershing and Bliss awaiting us. I had a preliminary conversation with Clemenceau and confided to him that I thought that the Doullens arrangement was too vague and that it was imperative that Foch should be endowed with greater and more direct authority over the Allied forces. Clemenceau, having already been approached by Foch on the subject and convinced by him, was of the same opinion. He began the conference by explaining that though the Doullens agreement had worked well up to a point, "the situation was, however, developing and a stage had been reached when it was necessary to define, with greater precision, the position of the 'General of the Coalition', as he would call General Foch." In fact, a decision was required as to whether the Doullens arrangement should stand as it was, or whether it required widening. He then called on General Foch to explain his views. Before he did so I asked that General Foch, in giving his views, would particularly specify in what respects he considered that the Doullens arrangement conferred insufficient authority on him to coördinate the action of the two armies. General Foch in reply —

. . . reminded the Conference that the Doullens arrangement stated that he was charged with coördinating the action of the Allied Armies on the Western Front. This implied that if there were no action, there was nothing to co-ordinate. If the French were taking no action, and if the British Army were taking no action, it was impossible to co-ordinate their action. Consequently something more was now wanted. He required the power to imply an idea of action to the Commanders-in-Chief, and to have this action carried out. In fact, before coördinating he must have the power of creating action. For this reason the text of the Doullens arrangement was insufficient, and should be made to include "power for the infusion of an idea of action." Moreover, it was not so much necessary to coördinate the action itself as the preparation of action. In quiet times it was necessary to create an idea around which the preparations should be made in coördination. On the 26th March at Doullens, the situation was very different from what it was on the 3rd April at Beauvais. On the former date it was a question of co-ordinating action which was in full swing. On the latter date it was a question of coördinating our preparation for future action. On the 26th March our armies were submitting to a battle imposed on us by the enemy, but to-day at Beauvais, we were thinking of our own action. In this latter case the powers of mere coördination of action were insufficient.

Sir Henry Wilson, who now that he had exchanged Versailles for Whitehall had rather modified his Versailles outlook, and had discussed the question with Haig in his car on the way to Beauvais, thought Doullens gave Foch all the powers he required and that there was no need for extension. Foch replied —

. . . that, if there was no action, or no movement, there was nothing to coördinate. His requirements would be met by the insertion of some words such as "order" (*"ordonner"*) or "to give orders" (*"donner des ordres"*).

From Foch's statements I realised that the Cabinet had not been fully informed by the C.I.G.S. as to the main defect in the working of the Doullens agreement. Foch's complaint was not so much in respect of differences which had arisen on particular sections of the battle front and which needed adjustment, although it was not functioning altogether smoothly in that direction. It was a much more important issue. His thoughts projected beyond the arrest of the German attempt to break through at Amiens. Foch's mind was not so much on the German offensive which had now been checked but on the great counter-stroke which he had sketched in his famous January Memorandum on the plan of campaign for 1918. He was thinking of the next step — of the necessary preparations for fighting out to a final decision the vast battle which had commenced. In this essential task he found himself hampered by lack of real authority. As he was the only General in the field with the necessary vision and decision to plan out such a campaign I decided to take all risks to secure for him the requisite power. If I felt that I could not, there and then, commit the Cabinet the whole way in view of the misgivings they had revealed at their last meeting, I resolved to go as far as I could to-day and on my return carry the Cabinet with me the rest of the way.

I therefore followed Foch in this strain: —

Mr. Lloyd George said that, speaking on behalf of the British public, they were very anxious to ensure that divided counsels should not end in disaster. A real effort had been made to co-ordinate the action of the Allies by means of the Supreme War Council and the Permanent Military Representatives at Versailles, because it had been realised that the Germans had one army and the Allies had three. Even last year the Allies on the Western Front had two strategies: Field-Marshal Haig's and General Pétain's.

Field-Marshal Haig interpolated that last year, he was under the orders of General Nivelle.

Haig was flushed and by his voice and manner I saw he was very angry at the line I was taking.

Mr. Lloyd George said that he did not refer to that period, although he reminded the Conference that General Nivelle's strategy had achieved the most valuable results, so far as the British Army was concerned, of the whole year's fighting, since it had put the Allies in possession of the Vimy Ridge and the country east of Arras. What he had referred to, however, were the operations later in the year, when Field-Marshal Haig had been fighting in Flanders and General Pétain's Army had been carrying out operations with limited objectives at considerable intervals. The consequence was that, although the Allies had had a superiority against the Germans of something approaching three to two, they had, in fact, achieved very little. In their recent offensive, however, the Germans, though probably not superior in numbers, had achieved very considerable results, and this was mainly due to their unity of control. Versailles had been set up with the object of securing a similar unity of action, but it had not been in full operation when this offensive commenced and none of its decisions had been carried out. Whatever had resulted from the recent actions must be credited entirely to the measures of coördination which had been achieved, but it was not sufficient.

What he was apprehensive of was that the Allied Governments would to-day merely reach a new formula without achieving any real unity of command. The British public wanted, and intended to know whether there was real unity. What we had now to decide was that General Foch should really have all the powers he needed. He said that the British public entirely believed in General Foch, as proved by the way in which his appointment had been received in the Press. Of course if General Foch should put the British Army in great peril, Field-Marshal Haig would appeal to his own Government, and no paper which could be drawn up could prevent this. Consequently, there was no objection to some words being put in to this effect. Unless he had the necessary power, however, General Foch would prove worse than useless. He said he would much like to hear the views of the American Generals on the subject, more particularly as General Bliss and General Pershing now had a special claim to attention, since the Army of the United States of America would be fighting side by side with their Allies under President Wilson's recent decision.

The ensuing discussion will give an idea of the different points of view of those who took part in the Conference: —

General Pershing said that it appeared to him that we had now reached a point in the War where entire coöperation of the Allied Armies should be assured. As a matter of principle, he knew no way to ensure such coöperation except by a single command. It was impossible for two or three Commanders-in-Chief, whose Commands were spread over such a huge front, by themselves to coördinate their activities unless the Armies were under one head. The experiments in this direction had already gone far enough. They had proved completely that coördination was impossible. Each General had his own responsibilities to think of. Success from now onwards would depend upon the Allies having a single command.

After this speech and another by General Bliss which gave to my proposal the powerful support of the two American Generals, Haig and Wilson saw that the Conference was not satisfied with leaving matters where they were, and that an extension of the Doullens arrangement was inevitable. Haig after consultation with Wilson then said —

. . . he was in entire agreement with what General Pershing said. There should be only one Head in France. His own instructions from the British Government were to take his ideas of strategy from the French Commander-in-Chief, although he was responsible for the safety of the British Army. Consequently he had always, subject, of course, to the orders of the British Government, looked to the Commander-in-Chief of the French Army for his strategical ideas. It would be very easy to insert in the agreement what General Foch required, and he thought that General Wilson's draft was satisfactory. What was really needed, however, was that the Commanders-in-Chief should work wholeheartedly and willingly in the closest coöperation with General Foch.

It was news to me that Haig was of opinion "there should be only one Head in France", and that he had "looked to the Commander-in-Chief of the French Army for his strategical ideas." It would have saved much tribulation and loss had he made it clear both in 1917 and in the early months of 1918.

M. Clemenceau then read a draft of a new agreement based on proposals made by General Wilson. Ultimately the following resolution was adopted: —

"The arrangement for the coördination of the Higher Command on the Western Front, concluded at Doullens on the 26th March, 1918, should be superseded by the following arrangement: —

"General Foch is charged by the British, French and American Governments with the coördination of the action of the Allied Armies on the Western Front. To this end all powers necessary to secure effective realisation are conferred on him. The British, French and American Governments for this purpose entrust to General Foch the strategic direction of military operations. The Commanders-in-Chief of the British, French and American Armies have full control of the tactical employment of their forces. Each Commander-in-Chief will have the right of appeal to his Government if in his opinion the safety of his Army is compromised by any order received from General Foch."

This Resolution carried matters much further than the Doullens plan. Foch was for the first time entrusted by the British, French and American Governments with the strategic direction of military operations and all the necessary powers were conferred upon him for that purpose.

As General Bliss afterwards wrote in his account of the Beauvais Conference: —

"It resulted in the nearest approximation to giving General Foch supreme command that was ever attained."

There is no better illustration of the difference made by the Beauvais Resolution in the development of the campaign than the discussion which took place at an Allied Conference held at Abbeville on May 1st and 2nd, 1918,[1] when Signor Orlando, on behalf of the Italian Army, raised the question of whether General Foch's functions as Commander-in-Chief should extend to the Italian Army and said that although he was prepared to accept the application of the Beauvais arrangement to the Italian troops that were in France at that time, he claimed that the Doullens agreement alone was applicable to the Army in Italy as that gave Foch the right to coördinate but not to command. As a commentary on the Beauvais decision and an exposition of the difference it made in the powers of Foch this discussion is worth perusing.

Foch was not altogether satisfied with this resolution. He thought that unless he had the power to issue orders to the two Commanders-in-Chief there would always be trouble in the interpretation even of the extended powers now conferred upon him. There was, according to him, no such office known to the Army as coördinator. In his characteristic way he said: "What am I? I am Monsieur Foch, *très bien connu* (with a smile), *mais toujours Monsieur Foch.*" I saw the force of his criticisms, and having regard to what happened after Doullens I thought his apprehensions were justified. I explained to him the difficulties I had, not only with Haig, but with national susceptibilities at home; but I promised that I would do my best to secure the assent of the British War Cabinet to making him *Général-en-Chef* and I asked him whether that would satisfy him. He said:

[1] Appendix, p. 47 (Abbeville Conference).

MARSHAL FOCH

à M. Lloyd George, au Premier Ministre
qui chassa les Nuages d'un Ciel fort orageux,
Cordialement,

F. Foch

11.10.18.

"That is a different matter altogether. If that were done there would be no more difficulties." On my return to England I sounded my colleagues and when I thought them ready for the suggestion I placed the whole matter before the Cabinet, and after some discussion they agreed to the appointment of Foch as Commander-in-Chief of the Allied forces. Unity of command was thus, after a great many vicissitudes, completely established, and for the first time the whole of the forces of the Allies on the Western Front were consolidated and united, not merely for defence, but for the great return blow that brought the War to a triumphant end. The disaster of the 21st of March had saved the Allies. Nothing else would have made it possible for us to overcome the natural susceptibilities and suspicions which had to be removed in order to enable us to achieve that unity which was essential to victory.

When Briand and I first made the experiment in unity of command in the spring of 1917, we encountered the resistance of two men, Haig and Robertson, whose most outstanding faculty was stubbornness. Their abilities were average, their obstinacy was abnormal. That type, in a narrow trench which had to be held at all costs, would have been invaluable; commanding a battlefield that embraced three continents their vision was too limited and too fixed. It was not a survey, but a stare. It was not that they were incapable of seeing anything except what was straight in front of them, it was that they refused to look at anything else and counted it a dereliction of duty to turn their eyes in any other direction.

In politics, in medicine and in religion one often meets the man with the fixed idea. Whatever the evil, there is but one remedy. It is the cure-all. Every other idea is a sideshow. It is a waste of time and energy to pursue them. It distracts attention and devotion from the saving principle. I discovered in the War that the military profession is no exception to the rule.

At the time of the Nivelle offensive in the spring of 1917, public sentiment in Britain was not in the least enamoured of the idea that a French General should have the supreme direction of a joint operation. Unfortunately, the risk of the experiment was not vindicated by the result. The operation failed on that wing of the wide battlefield where the Commander-in-Chief personally directed the attack. He was discredited in the eyes of his own Army, which mutinied against his leadership, and he was finally dismissed from his command by the Ministry which appointed him. This was an unhappy precedent to commend unity under a French General. On a smaller scale the experiment was repeated when six French divisions were placed under Haig at the Battle of Flanders. But even that limited effort at unity achieved nothing which served to recommend the idea of the united command. No one in urging his plan for a Generalissimo could point with pride and confidence to the sodden battlefields of Flanders and say, "See what unity has accomplished here."

There was the additional difficulty that the War had not yet thrown up a victorious General. With the exception of the Marne there had been no clear victory on the Allied side which had produced any decisive results, and there were many competitive claimants for the honour of that triumph.

Pétain never gave me the idea of a General whose personality or genius could lead huge armies to victory in a war where, at the right moment, a crashing attack was essential to defeat your formidable enemy. He was an able man and a good soldier. But he was essentially a Fabius Cunctator. He was careful and cautious even to the confines of timidity. His *métier* after the 1917 mutinies was that of a head nurse in a home for cases of shell-shock. The French Army after three years of unspeakable horror culminating in the shambles of the Chemin des Dames badly needed such attention. Pétain did it well and successfully. There is no other French General who could have done it as well. He did not irritate the frayed nerves of his patients with constant alarms and offensives. Nevertheless, Foch's summing-up of him to Poincaré will be acknowledged by those who knew him as accurate and fair: "As second in command, carrying out orders, Pétain is perfect, but he shrinks from responsibility, and is not fitted for a Commander-in-Chief." Both Poincaré and Clemenceau constantly complained of his pessimism. He was inclined to dwell on the gloomiest possibilities of a situation. Poincaré, in his Diary, said that in the German offensive Pétain was "defeatist." He would have made an ineffective Commander-in-Chief for Allied Armies confronted with the problems of 1918.

The French would not have agreed to the choice of Haig for the chief command of both armies. The fighting was on their soil. They could not have left to a foreign General the emancipation of French soil from the invader. Moreover, their Army was still much the largest. Apart from that they had no confidence in Haig's qualifications for such a position. They regarded him as a stout and stubborn fighter on conventional lines. But they knew only too well that he was devoid of the intellectual and personal gifts that make great commanders. He did not possess imagination, breadth or magnetism. For these reasons his name was never mentioned as a possible Generalissimo.

Who was left? Foch was known to be the ablest French General, but he had been withdrawn from the battle front for over a year. His intervention and guidance in the first Battle of Ypres had been superb. But the terrible losses sustained by the French in the Artois offensive in 1915, for which Foch was entirely responsible, temporarily destroyed the confidence hitherto reposed in his genius. His ruthlessness and his traditional belief in the policy of attack had cost his country dearly in French lives. The prolonged and bloody Battle of the Somme, when Foch commanded the French Army, showed considerable generalship which won much ground without undue losses, but it did nothing to recapture his prestige, for it accomplished nothing which satisfied French opinion. This offensive once more disappointed the hopes of a break-through. I saw Foch during that battle and I thought him a subdued and somewhat dejected remnant of the ebullient and triumphant Foch I first met. A severe motoring accident had shaken him badly. It took him months to recover fully. When his vigour was restored he was made principal military adviser to the French War Office in succession to a General of no distinction, General Roques. I remember talking to Albert Thomas about Foch about this date and he said to me: *"Foch est vidé et épuisé."* This remark exaggerated Foch's physical condition, but it fairly represented the general view formed of Foch's prospects at that period of the War. When a man of over sixty-five has been violently flung on to a windscreen you may well doubt his fitness to command in the field armies numbering millions at a critical stage in the history of the greatest war ever waged. He did not recover his old resilience and verve until the late autumn. Then they came back with the swell of a spring tide. When he accompanied the French Premier and myself to Italy after the Caporetto disaster I noticed for the first time that the dominating Foch of the first years of the War had sprung into full life and vigour once more. His inspiration vivified the Conference and propelled action.

After the Beauvais Conference of April 3rd was finished we returned to England the same day. As a mere matter of personal reminiscence I may here record two slight incidents which occurred on the return journey of the British Delegation. The Conference lasted till late in the afternoon, and as there was no place on the road where we could expect to have a meal, we decided to picnic on the roadside.

Clemenceau had brought a luncheon basket for himself and his Staff, but having lunched with the President before we arrived, he dispensed with his rations and passed them on to us. We feasted sumptuously on the *charcuterie* which had been provided for the Tiger. Mr. Winston Churchill, who had been to Headquarters discussing the replenishment of lost munitions, had joined us on the road. When we reached Boulogne, the town was in complete darkness, for there was a German air raid impending. We saw long columns of reinforcements marching silently in the dark, and when we came to the quay we witnessed the disembarkation of a number of young "kilties" about nineteen years old from the troopships by the light of a single torch. We got on to a "P" boat, a new craft invented to search for and to chase submarines. As soon as we left the harbour the bombs began to fall. There was not a light visible in the Channel, but halfway across there was a sudden illumination which lit up the water almost from shore to shore. A mile or two away we saw a ship which seemed to be on fire from stem to stern. Hull and halyards were all marked out in white flames. They had been smeared with a substance which illumined without burning. This was one of the new devices for detecting submarines that sought to take advantage of dark nights to thread their way between the vigilant greyhounds that were watching the tracks of shipping along our coasts.

Three days after the Beauvais Conference the first German push of the great offensive was arrested. It had failed to attain its strategic aim; but it was the most notable tactical success scored on either side on the Western Front, since the war of movement came to an end in 1914. Not one of the Allied offensives of 1915–16–17 can compare with it in the results achieved. In the course of little over a fortnight, the enemy had penetrated our lines on a 60-mile front and advanced a maximum depth of 40 miles beyond our front trenches. He had captured 975 of our guns, and inflicted on us 188,000 casualties, including 79,000 prisoners and missing. And he had achieved this result when his total forces on the Western Front were approximately equal in combatant strength to those of the Allies, and his gun power was less. Compare that with the Allied offensives in Champagne, on the Chemin des Dames, at Vimy, on the Somme, and at Passchendaele, when we had a heavy superiority in numbers. On the Somme, as a result of five months' fighting, we advanced a maximum depth of about seven miles, capturing 125 guns and 40,000 prisoners at a cost of 498,000 casualties to ourselves, not counting the French. At Passchendaele we spent nearly four months in winning five miles of useless and quaggy desolation — later to be abandoned in a single night without striking a blow — and in capturing 74 guns and 34,000 prisoners, at a cost of 400,000 casualties.

The total German casualties in their great March offensive, including their fight against the French, were 220,000. Even if their returns are held to be incomplete, and a percentage added to that total, the price paid for this success still remains far below what we paid on the Somme and in Flanders for gains which by comparison with those won in the German offensive had been quite trivial. All the same, for all practical purposes, this brilliant achievement was a costly failure. Amiens had not been captured. A gap had not been effected between the British and the French. The Allied loss had been repaired. The German Army with its diminishing reserves had acquired another useless salient to defend.

Ludendorff is entitled to claim that "it was a brilliant feat." I do not think anyone who has read fairly the history of the War can challenge his further statement that the Germans had accomplished what the English and French had not succeeded in doing, and that in the fourth year of the War. But the fact that the British Army sustained a heavy defeat must not blind us to what it accomplished in the face of great difficulties. The German Army had every advantage which good leadership could confer, the British Army was placed under every disadvantage in which bad generalship could land any troops. The Germans had prepared their plans with the greatest skill, they had worked them out with the greatest care. They massed their troops so that they should hit our line with the greatest force that could be concentrated at the front of attack, they assembled their reserves as close up to their first attacking troops as they conveniently could, so that no time should be lost in throwing them in wherever the need came either for further pressure or to relieve exhausted troops. When more reserves were needed either to overcome unexpected resistance or to exploit an unexpected advance, arrangements had been already made for bringing them up with the utmost celerity from other parts of the line. If the attack did not achieve its ultimate objective it was not through any lack of preparation on the part of the High Command.

What about the British Army? Although Headquarters knew the attack was coming, the preparations for defence were of the most slipshod character. As to preparing for counter-attack, which is an essential part of defence, it was bound to be ineffective for lack of reserves; and as for a counter-offensive, no means had been provided for it. Most of our troops were massed on sectors which, weeks before the 21st of March, G.H.Q. knew were not then to be seriously attacked, whilst the 42 miles of a line which, they were abundantly warned, would with the Third Army receive the first impact of an immense force, were lightly held. Most of our reserves were in and behind that part of the line which was the remotest from the battlefield. Although G.H.Q. was warned three weeks in advance that the greatest concentration of the enemy was opposite the weakest part of our line and that the shock would come there, it made no effort to strengthen it or to move any more of our reserves behind it. Haig rejected a proposal for building up a General Reserve of thirty divisions, two thirds of which would have been drawn from other armies and which would have been available to support our hard-pressed troops when attacked by overwhelming numbers. And we made no other arrangement for assistance from the French which could be termed a working plan for mutual support.

Taking the whole front the opposing forces were substantially equal, with a real mechanical superiority on the Allied side. But we so disposed our forces that for the first four days of the battle the enemy had an advantage of three or four to one in men and an even greater superiority in guns, most of our men and guns being kept at the extreme end of our line from the battlefield. The Official History tries to persuade us that Haig was right in keeping most of his army as far away as possible from the area of the impending battle. It seems a novel theory that the further reinforcements are away from the fight the more useful they are when they are needed! They are much more helpful when they are three days' journey from the battlefield than if they are only a few miles behind! How these great Generals presume on the ignorance of the common man!

The first reserves only came into action after our lines had been broken through by an overwhelming weight of men and guns. Our soldiers were never given a fighting chance of winning. Under such conditions there are plenty of historical precedents for the bravest men being seized with panic and running away from the battle. My great fear during all these anxious days was the recollection of Napoleon's saying at St. Helena, in explaining the *sauve qui peut* of Waterloo: "The bravest armies have all in turn been seized with panic, and the question then is whether you can rally them in time before they disperse." In the Battle of Amiens there was confusion, disorder, retreat, a muddle of broken divisions, but there was no panic, no *sauve qui peut*. There was no flight of terror-stricken mobs escaping from pursuing Death. They never ceased fighting. They sought opportunities for resistance right to the end. When out-flanked or driven from one position they looked out for another where they could make a stand. Officers rarely experienced any difficulty in lining them up for a fight whenever they found a suitable position where they could temporarily hold up the enemy. Their trouble was that there were so few prepared positions which they could occupy. An entrenchment or machine-gun emplacement which only existed on a notice-board was not a defensible position. And the shallow groove of spitlocked trenches was no shelter against artillery or rifle fire. G.H.Q. however could not afford to provide them with anything better, and concentrated the labour resources on favoured sectors which were not likely to be assailed. So the soldiers of the Fifth Army — the outcasts of Passchendaele — had to choose some convenient hump to shield them from the German guns whilst they were doing their best to delay the advance of the German infantry. The first day the line was ruptured, but the spirit of the troops was never broken to the end. When men were severed from their own units they joined up with others whom they found putting up a fight to hold up the German advance. Odds and ends of men who were not in the fighting ranks at all — engineers, labour companies, cooks, servants — picked up rifles, lined trenches, formed up little battalions and brigades of their own with the help of men who in the confusion of such a battle had strayed from their own units. The American engineers, who were helping us to throw up defences around Amiens, threw down their engineering tools, picked up their rifles and fought with valour beyond praise, side by side with an improvised gathering of strays, to arrest the enemy advance. There were many cases where the victorious masses of the enemy were held up by the heroic resistance of individual battalions and companies here and there on the battlefield, so that time might be gained for the meagre reserves that were tardily spared to creep up before the enemy could reach his final objective. This is not an imaginative picture, painted from reports made by British general officers anxious to minimise the episodes of the defeat. It is confirmed by much testimony from German eye-witnesses. It is worth quoting a few extracts from an account written by a distinguished German General,[1] compiled from reports which came to him. This is taken from his record of the opening day's fighting, March 21st: —

"In spite of the mist, the English artillery, firing by the map, yet managed to render good service to the infantry in their desperate struggle, and in many cases hung on till the last moment. The guns might well fall into the hands of the Germans, after they had been fought right up to the time when they were under German machine-gun fire! The battery officers with their crews then threw in their lot with the infantry, and helped to reinforce their weakened fronts. . . . The sturdy resistance of the English brought it about that already on the afternoon of the 21st the 39th Division (Second Line) had to join in the battle of the Lindequist sector. . . . The nearer the 126th Regiment gets to the Lagnicourt–Louverval–Doignies road, the stronger becomes the enemy artillery fire. After crossing this road, the right wing of the 3rd Company is forced to suffer heavily from the fire of an English machine-gun nest."

[1] Lieutenant-General Kabisch: "Michael."

On March 22nd: —

"Those in front who had sought and found in shell-holes or in trenches which they dug themselves, some shelter against the artillery and machine-gun fire of the English . . . had to satisfy themselves with the cold comfort of the bread they had brought with them through the night — the next morning the attack went on. . . . The resistance of the English was much tougher than it had been on the previous day. Hills and hummocks furnish for their innumerable machine-gun nests in and behind their second position the best cover and an excellent field of fire. Only with difficulty, pressing forward with a true contempt for death close behind the front line of the infantry, can the advancing shock batteries of the 2nd Field Artillery Regiment master some of these nests. At 8.30 A.M. the order had to be given to the rather thinned-out front line to dig itself in, in the positions it had reached quite close to the defences of the second English position! Hours pass of quite unbearable waiting. Cowering close to one another, the warriors peer gloomily forward, full of fury that an attack so promisingly begun should have been brought to a standstill. . . .

"Fresh artillery preparations and attacks alternate with counter-attacks by the English. The battle wavers hither and thither. Our brave comrades suffer terrible losses. The troops from the rear thrust forward into the fighting line. They too are shot down, without being able to achieve a change in the situation. At 6 P.M. the English along the whole front from Morchies to the Cambrai–Bapaume road renew a powerful counter-offensive. North of Morchies they also send their tanks forward. Bloodily repulsed they retire under fire of the German defences, back to the sunken road Morchies–Ziegelei. . . .

"Everywhere, in Morchies, and especially in the sunken road, savage hand-to-hand conflicts take place. Our men gain the victory. . . ."

Here is his description of the fight over an obscure village in the Somme area: —

". . . The gardens of the village were taken by storm, wire-cutters cleared the way through entanglements, the road dipped, and we were in the village. . . . By evening the 52nd Infantry Regiment succeeded in taking Falvy. . . . Then in face of the fire of enemy artillery and machine-guns the attack was brought to a standstill. At 4.00 in the morning of the 24th March the 12th Grenadier Regiment began the crossing by Bethencourt, but a strong machine-gun fire smote it from the houses of the village. . . ."

March 24th: —

"An English attack was beaten off. The English withdrew, as the mist cleared, into the houses of Bethencourt, about 200 metres distant. From thence they maintained a stubborn, heavy fire against the garrison of the bridge-head. . . ."

March 26th: —

"But the big result cannot be so soon achieved. The English pull themselves together again. A fight comes, in which the situation of the quite isolated 28th Infantry Division, divided into two groups, grows at times very serious. It is attacked in the morning twilight. The attack against the front and two wings was beaten off with heavy losses for the enemy. On the other hand, the enemy, thrusting forward from Bouchoir, succeeded in pressing back the right flank up to and east of Erches. Parts of this group appeared right behind the division. The batteries standing immediately behind the front line gave rapid fire at point-blank range. The 2nd Section of the 65th Field Artillery Regiment, and 1st and 3rd Batteries of the 55th Foot Artillery succeeded through their fire in compelling the enemy, who were advancing close up to the batteries, to take shelter in the trenches and shell-holes of the Somme position. . . ."

March 26th: —

"In Saulchoy meantime, three companies of the 1st Grenadiers/109 with the 7th Battery of the 14th Field Artillery were fighting independently against repeated fierce English attacks. Midday came. Where was the big success hiding? The battalion had to face the decision, whether to hold out in Saulchoy and defend the place against the thrusting attacks of the English, or to fight its way through in the direction of Erches to rejoin its own forces. It decided to stick in Saulchoy. . . ."

March 26th: —

"If the divisions were thus able continually to smash through the constantly renewed resistance of the enemy, they owe thanks for it not least to the accompanying batteries, whose sacrificial help was beyond all praise."

These extracts show clearly enough that the German advance was anything but a walk-over. It was achieved by immense superiority of men and artillery against an unremitting resistance. When it had proceeded so far that its effective superiority dwindled, it slowed down and stopped. The "obstinate British soldier", to quote Wetzell, had fully justified the quality of "toughness" with which he had been credited. But it is fair to add that the French troops had been worthy of the reputation they had acquired for their skill and gallantry when they dashed into the fight to help the overwhelmed remnants of the Fifth Army.

The German advance was thus delayed until time was given the two Allied Headquarters to make up their minds as to which of them should send the reinforcements that were needed. Great losses were inflicted on the Germans so that they found the immense reserves they had massed behind their lines were insufficient to crush and sweep away this disordered assortment of tough British soldiers from all sorts of battalions and services who would not run away to let the enemy through in time.

In the end Amiens was saved — the Haig-Pétain prospect of a British Army rolled up to the north and the French

Army rolled up to the south (which was also Ludendorff's plan) never materialised. There was no gap made between the British and French Armies and the main purpose of the first great German push had been thwarted. This was achieved by the unbeatable fortitude of the ordinary British soldier and the fighting officer who led him. Whoever was responsible for the retreat, they were blameless. By their undaunted valour they redressed the defects of their superiors. It was a soldiers' battle. The credit and the honour were entirely theirs. Wetzell was right in warning Ludendorff not to risk his last chance of restoring the fortunes of the Central Powers on the hope that, profiting by the strategical clumsiness and tactical stupidity of British Generals, he could crush the staying powers of the British soldier.

But the great offensive was by no means over. The first onrush had been checked, but the losses inflicted on the Allies had been heavier than any sustained by them within an equal period in any single battle on the Western Front since the beginning of the War. There were other great attacks coming, other great battles to be fought, other great defeats to be sustained, other heavy losses to be endured. When the Allies had survived this period of discomfiture, there was the problem of converting defeat into decisive victory and of driving the Germans in headlong retreat out of the country they had occupied for four years. The Germans for over three years had repelled every effort to dislodge them from positions so skilfully engineered that they successfully held them even against an enemy with a superiority of 50 per cent. in numbers. Each year these positions had been strengthened by every device of which military engineers were capable. Could they be stormed now when the Allies could not at best anticipate a superiority in numbers comparable with that which they enjoyed in 1916 and 1917? The Russian collapse and the Brest-Litovsk Treaty had released so many German divisions that the expected reinforcements of American troops could not sufficiently redress the balance to give the preponderance that the Allies possessed during the years of the Somme, of the Chemin des Dames and of Passchendaele. Was there any hope in these circumstances of securing a decision in 1918? At that date I met no one, military or civilian, who believed it possible. Any optimism which any of them felt earlier had vanished. No one quite realised the change that was effected when the armies of the West were placed under one Commander, and he the one man with the quality of military genius on the Allied side. We were soon to perceive the difference it made in the effective striking force of the French and British Armies.

2. THE BATTLE OF THE LYS

Ludendorff launches "Georgette" attack in Flanders — The Portuguese — German thrust successful — Attack underestimated at first — Foch promises French troops — Maurice's arithmetic — Our superiority in mechanised arms — Foch not anxious about Lys attack — Germans trapped by their own success — British anxiety — Flanders mud holds up the Germans — Plumer abandons Passchendaele salient — Foch's hopeful message — Flanders battle drags on — We learn of exhaustion of German reserves — Further French reinforcements: Battle of Kemmel — Villers-Bretonneux — British plans in event of German success — Views at Abbeville Council — Lys offensive a strategical blunder — German Army exhausted.

Ludendorff came to the conclusion by the 1st of April that he could not make real progress in the direction of Amiens and that the time had come to carry out another part of his plan, and strike a blow at another point of the British line. He chose the plain of the Lys — a variant of the original German plan for a thrust on the Flanders Front towards Hazebrouck and St. Omer, to which the code name "St. George" had been given by the High Command. This secondary version was called by the Germans "Georgette." The part of the line at which he first struck was held by a Portuguese division. A good deal of unfair derision had been cast on the

Portuguese troops for the feebleness of their defence. Some time before this attack I saw a battalion of Portuguese soldiers marching to the front. As far as the rank and file were concerned they appeared to me to be of excellent quality — stocky, well-built, and of smart and soldierly appearance. But their officers were obviously not equal in stamina or efficiency to their men. They had either been ill-chosen or lacked the necessary training. Wellington found that the Portuguese peasant made a first-rate soldier when disciplined and led by good officers: many of them drawn from our own veteran army. The victory of Busaco was largely due to the fine resistance they offered to some of the best troops of the *Grande Armée,* led by one of Napoleon's most famous Marshals. Their officers in this war, whatever one may think of their intrinsic merits, had never received the training which fitted them for leadership in a great war. Moreover, the Portuguese contingent had suffered recently from the effects of political changes in their own country. The Ministry that had brought Portugal into the War had been overthrown. Their successors were not overzealous in its prosecution. The result was that the little Portuguese Army in France had been let down during the past few months in recruits and equipment — worst of all in encouragement. But even if they had been the best officers and most efficiently equipped divisions in the field, they could not, in the circumstances in which they were placed, have put up a successful resistance against so formidable an attack. There were in the Portuguese Army a certain number of officers and men who were in sympathy with the point of view held by the new Minister in Lisbon. They were against the War. But that was not the sole reason of their flight. An incomprehensible piece of carelessness on the part of our Army Command was directly responsible for what happened. General Horne, the Commander of the Second Army, being warned that the next general attack would come in that sector, decided to withdraw the Portuguese Corps from the line and substitute two British divisions. Foolishly, he only withdrew one Portuguese division (the second) without substituting a British division and then left a forward position, which had been held by a corps of two divisions, to be defended by only one of the two Portuguese divisions, with a brigade of the other division in reserve. It was intended to withdraw these on the 9th when the two British divisions would take their place. The attack came suddenly before the change had been effected. What followed was inevitable with any troops.

The Portuguese were taken completely by surprise when they were about to leave. They were subjected to a heavy bombardment and an attack by masses of German troops who outnumbered them considerably. They broke, and no doubt their rout became a headlong flight.

But it is rather hard on a small nation, which has a long and honoured record for a valour and intrepidity on sea and land which enabled them for centuries to maintain the independence of their mountains against a powerful military neighbour and to become the pioneers of Western exploration in unknown seas and lands, that they should have to bear the stain of reproach for a defeat which was entirely attributable to the crass stupidity of a General from another race.

The British division on either side of the Portuguese had their flanks uncovered, and a retreat along a considerable front became inevitable. The Germans penetrated a distance of six miles in a single day. The battle extended on a wider front to the right and the left. The enemy was aiming at the only railway from South Flanders behind the British Front. Its capture would have been serious. It would have very gravely hampered the defence of the British Front by making it difficult to bring British and French reinforcements up rapidly to the point of attack. Fortunately, on our right flank, the German attack on Givenchy completely failed. Had it succeeded, the Germans might have accomplished what they had already failed to achieve when they made their first great attack south of Arras. They would have turned the flank of the British forces and have been able to start rolling them up. But the fierce German onslaught at this point was driven back with great loss owing to the magnificent resistance put up by the 55th West Lancashire Division, under General Jeudwine. It was one of the finest feats of the War and contributed to a considerable extent to the failure of the great German offensive. Lancashire has good reason to be proud of the part played by its troops in these battles — the stand made by the Manchesters during the attack on the Fifth Army, which helped so much to delay the German advance in March, and the resistance of the Lancastrians at Givenchy which thwarted one of the chief aims of German strategy in April.

But although the German attack failed at this critical point they advanced with alarming strides at other points on that front. At first it was thought that the attack was only a demonstration, and as such it was reported to the Cabinet, who were informed that our front was strongly entrenched. By the next day the reports from G.H.Q. stated that the attack was "more important" than had at first been thought. The reports we received from Headquarters as to the progress of the battle called to mind those first optimistic reports that came of the battle of March 21st. The first day or two of the Battle of Amiens there was "no cause for anxiety." Two days later our only hope was to let the Germans through and re-treat towards the north. Here also we had the same swing of the pendulum of hope and panic. One moment the attack was only a feint, then G.H.Q. rushed to the other extreme of pessimistic foreboding and came to the conclusion that the rapid advance of the Germans placed the Channel Ports in imminent jeopardy. The Cabinet were naturally anxious when these latter reports reached them and decided to impress on Clemenceau that they considered it essential that the French should treat our portion of the line as part of their battle front. We also resolved that "if we were satisfied on this point, the less the Generals were interfered with the better."

When Foch heard what had happened, he immediately dashed off to our G.H.Q. He did not quite share our apprehensions and he was very loth to part with any of the reserves which he was building up for his counter-stroke. He, however, promised French help. Our C.I.G.S. was satisfied with this undertaking. But even on the second day the reports did not indicate any overwhelming danger. The weight behind the offensive was not great. It was stated that the Germans had only eight divisions in the attack and our flanks were reported to be holding well.

When this offensive started Foch had only just received his commission as Commander-in-Chief of the three Allied Armies on the Western Front. Until he received his appointment he had not been in a position to give the necessary orders for the formation of a reserve. Now he acted promptly, and ordered the movement of five French divisions in support of the British Army.

In view of the Press and Parliamentary attack made on the Government at the instigation of Sir Frederick Maurice it is interesting to quote the report given to the Cabinet by him as D.M.O. on April 10th on the comparative numbers of the German and Allied infantry on the Western Front at that date.

The Director of Military Operations gave some particulars as to the relative strengths of the Allied and enemy armies at the present time on the Western Front. Reckoned in divisions, the enemy had 199 divisions compared with our 167. Assuming the enemy casualties to be about 200,000 they would now have 1,370,000 infantry. The six or seven divisions which had been brought across from Russia since the beginning of the battle might be regarded as compensating for their casualties.

This was an astonishing calculation. Seven divisions, even if they were complete, would not number more than 63,000 infantry. How could they compensate for losses aggregating 200,000 men?

On the Allied side, the French had brought in two divisions, and we had brought in one, but five of ours, and the Portuguese division, had been knocked out, which reduced the Allied rifle strength to 1,450,000 (a superiority, be it noted, of 80,000 men in infantry alone over the Germans).

The Director of Military Operations was of opinion that the enemy, in anticipation of this offensive, had prepared drafts to replace all casualties. They had 400,000 drafts available before the offensive started. In addition, it was possible for them to draw on their divisions in the East to the extent of 100,000 drafts. More-over, the Germans had taken all their troops that were serving in Macedonia and in Italy, which proved conclusively that they were concentrating every ounce of strength on the present battle. Against this, the French had 250,000 in depots, and we had 200,-000, including the men returning from leave. We had sent to France, since the 21st of March, 1918, 110,000 infantry and 20,000 to 30,000 others, over and above the men returning from leave.[1]

It was mentioned that, as regards the thinning of the divisions on the Russian Front, this might be counterbalanced by 100,000 United States troops due to arrive shortly in France.

Even this favourable report on the comparative strength of the rival forces was confined to infantry. It did not take into account our decided superiority in both men and

[1] That meant over 200,000 men.

material, in guns, aeroplanes and tanks, which had been increased since March 21st, and it certainly ignored altogether the important circumstance that our men were much better fed. The military importance of this last factor was revealed during these two offensives by two striking facts. The first was that the advance of the German infantry was seriously delayed by their raiding of captured stores which contained rations with which the German soldiers had not been acquainted for many a month — either in quantity or in quality. The second was that when the influenza epidemic, which swept over the world and caused more deaths than even the Great War, reached the German trenches, the inferior nourishment of the troops made them more vulnerable than the well-nourished British troops to the ravages of a specially malignant germ. Their casualties from this disease were therefore exceptionally heavy.

At the same meeting of the Cabinet the Secretary for War reported that our total estimated casualties in the great battle between March 21st and April 6th were 150,000. Our losses had been already made up by the men we sent to France since March 21st and those which had been brought from Italy.

Foch never took the same serious view of this offensive as he did of the March attack. The latter had taken the Germans weeks of elaborate preparation. They had brought sixty-three divisions close up to the front of attack. They had massed behind their attacking troops thousands of guns with huge ammunition dumps, new aerodromes and hospitals, all prepared for months in contemplation of a gigantic offensive in one definite area. In the Lys offensive there were no apparent preparations for a great attack. There were eight German divisions in the first assault with no great reserves immediately behind them. There is considerable evidence in favour of the view that this offensive was

originally only a limited attack on a weak part of our line
intended to attract French and British reserves from the
zone where the next great offensive was to be propelled. To
this extent Haig's first estimate of the attack as a demonstration was justified. Foch held the same view. That is why he
never lost his head when the offensive was an unexpected
success owing to the Portuguese episode. He was reluctant
to play the German game by sending more French divisions
to the north than were absolutely necessary to prevent the
Germans from breaking through to the Channel Ports. The
Germans were enticed out of their original plan by the ease
with which they pushed through the gap created by the
Portuguese retirement. The result was that an offensive
which was intended as a bluff to frighten the Allies into withdrawing their reserves developed into a great battle, with
the capture of the Channel Ports as its ultimate objective.
The Germans brought up their reserves from the south to
exploit the advantage they had won. They were caught in
a trap which they had laid for the Allies. More reserves were
spent in attack than in defence. Foch had refused to walk
into the pitfall dug for him by Ludendorff, but the German
Commander himself, in a moment of exaltation produced by
his easy victory over one Portuguese division, had tumbled
headlong into his own pit. He was not the first military
leader to be led to his doom by a flying foe.

The lure of the Channel Ports was a dazzling one. Apart
from the crippling effect which the occupation of these ports
by the Germans would have on the transport of our troops
and material to France and also on our anti-submarine campaign in the Channel, it would have its moral value for the
Germans in the dismay and disarray which would be created
in England. Had the ports been captured the Channel could
have been closed for our through shipping for London, in itself a serious matter. The occupation of Calais and of

Cape Gris-Nez by the Germans would for the first time have placed England within range of German guns. Paris was being bombarded by a gun that fired its shells from a distance of over 50 miles. Naval guns could have fired across the Channel. It is for this reason that the second German offensive made an almost deeper impression on the public mind in our country than even the first. The Germans at Amiens would be bad enough, but the Germans in possession of territory in view of our own shores was an infinitely more alarming prospect. And as their Army pressed forward with a thrust that seemed for three weeks to be irresistible — one well-known town after another falling into their hands (Armentières, Merville, Neuve Chapelle, and Bailleul were much more familiar names in Britain than Montdidier, Bapaume, Villers-Bretonneux, or even Amiens) — a certain alarm spread throughout the country. It was then that Haig penned his famous appeal to his troops, in which he said that they "must fight with their backs to the wall." By April 12th he was profoundly disturbed by the position and his uneasiness was communicated to the Cabinet at home. Hence the representations they made to the French Government as to the urgent need for French reinforcements. Foch, however, maintained his composure and took not only a calm, but a hopeful view of the German advance across the Lys. He held strictly to the view that the Germans were playing the Allied game and he resolutely declined to be fussed into having his ulterior plans upset because the Germans were wasting their reserves in gaining futile and costly victories in a direction where he was convinced they could be stopped before they reached anything vital. In adhering to this opinion he took risks, but war is always a choice of risks, and sound strategy and tactics consist in knowing the right risk to take. He sent five French divisions to the north. Later on he dispatched a few more, but by that time the

Germans had withdrawn their best reserves from the south in order to exploit a blunder — this time their own. He was fully justified by the event. The Lys offensive destroyed the German scheme of a second offensive towards Amiens. Foch maintained that the Germans had no chance of breaking through to the ports. At best their numbers were only equal to those commanded by the Allies. In the March offensive, when the Germans were thoroughly prepared and the Allies were not — when the latter were weakened by distracted counsels amongst the Commanders — they only penetrated a maximum of 40 miles into the Allied lines and were then stopped. There was small chance for such a penetration with weaker forces and hasty preparation. And the terrain was much less suitable for attack. In the north they could be held up by inundations and the plain of the Lys was boggy at that time of the year. Hindenburg describes the difficulties experienced by the German troops in their advance: —

"Our storm troops rose from their muddy trenches on the Lys front from Armentières to La Bassée. Of course they were not disposed in great waves, but mostly in small detachments and diminutive columns, which waded through the morass which had been upheaved by shells and mines, and either picked their way towards the enemy lines between deep shellholes filled with water, or took the few firm causeways. . . . It was only with the greatest difficulty that a few ammunition wagons were brought forward behind the infantry."

As they advanced further their troubles increased: —

"The difficulties of communication across the Lys Valley which had to be overcome by our troops attacking from the south had been like a chain round our necks. Ammunition could only be brought up in quite inadequate quantities, and it was only thanks to the booty the enemy had left behind on the battlefield that we were able to keep our troops properly fed."

In these positions: —

"Our infantry had suffered extremely heavily in their fight with the enemy machine-gun nests, and their complete exhaustion threatened unless we paused in our attack for a time."

Their losses were much heavier than those sustained by the defenders and they were losing heavily in their picked officers and men who were irreplaceable. This was the vindication of Foch's strategy. German reserves and drafts were being wasted in an offensive that consumed valuable time of which they had not a week to spare and weakened their reserve for future efforts beyond the possibility of redemption.

After a short respite to recuperate and reinforce their exhausted troops the Germans renewed their attacks mostly towards the north. They brought in fresh divisions from the south and for a time their attacks once more prospered. It was then that General Plumer took over the whole front of defence from La Bassée to the sea. His first measure was reluctantly to withdraw all the troops from the Passchendaele salient and occupy the line held by the British troops before that costly battle was ever fought. This step not only increased the reserves at his disposal but it upset the German plans on the extreme north of our front. They had contemplated making a great coup by pinching out the salient and capturing the divisions that garrisoned it. The evacuation was completed the night before the German attack, without their knowledge. The worthless territory which it had taken four months' terrible fighting and 400,000 casualties to capture was abandoned in a single night. The conquest was a nightmare, the relinquishment of it was a relief and an inspiration. When the encircling troops reached Langemark they found nothing before them to capture but the muddy triangle on which the British Army had been flogged to tatters for five months.

It was at this stage that Foch sent me a personal message which was significant of the degree of confidence he felt in the outcome of the struggle. In course of conversation with him at Beauvais I asked him whose hand he would prefer playing at that time — his own or Ludendorff's. He promised to let me know as soon as he had authority to look into the whole position and time to weigh the resources of the rival armies. That was on April 4th. On the 17th I received a message from him that "if he had to choose between playing his own hand and that of Ludendorff's, then if he had to get to Berlin he would prefer Ludendorff's hand, but as his mission was to beat Ludendorff, he would prefer his own."

But the battle of the north was by no means over. Whatever was the original intention of the German High Command in the initiation of this attack it had now developed into a major offensive with an objective which reached far beyond the first avowed purpose of eating up the Allied reserves and withdrawing Allied divisions to the northern end of the line where their communications were inferior to those possessed by the enemy. Even at this date their objective was not clearly defined in the minds of the German Commanders. It was rather of the "you never can tell" expectation. The British Army might at last be broken, the Channel Ports might be captured, and at least the French might be forced to send their reserves to the northern end of the front in order to avert disaster — in fact anything might happen when one secured the upper hand over an enemy. With these unexpressed hopes in mind large reinforcements were brought to the attacking force partly from Russia but mostly from France by the process of *roulement*. Gradually they pushed us back in the direction of Hazebrouck. They had already captured the Messines Ridge;

they now attacked and took more of the high ground to the northwest. As these conquests overlooked the plains of the north the situation became graver. Foch under the pressure of these events sent fresh reinforcements from the French Army to relieve some of our hard-pressed divisions. The Germans once more made a desperate effort to widen their left flank by a second attack on the Givenchy Front. It was repulsed with heavy losses by an inferior British force. On the other flank the German push was more successful. Orders were given that the inundations that protected Dunkirk and Calais against an attack from the direction of the Yser should be started.

In the middle of our anxieties the Cabinet received information from the War Office Intelligence which showed that whatever might be our worries, those of the Germans must have been even greater. In this vast struggle an equivalent of 208 German divisions had already been used against the British and the French. Of these 151 had encountered British troops and 57 had engaged the French. The Germans had still 63 divisions available for *roulement* but the British and French had 66. This estimate did not take into account the four divisions of American troops already in the front line, nor did it reckon the American reinforcements, some of which were already completing their training and equipment in France and would have been available in an extreme emergency to fill up depleted divisions. Under our new shipping arrangements, 30,000 a week of young American recruits were pouring into France. There would soon be 40,000 a week. As the attack so far had been entirely on the British Front, our troops had borne most of the brunt. But the Allied reserves were now definitely larger than those which were at the disposal of the Germans. It was therefore a question of increasing this superiority without taking too great risks for the next fortnight. In spite of

that vital consideration Foch came to the conclusion after a
visit to the battle area that he must spare a few of his reserve divisions for the British Front. The apprehensions
felt by the British Commander-in-Chief were naturally a
little exaggerated but by no means altogether ill-founded.
And the anxiety was primarily his. In the event, the fresh
French divisions sent to the north were found to be necessary
to stem the fierce German onslaught on the vital bastion
above the Yser. The Germans captured the important height
of Kemmel Hill from a French division which had replaced
a tired British division. But further German progress in
that direction was arrested by a combined British and French
force. The last German effort to capture the high ground to
the north had thus been repelled by a combined French and
British force. A French counter-attack had in this decisive
battle driven the enemy a mile beyond the line from which
he had started. The Germans had put into this fight their
last fresh divisions on their Northern Front. Their losses in
the battle had been exceptionally heavy.

Meanwhile we had a gratifying testimony to the effect
this diversion of the German forces to an unintended offensive
had upon their original plans. The second attack which had
been contemplated originally by them — and expected by
us — in the direction of Amiens, dwindled into a comparatively small affair where four divisions were employed
to capture Villers-Bretonneux and to push the German Front
on to the high ground above Amiens. At first it achieved a
certain measure of success; it captured Villers-Bretonneux
and the Germans came in sight of the spire of the great
Cathedral, but there was no weight of numbers behind the
onslaught. Their reserves were bogged in the Lys morass.
A brilliant counter-attack by combined forces of British and
Australians recaptured Villers-Bretonneux.

By the end of the month of April the Germans had come

to the conclusion that their great offensive in the north had miscarried as far as its chief aims were concerned and that the time had arrived for calling it off. They had not succeeded in destroying the British Army or in reaching the Channel Ports. They must now turn their attention to the French Army. They had by their conquests added another salient to their fronts and for weeks paid heavy toll to the British artillery that bombarded them from three sides. The Allies were not aware for some time of the difficulties experienced by their redoubtable foe in making any progress across the boggy ground which they had conquered, and fears of a further push still remained to disturb the minds of those who were primarily responsible for organising resistance in this battle area. There were serious discussions amongst the Allies as to what course should be pursued by the British Army if the Germans succeeded in driving us so far back as to make the Channel Ports untenable. Should we fall back on Calais, Boulogne and Dunkirk and prepare for embarkation of troops and material to England or should our Army join the French Army in the south and leave the ports to their fate as the French and ourselves did in 1914? If the military decision were in favour of a retreat to the ports, then preparations would have to be made in time for this eventuality. Enough shipping should be assembled at convenient ports so that they might be available at the shortest notice. Sir Douglas Haig and Sir Henry Wilson were in favour of the latter course. The Admiralty were very insistent that the ports should be held to the last moment. If Calais fell into enemy hands, Dover could no longer be held as a naval base for our submarine operations in the Channel. I understand that Pétain favoured the 1914 precedent — a retreat southwards to join the French Army.

Whilst these discussions were pending a meeting of the Supreme Council was held at Abbeville to decide this issue

amongst others. The Generals present were each invited
to express their views at a confidential meeting held at
the Prefect's House before the Council met officially.
Foch took no part in the discussion. When he was asked
to give us his opinion on the matter his only answer was
a gruff *"Ne lâchez pas pied"* twice and thrice repeated.
He would not even discuss the possibility of a retreat. The
Allies must refuse to lift a foot. Every inch of ground must
be held. He would answer no contingent questions based on
the hypothesis of a forced retreat. Psychologically, it was
a fine and stimulating gesture. You cannot fight at your best
with a retreating mind.

At that moment when we were discussing the possibility
of a German break-through as a problem demanding pre-
cautionary measures of a practical kind, the Germans had
decided to postpone further operations in Flanders until
after they had dealt with the French Army. We know and
are very much alive to our own troubles, and for that
reason are disposed to exaggerate them. We are not always
so conscious of the embarrassments of others, least of all
those of our foes and we either do not suspect their existence
or are inclined to mistake their character.

The Battle of the Lys was one of the great strategical
blunders of the German High Command. Ludendorff had
been warned of the unsuitability of the ground up in the
north for a great offensive until the late spring. Nevertheless,
he sent the picked divisions of his last army squelching
through these water-logged meadows intersected with ditches
and drains. He admits that it was with difficulty he could
get artillery up to support the infantry and that many divisions had consequently failed to show a disposition to attack.
Even food could not be brought up, let alone guns and ammunition. Hungry troops lost time in scrounging for anything to eat. Speed was of the essence of success in such an

offensive as he was conducting. In a week's time the March offensive on the Somme had penetrated nearly 40 miles into the British lines. After three weeks' hard fighting on the Lys Front the farthest point of penetration was 12 miles. The German Commander ought to have learnt the lesson of the failure of our attack in Flanders the previous year. That should have taught him that rapid movement of modern armies with their ponderous equipment cannot be achieved in a swamp. It is a strange coincidence that two of the most powerful generals of the War — one British and one German — should have almost destroyed their fine armies by insisting on fighting great battles in a morass. Both were lured by the hope that the moment they captured the high ground beyond the rest would be easy. Had Ludendorff been asked in the summer and autumn of 1917 how he would have liked to see the British Army spend its strength, he could not have chosen a better method for it to throw away its opportunities than the campaign to which it was committed by its own leaders. Had Foch been asked how he would have wished to see the Germans occupy what was left of their immense reserves after the Battle of Amiens, he could not have selected a better plan than to send Ludendorff's best army on what he once picturesquely described as "a duck's march" in the Flemish lowlands, where celerity of movement was impossible because cannon and ammunition wagons got stuck. That would give him the time he needed to build up a great Allied Reserve for the final crash into the exhausted remnant of the enemy's strength.

Our losses in these two great battles were necessarily heavy, but those of the enemy were much heavier. We are no longer dependent on estimates for the figures of either our own or enemy losses. Official statistics are available on both sides. Ludendorff complains that owing to lack of drafts these losses were unpleasantly felt. On the Allied side

American reinforcements were beginning to arrive, and that more than made up the Allied deficit. The Battle of the Lys gave time for the newly arrived Americans to be organised into an effective army.

The German Army was so exhausted and so depleted that it had to take a month to rest and fill up ere it was ready for its next move. That month's respite was invaluable to our Army which had been fighting without cease for six weeks. Meanwhile not only were American troops — mostly fighting men — being carried to France, usually by British ships, at the rate of 250,000 per month, but those already in France were perfecting their training, so that by the time the Germans were ready for their next attack there were five American divisions, each of them treble the strength of a German division, ready to take part in the conflict. What was perhaps even more important was that Foch was given time to develop his plans for the great counter-stroke he was contemplating and to make the necessary preparations for delivering it when the time was ripe.

3. How the British Public Faced Defeat

No panic — A Scottish sermon — Labour studies the map — Joining up with their pals — Appendix A: Extract of a Report of the Second Meeting of the Fifth Session of the Supreme War Council.

A prominent American who visited this country a few days days after the news of the March disaster was astonished at the general composure with which it was received by the British public. There was no sign of panic or even of excitement. That certainly is my recollection of the general attitude of the people. The defeat was regarded as an unfortunate incident inevitable in a prolonged war; it had happened before many a time in our history and the Allies had sustained unpleasant set-backs in this war, but these mishaps were always overcome in the end. No doubt of ultimate victory crept into the region of the British heart. During 1917, the previous year, when I had an occasion to take a journey to Glasgow and Edinburgh, there was a great deal of unrest amongst the Scottish workers and the pacifist movement was growing. During the late spring of 1918 when things were going badly in the north, and the Channel Ports were thought to be in peril, I again visited Scotland. I found a complete change in the attitude and temper of all classes alike. It was visible everywhere — in the streets, in the works, as well as in public assemblies. There was a grim resolve imprinted on the faces of the people. There was very little pacifist talk and the workers were applying themselves to the tasks of the War assiduously without grumble or protest.

At the Sunday service I attended at a Scottish Church before going to see Admiral Beatty, the Minister of the Kirk took as his text: —

"Gad, a troop shall overcome him; but he shall overcome at the last."

That passage from Holy Writ represented faithfully the temper in which the nation met defeat.

I was given two or three illustrations of the change wrought by disaster in the public spirit. I have already set forth in another chapter the difficulties we were experiencing with the Unions in effecting a searching comb-out of their men to provide recruits for the Army. Amongst other Labour organisations, we experienced a reluctance amounting to practical resistance on the part of one of the most powerful — the Miners' Federation. We had decided to take 50,000 young men out of the mines, but had hitherto failed to secure the effective coöperation of the Union. After the March defeat I invited the miners' leaders to an interview at 10, Downing Street. I was informed that they were still somewhat difficult. I had a map carefully prepared to show the depth of the German penetration on the British Front and the number of the divisions they had massed opposite our lines. Before starting any conversation I asked the leaders to accompany me to examine this map. They studied it with increasing gravity of mien. They saw its implication before I explained it and emphasised what it meant to their comrades in France. When they resumed their seats after a thorough examination of this startling chart, I saw at once that I should experience no further difficulty in securing their assent and assistance. Their chairman, Robert Smillie, was one of the most remarkable Labour leaders of his generation. He was inflexible and indomitable, but he was a sincere patriot and he was deeply moved by the irrefutable testimony of the map as to his country's dire need. He made no further objection to our request and it was evident to all present that he carried with him the judgment and emotion of all his colleagues.

Subsequently when the actual process of combing out in the mines had started, I had alarming appeals, not from the miners themselves, but from the Coal Controller as to the disastrous effect upon the production of coal. One protest entered by the Controller at a Cabinet meeting throws a remarkable light upon the spirit in which the workers faced a national emergency. He came to the War Cabinet to complain that he was encountering considerable trouble in the mines, not on account of the resistance of these men to being thrust in to khaki, but because when a miner was taken out of the pit and sent to the Army, his "pals" wanted to join him. He informed us that there were so many incidents of this kind that it was becoming a serious embarrassment to the Managers.

APPENDIX A

EXTRACT FROM A REPORT OF THE SECOND MEETING OF THE
FIFTH SESSION OF THE SUPREME WAR COUNCIL, HELD IN
THE CHAMBRE DES NOTAIRES AT ABBEVILLE ON THURS-
DAY, MAY 2ND, 1918

M. Clemenceau said that he understood that Signor
Orlando was anxious to raise the question of the Beauvais
Agreement. This agreement had not been formally presented
to the Italian Government for their acceptance. The French,
British and American Governments had agreed to nominate
General Foch as the soldier in supreme command of the
Allied Armies in France subject to certain conditions. General Foch had to this effect a letter of appointment written
by M. Poincaré and countersigned by M. Clemenceau. The
question was whether General Foch's powers should be extended to Italy, and whether the Italian Government would
agree to this extension.

Signor Orlando stated that he had already agreed. When
the armies fighting in Italy reached the same condition as
those fighting in France, Italy agreed to a single General
Commanding-in-Chief, and this General should be General
Foch.

M. Clemenceau said that this formula was too vague.
Who was to judge? He thought that there was no objection
to the course proposed, provided always that in the event
of General Foch giving an order which the Italian Commander-in-Chief regarded as contrary to the interests of
the army under his command he could appeal to his own
Government. That proviso existed in the case of the Beauvais
Agreement. Further, the agreement concerned the command

of the Allied Armies in France only — not in America or Great Britain.

Signor Orlando thought that the whole question depended largely on the spirit of accord existing between the Generals concerned.

M. Clemenceau thought that as the American Government had accepted General Foch's jurisdiction over the American troops in France there was no reason why the Italian Government should not equally fall in line.

Signor Orlando pointed out that the above agreement as it stood applied to the three Armies in France. If at any time there were three Allied Armies in Italy which had to meet a big enemy offensive, then he thought that his Government would accept the principle of a supreme commander.

General Foch said that Signor Orlando had stated that if at any time the Allied Armies were fighting side by side in Italy, then there should be a Commander-in-Chief in supreme command. But even if that were not the case, in his view it was most important that Italy should accept and adopt the same system of coördination as the other Allies had in France. It was greatly to the interest of General Diaz to know what was the situation at any time in France, and what were the plans of the Allied Commanders there; similarly, the officer in supreme command in France must know exactly what the situation was in Italy so that he could make his plans accordingly. The only thing to his mind was to apply the system of coördination to Italy. This did not at all mean the application of the supreme command to Italy, but only a complete coördination of system.

Signor Orlando stated that he had tried on the previous day to express his views clearly by saying that the Beauvais Agreement could be considered from two angles of vision: —

1. It established the principle of an effective command of the Allied troops in the same theatre of war. This did not

at present apply outside France, but he would accept the principle when it was thought necessary to apply it to Italy.

2.   The application of the principle of coördination to all the Allied Armies. This also he was prepared to accept, but he wished to point out that so far he was only a third party to the bargain and not one of the contracting parties in respect of the Beauvais Agreement.

Mr. Lloyd George said that he drew a distinction between (*a*) coördination, (*b*) the functions of General Foch as supreme commander. The agreement decided upon at Beauvais marked a notable advance upon that which had been accepted at Doullens. General Foch as Generalissimo had functions in France which did not apply to the Italian Army. General Foch actually gave orders as to the disposition of the troops in France. He thought that they should invite Signor Orlando not to accept the Beauvais Agreement as extended to cover Italy, but the Doullens Agreement which merely coördinated the combined efforts of the Allies from the Channel to the Adriatic.

M. Clemenceau said they were all agreed about General Foch's powers in France, which covered the French, British and American troops there.

General Foch pointed out that the Doullens Agreement was a dead letter and had been superseded by the Beauvais Convention. He deprecated the resuscitation of a buried agreement.

Mr. Lloyd George thought that the Council at present was arguing about two different matters. He thought that Signor Orlando would certainly agree to General Foch commanding such Italian troops as might be in or be sent to France, but he himself would go further, and he would ask Signor Orlando to accept the principle of coördination under General Foch extended to the shores of the Adriatic.

M. Clemenceau said that that was all he himself desired.

General Foch said that the Doullens Agreement was to coordinate the actions on the Western Front. The Beauvais Agreement, however, went further.

Signor Orlando said that the Beauvais Agreement was dual in character; it covered both coördination and the principle of supreme command. He himself accepted the principle of coördination.

CHAPTER II

THE MAURICE DEBATE

AFTER the second German offensive of 1918 had been successfully fought to a standstill a controversy arose as to the conditions that led to the March defeat. This controversy threatened the life of the Government and in the sequel had a disruptive effect upon the fortunes of the Liberal Party.

Those who were anxious to escape from their responsibility for the heavy defeat which our Army had sustained in the first spring offensive attributed it entirely to the neglect of the Government to provide the necessary quota to make up the heavy losses sustained in the autumn by our fighting forces in Flanders. It was represented that the British Army had on March 21st been overwhelmed by an enemy which considerably outnumbered them and that there were no reserves available to support our hard-pressed Army. As Haig put it when he met Gough after the defeat, "We cannot fight without men." Most fantastic figures were in circulation as to the wretched remnant of troops with which Haig had been expected to fight the greatest battle of the War against the whole might of an immense German Army. A

conspicuous example of this pernicious gossip is a statement made at this time by Mr. Arnold Bennett — which
constitutes one of his most imaginative "Old Wives' Tales"
— that the British infantry had been reduced to 250,000
men!

The militarist Press took up the cue. There was a
propagandist campaign organised in the Press, in social
circles, in the clubs and in the Lobbies of the House, and it
ultimately culminated in the cabal which, after working
assiduously but in vain to overthrow the Government for
attempting to organise a General Reserve behind our
threatened Army, thought that, after repeated failures, their
opportunity had at last arrived. Since the War the apologists
of G.H.Q. have repeated the censure without giving to it
any statistical support. I feel therefore that it is incumbent
on me to dispose finally of this calumny by giving the official
figures supplied to the Government by the War Office. I
shall quote no figures except those officially supplied by the
appropriate military authorities at the time. My principal
witness will be Sir Frederick Maurice, the fizzling cracker
that was chosen to blow up the Government.

I have already stated very fully the difficulties experienced by the Government in raising fresh recruits for
the fighting forces. It was the common experience of every
belligerent country in the fifth year of the War. In each and
all of those countries the military Staffs were exerting the
whole of their influence to extract the last available men for
the shambles. In every country they criticised and bullied
their Governments for keeping fit men at home to do essential
work instead of sending them to the Army. In Germany
Ludendorff complained that there were not munitions for
the front and that the enemy were much better supplied.
In the same document he grumbled that there were too many
fit men in the workshops and that they ought to be pulled

out and sent to the army. These contradictory attacks on politicians were only the common form of insensate nagging by those who have failed to make the best use of the material placed at their disposal. They ascribe their own shortcomings to defects in quality or quantity of the means with which they have been so lavishly equipped. What were the charges brought against the Government by some of our armchair soldiers?

1. That we ought to have combed out more closely the essential industries of the country to make up for the abnormal and underestimated losses of Passchendaele.

2. That we had deliberately and knowingly left our Army to face vastly superior numbers of Germans without taking the necessary measures to reinforce them, because we had not the courage to face the labour clamour that might ensue.

3. That we wasted a needlessly large number of troops on "side-shows" which were not in the least helpful to the winning of the War.

As to the first charge, I have dealt with it fully in my chapter on man power. I claim that there I have shown that from the point of view of the effective prosecution of the War, the Government made a much more effective use of the man power of the nation than the Generals made of the fine manhood placed at their disposal. We did our best to avoid wasting this valuable asset of the nation. Will anyone who has fairly read the grim story of our military futilities make the same claim for the Allied Army leaders — in Russia, France or Britain?

As to the second charge, that the Government, either through carelessness or cowardice, had allowed our troops on the Western Front to be so outnumbered that they had no chance to put up a successful fight against the German onset, I will now give the actual figures supplied to me at the time by the very men at the War Office who, when they were disgruntled by supersession, became our principal critics. Sir Frederick Maurice, who subsequently instigated the Parliamentary onslaught on the Government, was up to the end of April on the Staff at the War Office as Director of Military Operations, and it was he who kept the Cabinet informed from time to time as to the relative strength of the German and Allied forces on the Western Front. On the 13th of March — a week before the great battle — he imparted to the Cabinet the information that "the enemy on that front had an approximate rifle strength of 1,370,000 men with 15,700 guns while the total Allied rifle strength on the Western Front numbered 1,500,000 infantry and 16,600 guns. The relative strength of a British division was slightly larger than that of a German division." This gave us a superiority of 130,000 men in infantry alone. If the numbers of men employed in the artillery, in tanks and in aeroplanes are added, the superiority was then considerably greater. On March 23rd, the third day of the great battle, we were given fresh figures. War Office statistics were always like the desert sands. Any change in the wind either converted humps into hollows or hollows into humps — according to the direction of the wind. Here they are as they were given to the Cabinet by Sir Frederick Maurice, this time corroborated by a less mercurial arithmetician, General Macdonogh, the Director of Military Intelligence: German rifle strength 1,402,800; Allies 1,418,000: a superiority still which was the equivalent of two German divisions. This is without reckoning our supremacy in the air, and in guns, ammunition, machine-guns, tanks and transport, all involving a highly effective addition to our combatant strength in men.

I have already quoted the War Office figure as to guns. On the 20th of March they furnished us with a comparison of Allied and enemy strength in other arms.

Machine-guns

    Allies 100,000

    Enemy 64,000

Cavalry

    Allies 84,000

    Enemy 38,000

In the battle dismounted cavalry formed a valuable reserve. Without their horses the cavalry proved to be an efficient fighting force. In tanks we had an overwhelming advantage. In at least one great battle this superiority gave us the victory. On April 10th, after the Battle of Amiens had been fought to a standstill and the British Army were facing the second day of a second battle on the Western Front, Sir Frederick Maurice gave to the Cabinet what he called "some particulars as to the relative strengths of the Allied and enemy divisions at the present time on the Western Front." He assumed that the Portuguese divisions were "knocked out." They would therefore not be in the computation. The enemy infantry was given as 1,370,000; the battle and the loss of the Portuguese had reduced the Allied rifle strength to 1,450,000 men. Six or seven German divisions had been brought from Russia since the first battle began. Maurice reported these as compensating for German losses in the attack. He put these losses at 200,000. Seven full German divisions would not make 60,000 men — barely 50,000 in rifle strength. In all these estimates there is a straining to exaggerate enemy strength and to minimise our own. On the other hand, full allowance is made for our own losses and there is the choice of rifles as the basis of comparison, which gives no fair idea of our real superiority in combatant power. Nevertheless, after a disastrous battle in which Haig complained that he could not fight without men, the Allies on the Western Front had still an infantry superiority of 80,000. Had the superiority of men employed in artillery, tanks, aircraft and cavalry been included, it would have been at least 150,000. And yet our Commander-in-Chief could not hold entrenchments dug and wired against an attack from inferior numbers of troops which he had described as being of poor quality. Why? Because he had not enough men, forsooth! It is an insult to the British and French soldiers who fought with such incredible valour. If the Allied superiority in men and mechanical power was not organised in such a way as to be utilised to the best advantage on the day of the battle, whose fault was that?

These figures were volunteered to the Cabinet by Sir Frederick Maurice on April 10th. We had no further reports which would disturb the confidence created by General Maurice's careful and encouraging analyses of the intelligence received from G.H.Q. as to the statistical position. On April 18th the C.I.G.S., who said he had "only just returned from France", reported that the British and French had three more divisions in reserve than the Germans. This did not include the Americans who had two or three complete and trained divisions in reserve. Alas! all of a sudden our superiority disappeared in a week-end! I woke up on Monday, the 22nd of April, to read in the Weekly Summary prepared by the General Staff that an Allied superiority of 86,000 rifles had been converted into a German superiority of 330,000! Had some catastrophe befallen the Allies unawares, like the pestilence that destroyed Sennacherib's army in a single night? Our reports from France showed that the Germans were suffering much heavier losses than the Allies. The German official figures when they reached us later confirmed our estimates. But the disaster that tore such a yawning chasm in the Allied battalions occurred not on the blood-stained fields of France or Flanders but in a carpeted chamber of the War Office. The devastation of our ranks was not wrought by German artillery but by a British fountain pen. What had occurred to precipitate such a calamity? Sir Henry Wilson was desirous of securing a D.M.O. in whom he had greater confidence than he had in the then occupant of that office — so he substituted General P. de B. Radcliffe for General Sir Frederick Maurice. I do not wish to discuss the comparative merits of these two officers. I am only concerned to point out the shattering effect of the change upon our poor harassed infantry in France and our humbugged public at home. The Germans had an unexpected reinforcement of 200,000 bayonets, and 120,000 of our riflemen dissolved in the mist. And the American divisions had been wiped out altogether or relegated to a footnote as unconsidered trifles. What unheard-of disaster! I was naturally staggered at this inexplicable transformation. I realised that the battle had been transferred to the Home Front. I therefore dictated the following Memorandum for the General Staff in order to obtain from them some explanation of this catastrophic change in our military position.

"SECRETARY OF STATE FOR WAR

"I am entirely at a loss to understand the figures of Allied and enemy rifle strength printed in last week's summary of the military situation. Before I made my statement on the introduction of the Man-power Bill in the House of Commons I asked the Staff to supply me with information as to the strength of the opposing forces on the Western Front at the commencement of the battle. Those figures showed a slight Allied superiority in infantry, a three and a half to one superiority in cavalry, a considerable superiority in artillery, a very considerable superiority in machine-guns and also a decided superiority in aircraft. No figures were however supplied of the numbers of aeroplanes on either side. Now I am told that after four weeks of the fighting, the enemy rifle strength is greater by 333,000 than that of the Allies. What possible explanation can there be of this? The attempted explanation is surely an inadequate one. What is it? 'Since then the situation has been materially altered by the reduction of six British divisions, the disappearance for fighting purposes of the Portuguese contingent and the arrival of 18 more German divisions from Russia, Italy and the Balkans.'

"1. This is the first I have heard of 18 divisions having arrived from the East and the Balkans since the battle began, for the figures supplied me by the Staff were figures of the forces on 21st March. However, even assuming there were 18, the net addition to the German strength does not even approximate 333,000 rifles.

"The disappearance of the eight Allied divisions at the outside represents a loss of between 70,000 and 80,000. The addition of the 18 German would represent another 135,000. Add this figure to the 80,000 minus on the Allied side; the total is 215,000.

"But the writer of this paragraph has given no credit for the divisions that have arrived in France on the Allied side since 21st March. There have been two British and four French. These represent at least 50,000 rifles. Deduct that figure from the 215,-000. That leaves 165,000, which is exactly half the superiority claimed for the Germans at the present date. Unless therefore the figures supplied to me by the Staff a fortnight ago were deplorably misleading, this paper ought instantly to be revised and the Ministers amongst whom it is circulated warned of the serious error for which it is responsible. If on the other hand I was misled a fortnight ago and the House of Commons and the country through me, then it is time that the Department responsible for information should be thoroughly overhauled.

"2. But my criticism of the figures in the summary of military information does not end here. Machine-gunners have been cut out as if they were no addition to the rifle strength of the forces. Why is that? Is it because the Allies happen to have a very considerable superiority in machine-guns and it does not suit the writer of this paper to insert any figure which minimises the German superiority? The same observation applies to this omission to include the cavalry. Many French, and I believe British, cavalry divisions have been added to the rifle strength of the Allied

Armies, and are now fighting in the line as infantry. Our superiority in cavalry is between 40,000 and 50,000. Why should that be left out?

"How does he make out that 205 enemy divisions represent 1,617,000 rifle strength? I understand that the enemy have nine battalions in each division and that each battalion is 750 strong. That comes to less than 1,400,000 rifle strength. Something was said about a week ago about the battalion strength of the enemy being increased to 850 before the battle. If that were done it must have been either by the addition of machine-gunners or by taking 180,000 men out of the depots behind the line. Should it be the former then machine-gunners ought to be added to the calculation of the British and French rifle strength. Should it be the latter, then 180,000 ought to be deducted out of the 400,000 reserves which the Germans are supposed to have had ready for drafts at the commencement of the battle. If the latter should turn out to be the case, then taking the German casualties at 300,000, even assuming the whole of their 400,000 drafts were infantry men — which is a big assumption — the Germans must already be 80,000 short in the rifle strength of their divisions.

"From any point of view this document is extraordinarily slipshod, and I suggest that a thorough investigation be made as to how it came to be prepared and who is responsible for editing and issuing it.

D. Ll. G."

"22.4.18."

That day I brought the amazing production of the War Office Staff before the Cabinet and demanded an explanation from the C.I.G.S. Neither Maurice, the late D.M.O., nor Radcliffe, his successor, was present. Sir Henry Wilson did not seem to have seen the report and was quite unable to explain the discrepancy between the figures submitted by Maurice to the Cabinet a few days since and those which appeared in the Weekly Survey. He disclaimed all responsibility for the revised figures, but promised to institute inquiries and report later on. I found that the Director of Military Intelligence, to whom all reports of enemy strength were brought, and by whom they were carefully sifted, knew nothing of this fresh estimate. The new D.M.O. was not in charge at the time it was prepared. At that time Maurice was responsible. It was said of Wellington that his long nose was worth so many thousands to the British Army. Of Sir Frederick Maurice it could be said that when his nose was put out of joint it was worth 400,000 bayonets to the enemy.

It was understood that Maurice was hopeful of receiving either a Command or a Staff appointment in France, but Haig was not eager to be so patently associated with a political intrigue in England, especially over a personal quarrel which did not concern him. The fate of Robertson had not moved him. Why should he worry over a much smaller man? So Maurice did not go to France. He spent his unsought vacation in caballing against the Government with its enemies in Parliament and in the Press. His judgment was never specially sound and now that he was deprived of his responsible post on the Staff it became for the time being completely unhinged. There is no other charitable explanation for his conduct. He may have taken counsel with friends: if so, those may have been somebody's friends, but they certainly were not his. He wrote to the papers for publication a letter which condemned as inaccurate a statement made in the House of Commons on military matters by two members of the Government — Mr. Bonar Law and myself. He was still in the service as an officer. Such knowledge as he possessed on these questions must have been acquired as a member of the Staff. In fact, he claimed that his knowledge on one point arose from his being present at a War Council. He did not seek permission to reveal it. Had he been an officer in the British Expeditionary Force and written a letter challenging the accuracy of an official *communiqué* which he alleged misrepresented the truth about a battle in which he had taken part, he would have been promptly courtmartialled. That his allegations were false, of course aggravated the offence. The terms of Sir Frederick Maurice's letter to the Press were as follows: —

"To the Editor of —— :

"Sir, — My attention has been called to answers given in the House of Commons on 23rd April by Mr. Bonar Law, to questions put by Mr. G. Lambert, Colonel Burn and Mr. Pringle as to the extension of the British Front in France (Hansard, Vol. 105, No. 34, p. 815). These answers contain certain misstatements which in sum give a totally misleading impression of what occurred. This is not the place to enter into a discussion as to all the facts, but Hansard's report of the incident concludes —

" 'Mr. Pringle: Was this matter entered into at the Versailles War Council at any time?'

" 'Mr. Bonar Law: This particular matter was not dealt with at all by the Versailles War Council.'

"I was at Versailles when the question was decided by the Supreme War Council to whom it had been referred.

"This is the latest of a series of misstatements which have been made recently in the House of Commons by the present Government.

"On 9th April the Prime Minister said: —

" 'What was the position at the beginning of the battle? Notwithstanding the heavy casualties in 1917 the Army in France was considerably stronger on the 1st January, 1918, than on the 1st January, 1917.' (Hansard, Vol. 104, No. 24, p. 1328.)

"That statement implies that Sir Douglas Haig's fighting strength on the eve of the great battle which began on 21st March had not been diminished.

"That is not correct.

"Again, in the same speech the Prime Minister said: 'In Mesopotamia there is only one white division at all and in Egypt and in Palestine there are only three white divisions; the rest are either Indians or mixed with a very small proportion of British troops in those divisions — I am referring to the infantry divisions.' (*Ibid.*, p. 1327.)

"That is not correct.

"Now, Sir, this letter is not the result of a military conspiracy. It has been seen by no soldier. I am by descent and conviction as sincere a democrat as the Prime Minister, and the last thing I want is to see the Government of our country in the hands of soldiers.

"My reasons for taking the very grave step of writing this letter are that the statements quoted above are known to a large number of soldiers to be incorrect, and this knowledge is breeding such distrust of the Government as can only end in impairing the splendid morale of our troops at a time when everything possible should be done to raise it.

"I have therefore decided, fully realising the consequences to myself, that my duty as a citizen must override my duty as a soldier, and I ask you to publish this letter, in the hope that Parliament may see fit to order an investigation into the statements I have made.

I am,

Yours faithfully,

F. MAURICE, Major-General."

"20, Kensington Park Gardens,
    6th May."

I must enter into this transaction in some detail not only because it represented the last of a series of efforts made by the opposition and their military confederates to embarrass and overthrow the Government at a critical moment when we needed all our faculties of nerve and mind to deal with a grave emergency, but because it played a dominant part in the General Election at the end of the year and had a great deal to do with the rout which befell Mr. Asquith's followers at the 1918 Election. Neither Bonar

Law nor I alluded to the incident during the whole contest, but the electorate had not forgotten nor did they forgive those who engineered or took part in this conspiracy at such an anxious stage in the War, and the Mauriceites were annihilated at the polls.

It soon became evident that Sir Frederick Maurice was the tool of astuter men who used him for their own personal and partisan purposes. Before the letter ever appeared, questions were put in the House by bitter opponents of the Government based on information which had obviously come from military sources. When the Maurice letter first appeared, the Opposition Press hailed it as a justification for turning out the Government. The *Westminster Gazette* (since defunct), a paper inspired by Mr. M'Kenna, the Deputy Leader of the Opposition, promptly wrote, "There must be a drastic change in all this, and if it involves a change of Government that must come too." The Government had lost the confidence of the country, continued the article. It announced the first move of the Opposition — a Parliamentary Committee to institute a searching inquiry into General Maurice's allegations. The *Times* demanded that the inquiry should extend beyond those questions, and that it should include such questions as man power — whether the Army had made a proper use of the men the country had already provided — also the Versailles Council and finally the Unity of Command. I felt that such an inquiry conducted in the middle of a great battle would be highly dangerous. It would paralyse all war directions, for it would distract the attention of Ministers and of the Staff from urgent affairs; it would divide the nation, and such divisions would no doubt extend to the Army. I was therefore in favour of taking the Opposition challenge on the floor of the House of Commons at the earliest opportunity and having done with it one way or the other. Mr. Bonar

Law, however, felt that his personal honour was impugned, and he insisted on a tribunal of two judges to investigate the charges. Mr. Asquith demanded a Select Committee. Mr. Bonar Law offered a judicial Tribunal of Judges. This proposal was rejected by the Opposition. Upon which Mr. Asquith gave notice that he would move for the appointment of a Select Committee.

The motion for the Debate tabled by Mr. Asquith demanded: —

"That a Select Committee of this House be appointed to inquire into the allegations of incorrectness in certain Statements of Ministers of the Crown to this House, contained in a letter of Major-General Maurice, late Director of Military Operations, published in the Press on the 7th day of May."

This motion was acclaimed by the enemies of the Government as a direct challenge to its authority, and the Opposition Press canvassed in headlines the chances of the Administration falling and the possibility of forming an alternative Ministry. The Government, they argued, had accepted the principle of an inquiry by proposing a Judicial Tribunal. But the only verdict the Opposition would accept would be one by a Select Committee. The nature of the evidence to be examined was such that it could not be laid before a Select Committee. Therefore the Government must resign!

On the following day, May 9th, 1918, the Maurice Debate took place in the House of Commons. In proposing his motion, Mr. Asquith somewhat surprisingly disclaimed any intention of attacking the Administration. "Nor again," he declared, "is the Motion which I am about to make, either in intention or effect, as I have seen it rather absurdly described, a Vote of Censure upon the Government." Seeing that the newspapers supporting him had for the past two days been making it abundantly clear that the Government could not possibly accept the motion and retain office, this disclaimer deceived no one.

Mr. Asquith urged the merits of a Parliamentary Committee of Inquiry, and the demerits of any other kind of inquiry, and dramatically asked, "What is the alternative?"

"Get on with the War!" suggested Mr. Stanton, a Miners' Member; a remark which Mr. Asquith characterised as "very irrelevant." The interjection was, however, received with such a cheer as I have rarely heard in the House.

In my reply, I began by pointing out the inconsistency which had marked General Maurice's conduct.

"A General, a distinguished General, who, for good or bad reasons, has ceased to hold an office which he has occupied for two years, challenges, after he has left office, statements made by two Ministers during the time he was in that office. During the time he was in such office he never challenged those statements, when he not only had access to official information, but when he had access to the Ministers themselves."

General Maurice had been in daily contact with me. On the days following the speech he now challenged, he had been present at the War Cabinet. Neither at those meetings nor privately had he protested, either to me as Premier or to his own Chiefs, the Secretary of State for War of the C.I.G.S., about a matter which he now felt to be so vital as to warrant him in breaking King's Regulations and setting an example of indiscipline to the whole Army.

I then dealt with the issue of a Select Committee, proposed by Mr. Asquith. I pointed out that while the issue was purely one of fact, which two impartial judges could swiftly settle, it involved reference to a mass of confidential information, the official military secrets of ourselves and our Allies. It would be highly undesirable to have this exposed to a Committee of the House, particularly to one on which Party passions were certain to be running high. On the other hand, it had become clear since Tuesday that the judicial panel proposed by the Government was not acceptable to the Opposition. The hostile Press "which is egging on my right hon. friend, prodding him, and suggesting that he ought to do this and the other to embarrass the Government", had made it perfectly clear that no statement, no decision of any secret tribunal, would ever be accepted.

I had therefore abandoned the idea of arranging for an inquiry, and I proceeded instead to give to the House the essential facts in rebuttal of General Maurice's charges. In regard to the question of relative strength of the British Army on January 1st, 1917, and January 1st, 1918, I showed that the figures on which was based the reply to a question on this point on April 18th were obtained from a note supplied by General Maurice's own Department.

As a matter of fact — although I could not quote these figures to the House, as it would have involved publishing a secret War Office return — the official war figures, supplied by the D.M.O.'s own Department, on which my original assertion had been based, showed that the total ration strength of the B.E.F. in France on January 1st, 1917, was 1,594,000; and that on January 1st, 1918, it was 1,970,000. These figures are inclusive of certain non-military labour units — Chinese and Indian, etc. If these are omitted, the strength of the troops themselves, combatant and non-batant, shown in the published "Statistics of the Military Effort of the British Empire", is found to be: —

1st January, 1917	1,591,745
1st March, 1917	1,802,048
1st January, 1918	1,828,616
1st March, 1918	1,886,073

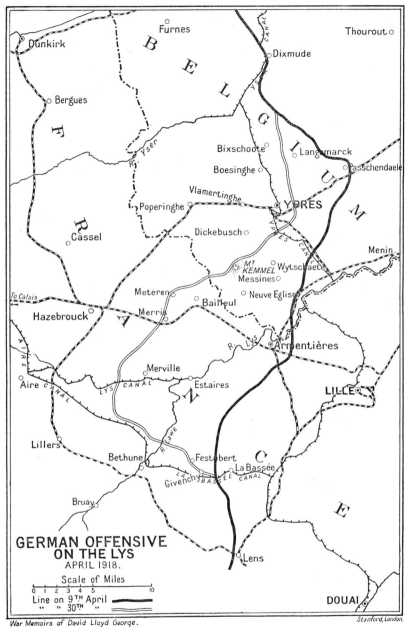

GERMAN OFFENSIVE
ON THE LYS
APRIL 1918.

Scale of Miles

0 1 2 3 4 5   10

Line on 9TH April ━━━━━
   " " 30TH "

War Memoirs of David Lloyd George.

Stanford, London.

The figures given me by General Maurice's Department on April 18th, showing combatant strength only in the B.E.F., France, were: —

> January, 1917 1,253,000
> January, 1918 1,298,000

I quoted to the House the conclusion of the covering Note from General Sir Frederick Maurice's Department, which ran: —

"From the statement included, it will be seen that the combatant strength of the British Army was greater on the 1st January, 1918, than on the 1st January, 1917."

On this I remarked: —

"This comes from General Maurice's own Department, nine days after I made that statement! I am not depending on the fact that all these men who were ruled out as 'non-combatants' are an essential part of the strength of the British Army in France. I have this statement, that, as regards those who were technically treated as combatants, we were better off on the 1st January, 1918, than on the 1st January, 1917. As a matter of fact, there was an increase as between the 1st January and March, 1918, but it just happened that I thought I would take the first month of the year."

I further pointed out that as regards our strength relative to the enemy in March, 1918, statements had been made by General Maurice himself on March 27th and April 3rd which had appeared in the American Press, declaring that —

". . . on the whole front, the opposing forces at the beginning of the battle were approximately equal, and therefore the readjustment of the balance on the battlefield is only a matter of time."

If there were in fact anything inaccurate in the statement made by me, which General Maurice had challenged, it was based on information and figures supplied by the General's own Department, so that Maurice would himself have been responsible for misleading the Premier and through him the public.

Passing to the question of the number of British divisions in the East, I said there was no doubt as to there being only one in Mesopotamia. As for the number in Egypt and Palestine, I had been informed in the Cabinet by the C.I.G.S., in Maurice's presence, that there were only three, which was at that time the official position, though I had since learnt that the reconstitution of the other divisions by the substitution of Indian for British troops had not then been fully completed. If there had been delay in substituting Indian for white troops the military authorities were responsible. The minute of the meeting, recording the C.I.G.S.'s statement had been submitted to Maurice, who suggested no correction. It was grotesque to charge me with attempting to mislead the public when I quoted an official statement supplied to me by the Department for which the General who was now impugning my accuracy was directly responsible.

As regards the extension of the British Front, I pointed out first that General Maurice was not, as he had alleged, himself present in the Council Chamber at Versailles when discussion turned on this issue, and that the implication deliberately given in his letter that he was thus present was false. Secondly, I made it clear that the extension of the British Front had been agreed between Pétain and Haig and according to Haig's own statement to the Council had already been carried out. The extension discussed at the Council was a further one, which never came into effect. And in the third place I dealt with the suggestion that the actual extension was one forced on Robertson and Haig against their judgment by the War Cabinet. Carefully choosing my phrases in order not to give offence to our Ally, I told the House how the French had insisted, as a military necessity, on our taking over more of the line; how Robertson had agreed to it, subject to its being left to Haig, in discussion with Pétain, to decide how much he felt himself capable of taking over; and how, far from the decision being made by the War Cabinet and forced on an unwilling military Command, it had proceeded from the urgent demand of the French military authorities, agreed to by our own, and carried out by the Commanders-in-Chief in joint consultation. In this connection I read to the House a Memorandum of October 18th, 1917, by General Sir William Robertson, confirming the fact that no decision had been taken by the political leaders behind Sir Douglas Haig's back. The Memorandum was as follows: —

"At the recent Boulogne Conference between the Prime Minister, M. Painlevé, General Foch and myself, the question of extending our front was raised by the French representatives. The reply was given that, while in principle we were of course ready to do whatever could be done, the matter was one which could not be discussed in the absence of Sir Douglas Haig, or during the continuance of the present operations, and that due regard must also be had to the plan of operations for next year. It was suggested that it would be best for the Field-Marshal to come to an arrangement with General Pétain when this could be done. So far as I am aware, no further formal discussion has taken place, and the matter therefore cannot be regarded as 'decided.' Further, I feel sure that the War Cabinet would not think of deciding such an important question, without first obtaining Sir Douglas Haig's views. I am replying to him in the above sense."

I also quoted from the War Cabinet Minutes of October 24, 1917, to show that the decision they then took with regard to the extension of the front was to approve the policy suggested to them in this matter by Sir William

Robertson. I sketched the further history of the matter, which confirmed the fact that while Sir Douglas Haig had enjoyed the full approval and authority of the War Cabinet in the steps he had taken to extend his line, the measure had been the result, not of Cabinet dictation, but of the pressure of the French Government and military authorities — pressure which he could not well resist.

The real moral of the discussion about extension of the British Front was the necessity for unity of command.

"That question of the extension of the line would never have arisen if we had had that unity. Instead of one Army and one Commander responsible for one part of the line and another Army and another Commander responsible for another part of the line, one united Army — one united Command — responsible for the whole and for every part was the only method of safety. I am glad we have got that at last. It was not so much a question of the length of the line held by one force, and the length of the line held by another. It was a question of the reserves which were massed behind. If we put two or three more divisions into the line, there were two or three fewer divisions which we could put into the reserves, but the French had two or three more divisions which they could put into the reserves."

I expressed regret that Mr. Asquith should have failed to deprecate General Maurice's grave breach of discipline, which set a most subversive example to the Army at large. I concluded by appealing for national unity in face of the very serious situation with which the nation was confronted. This kind of controversy wasted time and energy which the Government should be using to prepare for a fresh German onslaught.

"I really implore, for our common country, the fate of which is in the balance now and in the next few weeks, that there should be an end of this sniping."

Sir Edward Carson appealed to Mr. Asquith to withdraw his motion, but in vain. No doubt he had given his followers pledges to take it to a division, and could not draw back. It was defeated by 293 votes to 106. The Opposition Press could not conceal the fact next day that they had been defeated, not only by votes, but by the circumstance that on examination they had been shown to have no case.

General Maurice was dealt with by the military authorities, who forthwith placed him on retired pay.

CHAPTER III

STROKE AND COUNTERSTROKE

1. THE GERMAN SUMMER OFFENSIVE

By the middle of May the tremendous German assaults on
the British line had been brought to a standstill without their
achieving any of their objectives, cumulative or alternative.
The British Army had been beaten back, but it had not been
broken. At the end of the two battles it still presented an
impenetrable front of resistance to its redoubtable assailant,
and owing to reinforcements of men and material it was on
the whole stronger than it was when the offensive began.
The German onslaught had not succeeded in its efforts
either to create a gap between the British and French Armies
or to reach the Channel Ports, and it had completely failed
to destroy our Army. Ludendorff's brilliant tactical triumphs
had accomplished no strategic purpose. In fact, they weakened the German Army by the heavy casualties that it

sustained and by considerably extending its front at a time when it had no reserves to spare. These failures ultimately proved fatal to Ludendorff's last chance of forcing a decisive battle before the Americans were ready to throw in a sufficient number of troops to convert an approximate equality in numbers into a definite and widening inferiority for the Germans. Time was on the Allied side. Two precious months had already been expended in vain attempts to compel a decision. The enormous reserves, which had been carefully and skillfully assembled in order to overwhelm the British Army before the French could come to its aid, had been largely dissipated. The German casualties were enormous, and the fresh divisions brought up from Russia since the 21st of March were insufficient to fill the gap. Never again could Ludendorff mass so formidable a striking force.

The Reichstag Report on the offensive and its failure puts the position quite fairly: —

". . . Strategically the great offensive did not succeed. But the tactical results were extraordinarily large. The attackers had broken through the enemy positions in a few days to a depth of 60 kilometres — far deeper than the English and the French had ever advanced in massed battles lasting for months. The booty was immeasurable; 90,000 prisoners had been taken. The method of attack had been brilliantly justified, and the troops too had fought magnificently. But the great tactical victory had involved a heavy sacrifice. Some 90 divisions altogether had had to be thrown in. That was the big shadow which fell across the victory." [1]

General Von Kuhl, in his report to the Reichstag, speaking of the spring offensive, said: —

"With every month the hostile superiority increased, while the reinforcements of the German Army became continually scarcer and were no longer adequate to make good even approximately our losses. . . .

[1] "Die Ursachen des Deutschen Zusammenbruchs im Jahre 1918", Vol. III, p. 137.

"Only a limited number of divisions could be adequately equipped for the attack, while the weak divisions holding the front stopped permanently in the line, without getting time for rest or training. Thus the troops were gradually getting used up, while the enemy was getting a substantial addition to his fighting strength through the arrival of the Americans and through the new fighting weapon of the tanks." [1]

Our military advisers, in their computation of the relative strengths of the armies, always ignored the immense advantage which our undoubted mechanical superiority gave to us in fighting strength. This amateurish insistence upon numerical rather than mechanical strength is surprising in a body of men who were supposed to be experts. But the Germans realised only too well its shattering effect upon their troops. Both the Reichstag Report and Hindenburg in his Memoirs dwell sadly upon the disastrous results of our superiority not merely in tanks but in guns, in ammunition and in aeroplanes.

But the German failure was not entirely attributable to these causes. There were other elements. It was undoubtedly the newly achieved unity of command on the Allied side which enabled the Allies for the first time to make the fullest use of all their resources in men and material. When the Germans found that Foch in his new capacity could treat the front as one, and from south to north swing fresh and vigorous French divisions to reinforce the British line — as happened in Flanders in April — or send British divisions from north to south to support the French if they were hard pressed, they realised that they were confronted with a novel factor which would profoundly influence the Allied strategy. There was an end to the condition of things which existed before the first offensive and which one of the German Generals had summarised when he said: "The

[1] *Ibid.,* pp. 188 and 189.

French will not break their legs in their hurry to help the British." That calculation had inspired their strategy. They could depend upon it no longer.

The Reichstag Report acknowledges the part which unity of command played in the German defeat: —

"The German attack had utterly smashed up the English Fifth Army. On the English side this was described as the biggest defeat which the English had suffered in their history. A wide gap appeared between the English and the French. Field-Marshal Haig made up his mind to withdraw in the direction of the sea, General Pétain thought above all about covering Paris. Preparations had already been put in hand for evacuating Paris, and calculations made about the embarking of the English Army. The separation of the English from the French was imminent. . . .

"The phenomenon, which appears in almost all coalition wars, had been repeated: in a moment of acute danger, each of the Allies thinks of his own interests. For this cause it marked a turning point in the War, that in this extremity the Entente was successful in setting up unity of command. . . .

"The Entente has to thank General Foch for successfully subordinating the divergent interests of the Allies to a higher, united purpose, for closing the gaps and organising resistance to the separation of the English and the French." [1]

The German Supreme Command still adhered to its conviction that their only hope of achieving victory was to defeat the British and drive them away from the Channel Ports. Ludendorff's memoranda show clearly that at this stage he was solely concerned to deal us such a blow as would make us willing to consider a peace without victory. The French people, fighting desperately on their own soil, were bound to continue the struggle as long as they could hold out and retain the support of their Allies, and their leaders

[1] "Die Ursachen des Deutschen Zusammenbruchs im Jahre 1918", Vol. III, p. 138.

were bent on recovering Alsace-Lorraine; but if Britain failed them the French would be compelled to consider terms. Ludendorff was quite clear that we were the backbone of the Entente and that no German victory was possible without our defeat. As he put it in a memorandum earlier in the year: —

"The insistent question is — how is it possible to defeat England in the field and exploit this blow to bring about a simultaneous collapse of the English war machine, even at home?"[1]

But before launching another attack on the British positions in the north, Ludendorff decided that his next stroke must be further south, in order to draw away the Allied reserves from the north.

At a council of war held between Ludendorff and the Chiefs of the General Staffs of the army groups of Crown Prince Rupprecht and of the German Crown Prince after the practical abandonment of the Lys attack, it was decided that the next stroke should be an attack on the French, on the Chemin des Dames sector. It was a quiet part of the front, and Ludendorff hoped by breaking through it to compel Foch to withdraw his reserves from the north. The order issued by the Supreme Army Command on May 1st, 1918, stated that —

"This attack has for its aim to break up the present united front of the Entente opposite Crown Prince Rupprecht's Army Group, and therewith create a fresh possibility for a successful renewal of the offensive against the English."[2]

The great offensive against us was to follow as soon as possible after the diversion at the Chemin des Dames had achieved its purpose.

[1] "The General Staff and Its Problems", Vol. II, p. 552.
[2] "Die Ursachen des Deutschen Zusammenbruchs im Jahre 1918", Vol. III, p. 558.

There was considerable discussion as to what part of the British Front was to receive the ultimate blow. At first Ludendorff favoured a renewal of the attack on the Amiens Front, in the direction of Doullens, as the Flanders Front was too difficult and too strongly held. But after further discussion, the greater advantages to be reaped by an advance further north brought down the scales in favour of a fresh Flanders offensive when the weather improved. This next attack on the British line was to be postponed until the summer and preparations were made for it all through May and June.

Between the closing of the German attacks in Flanders at the end of April, and the renewal of their offensive on the Aisne on May 27th, both sides were busy licking their wounds. We were painfully conscious of our losses, and were straining every nerve to make them good, combing out recruits, calling up classes of older men, for the first time during this war sending men of the "B" class to fill up gaps in divisions holding the quieter parts of the line and, above all, making unparalleled efforts to bring across as many troops as possible from America, which alone offered an unexhausted reservoir of vigorous man power. The flow from it had so far only just begun. What was achieved in these directions I have dealt with in other chapters. We also made immense efforts to strengthen our defences along the whole of our front. The output of barbed wire in this country increased from 800 tons to 1,100 or 1,200 tons a week. In addition, a large order was placed in the United States. This will give some indication of the strenuous efforts made to improvise new defences and improve the old. Still, the enemy had lost more heavily then we in the spring offensives, and his reserves of available men were more depleted than ours. Every available source had already been combed and recombed. On May 15th, a fresh order was issued that 30,000 men for the infantry were somehow to be extracted from the already much depleted personnel of the German Quartermaster-General's Department, a similar number from the Air Force, and an equal number from the ranks of the signallers, field railways and motor transport. But there was small hope that the order could be carried out. General von Kuhl stated in his evidence before the Reichstag Commission: —

"The course of the fighting in the March offensive made it clear that our losses could not be made good by reinforcements. So in April certain regiments of mounted rifles were broken up; and in May, two divisions were placed at the disposal of the Army Group to be broken up and distributed between the other divisions. In spite of this, we were unable in April and May to fill up the gaps caused by the offensive on the Armentières Front, and to maintain our attacking divisions at full strength. The average field strength of the battalions, which at the end of February still amounted to 807 men, had sunk by the end of May to 692 men."[1]

One hears a good deal of the fog of war, and having taken an active part for years in the administrative direction of the greatest war in history, I can well understand what it means. Despite aeroplanes crossing and re-crossing the lines, the endless observing and photographing of German positions and stations, and the watching of German movements; despite also an elaborate system of intelligence depending on spies and examination of prisoners and of deserters, the gaps in our information were incomprehensibly great. On re-perusing the reports that came up from day to day through the War Office from Headquarters in France and other sources, it is evident that we had no clear realisation in May of the extent to which the tremendous battles of March and April had crippled the Germans and incapacitated them from organising any further offensives on a scale which even

[1] "Die Ursachen des Deutschen Zusammenbruchs im Jahre 1918", Vol. III, p. 209.

approximated to the magnitude of their attack in the spring.
Whilst they were unable to patch up the rents torn in the
ranks of their armies, we were under the impression that by
withdrawing fresh divisions from Russia they were increasing their strength week by week, and that they would shortly
be in a position to launch a greater attack than ever upon the
Allied Front. French and English Staffs might differ as to
whether the attack would be on the British or French lines,
but they were in agreement as to the immensity of its scale.
Haig reported to the C.I.G.S. that he anticipated in the near
future an attack on his front by the Germans with a force of
80 divisions. Foch did not agree about the locality of the
offensive. Sir Henry Wilson reported to the War Cabinet
ten days later that "by the second week in June the Germans
would have reached their maximum available force, and
might attack with *at least* 100 divisions which would be a
larger force than that which took part in the offensive of
21st March."

The events of June will show how completely these estimates and forebodings as to the German numbers were falsi-
fied, but at the time the Allied Staffs assumed that the German Army had a decisive numerical superiority greater than
that which they possessed when they made their first attack
in the spring. How came they to make that mistake?

I have already pointed out that common arithmetic does
not seem to constitute a part of the training given at Staff
Colleges. One illustration of this kind of miscalculation was
the understatement of the numbers of the American Army
which had already reached France. During the month of
May alone 160,000 American troops reached France. Of
these 60 to 70 per cent. were infantry and machine-gunners,
the rest being field engineers, signallers and ambulances.
Reckoning the infantry alone on the basis of a full German
or British division, this would have been equal to a reinforce-

ment of nearly twelve divisions. The mechanical support in artillery, aeroplanes and tanks could have been supplied by the French and British Armies. In the event of a serious emergency arising these men would have been available as infantry to help us in holding the line. Territorials who had not had any more opportunity for training had been put in the trenches to hold the line in the winter of 1914 and the spring of 1915, and a mixed crowd of men who had received no training as infantry had helped to arrest the German advance on Amiens.

It was not only that the German reinforcements from home and from the East were insufficient to make up the losses, but also that the quality of these reinforcements was comparatively poor. The best men had already been brought from the Russian Front; what was left was the poorer material. The recruits combed by the Germans out of industry and agriculture were deficient in training and there was no time to fit them for the terrible task in front of them.

Despite their increasing weakness, or rather because of it, the Germans dared not let the initiative pass out of their hands. Unless they could score a decisive success before the autumn, they were doomed. And, as for the moment there was no hope of such success on the strongly held British Front, they launched their diversion against the French on May 27th. They attacked on a front of 50 kilometres between Rheims and Soissons.

They achieved what proved for them another brilliant tactical victory which, just like the triumphs they had won on the British Front, turned out to be damaging to their chance of ultimate success. In contrast to the offensive of the 21st of March they depended not on numerical superiority at the point of attack but on surprise. There is the usual discrepancy between the reports given by the French on one hand and the Germans on the other as to the numbers engaged on both sides. The Germans assert that they attacked with inferior numbers. The French, on the other hand, assert that the attackers were much more numerous than the defenders. British official reports to the War Cabinet gave the number of German divisions as "uncertain but it was clear in any case that the numerical superiority of the enemy was not sufficient to account for his rapid advance." By the third day of the battle only 16 German divisions had been identified. Between the French and ourselves the Allies had by then more divisions in that sector. Even the number of German divisions given by the French to explain their defeat falls a long way short of the anticipated 100 divisions which were expected to take part in the next German offensive.

At the time of the German thrust, four British divisions were recuperating in the "quiet" sector near Soissons after being knocked about in the spring battles, and although they were largely formed of fresh drafts, including many rather raw recruits, numbers of them gave a splendid account of themselves, hanging on to their positions till their flank was uncovered through the French on their left retiring, and still holding up stubbornly the shoulder of their line which guarded the west of Rheims. This is the report of the part played by the British divisions in the battle which was given to the War Cabinet by Sir Henry Wilson, who had had a conversation with General Hamilton-Gordon, who was in command of the corps: —

"General Hamilton-Gordon had three divisions of the IXth Corps in the front line on the 27th May: the 50th Division on the left, the 8th in the centre and the 21st on the right, in the Berry-au-Bac area. The first news of an impending attack came on the night of the 25th–26th May from a deserter. The battle started with heavy gas shelling, especially of the back areas, followed by an intense bombardment for two and a half hours. The wire having been cut by trench mortars, the enemy attacked in the usual way, with the assistance of tanks. The 50th Division was left "in the air" by the retirement of the 22nd French Division on the left, without warning to the 50th Division. The Germans were already in the town where the Commanding Officer of the 50th Division was quartered when he received the first intimation that the French had fallen back. The Germans came through the gap left by the 22nd French Division, and got behind the 50th Division, which suffered severely. The German tanks were used mainly at the point of junction of the 50th and 8th Divisions, and succeeded in working along a valley and getting behind the 8th Division. The 21st Division made a very good fight, but, owing to what had happened to the 8th Division, it had to withdraw eventually behind the Aisne. The 25th Division, which was in reserve, was put, by order of the French Army Commander, into the second position, and was overrun by troops coming back. All four divisions suffered heavily. The faulty French lateral communications, and especially the failure of the 22nd French Division to warn the 50th British Division, were important factors in causing the retreat."

The British casualties were heavy — they were estimated at 10,000.

The French were not warned of an impending attack by a concentration of troops behind the German lines. Nor was there any evidence of a contemplated offensive at that point. But like the 21st of March it started by a violent but short bombardment of the French trenches without any preliminary registration, and the movements of the attacking force were concealed by a morning mist.

Apart from the element of surprise, the bewildering collapse of the French resistance was accounted for by the blunders of the General who was in command on that part of the front. Blind to the experience of the War, and deaf to the orders of Pétain, he insisted upon keeping the bulk of the troops massed in the forward positions, so that the intense artillery preparations with which the Germans prefaced their attack smashed the defenders to pulp, and few were left to resist. And by unduly delaying his orders for the destruction of the bridges over the Aisne, he suffered them to fall into the hands of the enemy, and thus made their advance easy. The centre of the attacked front caved in, and the Germans swept over the Chemin des Dames, down to the Aisne and across its unbroken bridges, and on to the Vesle, which they also crossed. During the first day they had advanced at the centre to a depth of 12 miles. This was far more than they had accomplished in a day, either in the St. Quentin battle of March or in their April attack in Flanders. It was in fact a startling and disconcerting success. The next two days they pressed onward right and left to widen their salient and reached the bank of the Marne. They were thus well on the way to Paris. In four days, Ludendorff had advanced over 30 miles, had taken 400 guns and nearly 40,000 prisoners. Ultimately in this battle they captured 55,000 prisoners, 650 guns and 2,000 machine-guns with vast stores of ammunition. The German losses were comparatively slight. As a feat of arms, it was magnificent. As a piece of strategy, it turned out to be suicidal.

This German victory and especially the ease and rapidity with which it was achieved had a depressing effect on the Allied morale. It was the third great battle in which the Germans in a few days had broken through the Allied line to a depth which the French and British offensives had never reached after weeks and months of laborious and costly effort. The prisoners and guns captured by the enemy in each of these battles exceeded the highest record of the Allies in any of their great offensives. The defeat of the 21st of March was capable of an explanation which was not derogatory to the powers of resistance of the British Army. Their defences were crude and imperfect and they were overpowered by an enemy who outnumbered the defenders

by three to one. But in the May battle the defences were
exceptionally strong and the numbers on both sides were
approximately equal. There was another reason for the general sense of dejection caused by this defeat. When we were
beaten in March the French were more than inclined to
ascribe the disaster to bad leadership on the part of our Generals, which they thought accounted for a lack of fighting
spirit in our soldiers. But when the French were at the first
assault swept out of Kemmel — a position which for years
had been well behind the British front line — doubts began
to creep into minds which hitherto had been confident of the
undiminished proficiency of the French Army. The heavy
defeat sustained by the French on the Chemin des Dames
and the Aisne and the poor fight put up by their divisions,
which enabled the enemy at one blow to advance within 40
miles of Paris, created for the time being a sense not only of
despondency but of something tantamount to dismay. This
was deepened by the nightly bombardment of Paris by
enemy aeroplanes. Another mysterious development caused
a panic in the French metropolis. Huge shells, emanating
from no one knew where, dropped on Paris. Buildings were
shattered and hundreds were killed or maimed. One of these
missiles dropped through the roof of a church where Mass
was being celebrated, killing scores of the congregation. At
first it was thought that a solitary aeroplane had flown over
the city and dropped a bomb here and there. When it was
discovered that the explosions were due to a gigantic gun
which fired from a distance of 50 miles, there was consterna-
tion amongst all classes. Multitudes fled from Paris to safer
environments.

   Just at the moment of deepest gloom the Allies held a
series of conferences at Versailles. We all knew that victory
or defeat in a war between adversaries who were fairly
matched would resolve itself ultimately into a question of

morale. The strain of continuous fighting under conditions of terror unexampled in character and duration was bound sooner or later to break the nerves of the bravest men. Which of the two rival armies would be pushed first across the frontiers of endurance? Victory would rest with the one that remained on the battlefield in howsoever exhausted a condition. In the spring of 1917 the French *poilu* was on the point of a complete nervous breakdown, but he was not so far gone that he could not be rallied to defend his trenches, and the Germans were not then in a position to press their temporary advantage. The Italian Army had a bad temporary collapse in the late autumn of 1917. Passchendaele had undoubtedly worn down the high spirit of the British Army. In the March and April 1918 fighting the Germans had overrun positions which in 1916 and 1917 would have been thought impregnable on either side. What about the French morale? Had it recovered enough of its old valiant ardour to face and repel the onset of masses of well-led veterans exhilarated by a succession of brilliant victories? Recent events had inspired doubts in men not ready victims to vague fears. When we assembled in the conference chamber at Versailles we could hear all day during our discussions the deep thud of the German guns at Château Thierry. In the evening the German aeroplanes flew over our heads and we heard the fierce crack of their bombs in the direction of Paris. The lakes in the gardens of Versailles were all camouflaged with a green cover of imitation grass so as to mislead hostile bombers. Lord Derby, who was then our Ambassador in France, reported to me that there was a wave of pessimism sweeping over Paris, and that there was special resentment felt against Foch, who had not realised extravagant expectations by immediately arresting the German advance after he had been placed in full control of the Allied Armies. In his opinion, unless there was an improvement in the situation and that soon, there would be an irresistible demand for a change in the Supreme Command. The only reason why Clemenceau did not share Foch's temporary unpopularity was the feeling that there was no one else to take his place. Probably there were no keen competitors for a position which in the circumstances had more risk than glamour attached to it. This report fairly represented the Parisian atmosphere. An important British official said to me during this conference: "This is the last occasion upon which we shall be able to hold our meetings at Versailles." If the French had so readily given up elaborate entrenchments when the Germans were advancing on their capital, what reason was there to expect that they would hold on to positions where there was no time to prepare adequate defences?

This general despondency came upon me with surprise. I did not anticipate it. I did not share it. I thought it quite unjustified. I was convinced we had got over the worst. I was confirmed in my impression by the attitude of Foch. He definitely did not share the prevalent pessimism. He was calmly preparing his great counter-stroke and making ready for it. He was disappointed with the poor show made by the French divisions in the last battle and he was conscious of the fact that the defeat interfered with his plans for the counter-offensive and postponed its date. Nevertheless, the whole of his mind was concentrated on the building up of such reserves as would not only enable him to beat off the enemy but to launch a counter-stroke that would hurl the Germans back and which would — once their retreat began — enable the Allied Armies to batter them without cease into a shapeless rout.

We had an entertaining demonstration of Foch's strategical plans during one of our adjournments for lunch. He and Mr. Balfour were out for a stroll in the garden. We could see them engaged in an animated conversation, *i.e.*, animated as far as General Foch was concerned. Mr. Balfour was evidently listening with deferential attention to the old soldier, interjecting an occasional question. We then saw the General standing in front of the statesman indulging in violent pugilistic gestures first with his fists and then with his feet. We discovered afterwards that he was illustrating the great plan of his counter-offensive. When it began, he would hit here and hit there — he would use not only his two arms but both his feet, hitting and kicking without cease so as to give the enemy no time to recover. It turned out to be a dramatic forecast of the method which the great soldier was soon to employ and which ended in complete victory for the Allies. Foch saw in this moment of apparently calamitous defeat that the Germans had helped his ultimate scheme by the apparent completeness of their victory. Once more it was for them a tactical triumph but a strategic calamity, for the deep salient that resulted could not be held without devoting considerable forces to this task — forces intended to carry out the "Hagen" attack upon the British Front. It was too narrow a salient to form the base for a further advance unless it could be considerably widened; and that meant that yet more troops must be used up in thrusting sideways at the bastion of Rheims, which still held out to the east, and at the forest of Villers-Cotterets and Compiègne, which hemmed the new salient in on the west.

The German offensive was only partially successful in its purpose of drawing the Allied forces to the south and thus weakening the British Front. Foch was well aware that Prince Rupprecht's Army was still intact opposite us in Flanders. He brought reinforcements from the troops south of the Somme, and eventually as the battle progressed he ordered down the French Tenth Army, which had been in reserve behind our First and Third Armies in the north. But by this time it was evident that the Germans were too deeply committed across the Aisne to be able promptly to transfer their attack to the north, while our forces there were rapidly regaining their strength. In the month from March 21st to April 20th, fresh drafts totalling nearly 200,000 had been sent by us to France, including, as a reserve of the emergency, the youths under nineteen. By June 1st the total British white forces, home and Dominion, in the B.E.F., France, were within 7,000 of their total of March 1st, and a month later they had passed it. Once again the Germans were in the position that they must draw the Allied reserves again to the south by a fresh attack there before they could hope for success with their "Hagen" attack in Flanders. And meanwhile they had extended the front they must hold in the south by the circumference of a deep and precarious salient.

The Germans were thus doubly committed to continue their offensive in the south — partly because the positions they now held were unsafe for defence unless the salient could be widened; partly because it was their only method of weakening the reserves in the north and making possible their long-planned Flanders offensive.

The Battle of the Aisne drew to a close on June 6th. Its last day was marked by a successful counter-attack by American troops, and another by the British. The fine performance of the Americans on June 6th was an omen of grim significance for the Germans and a revelation to the astonished Headquarters of their allies, who had been assured that nothing was to be apprehended from the American Army for another year.

Three days later, on June 9th, the Germans launched an attack on the Montdidier-Noyon sector. This, however, did not surprise the French, as Foch had anticipated that such an attempt would be made by a thrust on an adjoining sector to widen the German salient. The assault was held at its ends, but penetrated the French line to a depth of 6,000 yards in the middle. This, however, was insufficient to bring the enemy near to Compiègne, and a counter-attack by Foch on the 11th compelled Ludendorff to abandon his effort. A week later another attempt was made, this time against the eastern shoulder, by an assault to the east of Rheims. But it was on a small scale, and came to nothing. The German blows had lost their former vigour, while the French were recovering their confidence. Colonel Schwertfeger, in his evidence before the Reichstag Committee, said of this fighting: —

"Meantime, as a sequel to the offensives on the Chemin des Dames, the assault which we delivered on Compiègne had been started on the 9th June; but it had to be broken off on the 11th under the impact of a powerful French counter-offensive. The whole front from Montdidier to Rheims was placed on the defensive, and in the middle of June comparative quiet set in." [1]

For nearly a month there were only local operations on the Western Front. The Allied forces staged various minor attacks for the purpose of improving their line at different points and harassing the enemy. One of these, which occurred on the British Front, caused grave annoyance to the American Commander-in-Chief. This was an attack on Hamel, in the Fourth Army area, which was carried out on July 4th by Australian troops. The 33rd American Division was training with the British forces on this sector, and the Australians and Americans, who had both come from far across the ocean to fight the battles of the old Continent from which their forefathers had sprung, seem to have struck up a warm friendship. I visited the American camp shortly after the battle, and had the privilege of reviewing the troops. As

[1] "Die Ursachen des Deutschen Zusammenbruchs im Jahre 1918", Vol. II, p. 191.

they swung past they appeared to me to be as fine a body of men as I have ever set eyes upon.

From one of the officers I heard an amusing account of what happened over the Hamel fight. When the attack to relieve the pressure on Amiens was projected, it was arranged that Australians and Americans should both take a part in the enterprise. The young Americans were overjoyed with the prospect of entering into their first battle in the World War. A message, however, came from American Headquarters, forbidding their use for the fight. The reasons given for this peremptory order were that they were there for training, and were not yet ready to be put into action.

When the Americans heard of this order a wave of disappointment spread over their camp, and some of them passed the sad news to their Australian comrades. The latter promptly scoffed at the idea that they should be diverted from their purpose merely because an order had come from Headquarters, and they told their American comrades: "You don't mean to say that you take any notice of those blighters — we never do."

The Americans agreed with this view, went into action, and by all accounts I heard they fought with great dash and spirit. The only comment of the Australians was: "They are fine fighters, only rather rough!"

General Pershing records in his book, "My Experiences in the World War", his extreme annoyance with the British Army Staff for allowing the American troops to fight contrary to his orders. He says that the immediate result of this incident "was to cause me to make the instructions so positive that nothing of the kind could occur again." [1]

During this pause in the carrying out of major offensives, Ludendorff was engaged in reforming his damaged divisions with such material as he could scrape together. He was still

[1] Page 475.

counting on delivering that final blow in Flanders; but before he could do so he was under the necessity of widening his perilous salient on the Marne. On the 14th of June he ordered preparations to be put in hand for a double assault to be delivered on or about the 10th of July on both sides of Rheims, with a view to pinching out this cramping obstacle and straightening out the narrow salient. Presuming its success, the Hagen attack in Flanders was to follow ten days later.

Ludendorff further ordered that arrangements should be made, following up these offensives, for a big thrust between the Somme and the Marne, to capture both Amiens and Paris. But here a protest arose in his General Staff that there would not be troops enough for so big a simultaneous thrust, and on July 12th, Ludendorff announced that they would have to wait till after the Marne and Flanders offensives to decide whether to make their next attack on Paris or on Amiens.

Events were to save them this trouble. Ludendorff was not the only person making plans during June and early July. Foch had no sooner got the Germans pegged down in their vulnerable salient than he started to prepare a counter-stroke. There were now large numbers of American troops in France — by the end of June there were already twenty-four complete divisions, of which ten were in the line — and reinforcements were hurrying across the Atlantic at the rate of a quarter of a million a month. The Allies had once more a numerical superiority and Foch was a firm believer in the attack. He was accumulating reserves for a great thrust in in the direction of Soissons which would cut behind the German divisions occupying the Château Thierry salient. This was to be delivered as soon as the army of the Crown Prince was fully engaged in its projected attack to the east and

GENERAL LUDENDORFF

west of Rheims. These reserves Foch jealously preserved for the great opportunity that he had known for months would arise after the Germans had exhausted their strength in unsuccessful offensives. It was an essential part of the plan of campaign he submitted to the Military Representatives of the Council and to Pétain and Haig in January. It will be recalled how these two eminent military leaders scouted it as an impracticable proposition. When the rapid advance of the Germans to the Marne at the end of May seemed to threaten Paris, Pétain meant to draw upon these reserves to bar the German onrush, and had actually given orders that some of the divisions designed for the counter-offensive should move to the support of the French Armies who were barring the road to Paris. Foch however intervened and refused to allow them to be drawn away from their designated purpose. Pétain had to use such other troops as he could find to defend Champagne and the line of the Marne. The Reserve Army remained intact under cover of the woods, ready to pounce at the word of command from the Generalissimo.

Although the "Hagen" attack on Flanders was still pending, Foch rightly judged that it would not be delivered until after the further German assault on Rheims. In fact, nine of Prince Rupprecht's reserve divisions were brought down from the north for the new offensive against the French to the east of Rheims. Haig, who at first had been averse to despatching any troops to Champagne, subsequently accepted Foch's view and agreed to the withdrawal of eight French divisions from the reserves behind his front. He also supplied four of his own British divisions to strengthen the attack on the German salient.

On July 15th the last German offensive of the War was launched, east and west of Rheims. Foch was expecting it, and was prepared to give up a certain amount of ground on both fronts. Pétain's tactics of the elastic front, lightly held in the forward zone, which forced attackers to advance beyond the support of their trench mortars before they met the main body of the defence, muffled on this occasion the full force of the onset, which did not achieve any very spectacular gains during its first two days. On the third day, Foch struck. He had massed his army of attack under General Mangin, one of the most dashing Generals of the War, in the forest of Villers-Cotterets, on the west flank of the German salient, and thence they issued, with the first light of dawn, supported by a mass of tanks and with no preliminary bombardment. Mangin attacked with 22 divisions between the Marne and the Aisne, in an easterly direction, on a 50-kilometre front. Of these divisions, two were British, two were American and therefore twice the strength of the ordinary British or French division. The very existence of such a tremendous striking force on their western flank was skillfully concealed from the enemy; the first day the Allies penetrated to an extreme depth of ten kilometres, captured 16,000 prisoners and approximately a hundred guns. The lateral communications between Soissons and Château Thierry, road and railway, were thus brought under fire of the Allied artillery. The two American divisions were in the forefront of this attack, and in this, the first big offensive operation in which they took part, they covered themselves with glory. The part played by the British divisions in this attack was also noteworthy and contributed largely to the victory.

The British divisions attached to Mangin's Army were the 15th and the 34th. At the opening of the battle they were held in reserve, and were thrown in on the 23rd of July. On that and the following days they were fiercely engaged. A footnote in the published despatches of Marshal Haig notes in connection with this battle that: —

"The 17th French Division generously erected a monument to the 15th Division on the highest point of the Buzancy plateau, where was found the body of the Scottish soldier who had advanced the farthest in the attack of the 28th July." [1]

And Marshal Foch records in his Memoirs that during a resumption of the attack on August 1st, in conjunction with three French divisions: —

"The British 34th Division, supported by tanks, assaulted the heights of Grand-Rozoy, and in spite of furious resistance by the enemy, they carried the German position between Grand-Rozoy, the Signal de Servenay and the village of Cramaille at the point of the bayonet. Here they hung on in the face of numerous and powerful counter-attacks. This decisive action compelled the Germans to make a new withdrawal." [2]

It was an effective surprise. Ludendorff had already gone north to Tournai to supervise the preparations for the Hagen attack, to be met on his arrival with the news of the French break-through. Admittedly the Germans had received previous warning of the pending counter-offensive. But they had — quite correctly, as it happened — understood that Foch intended to launch it on or before the 14th of July, and when it did not come then, they supposed it had been abandoned.

The course of the battle for the first two days had lulled them into security as far as their western flank was concerned. A desperate battle was raging around the heights above Rheims and farther along towards the east. The Germans assumed that Foch had been compelled to throw in his reserves to help the hard-pressed French Army in those sectors. During these two days hardly a shot was fired between Soissons and Château Thierry, and the German troops in the salient were deluded into the belief that the danger of

[1] "Sir Douglas Haig's Despatches", p. 256.
[2] "Memoirs of Marshal Foch", p. 422.

an attack from that quarter had passed. To quote a brilliant German writer's [1] description of the tranquil state of mind into which these troops had subsided: —

". . . Night and day they have heard the fire from the actions going on about the Marne and in front of Rheims . . . they hear of successes: that we are fighting south of the river and have made some advance in the wooded hills. Then, too, the rumour is started that the enemy is everywhere in retreat — that he is throwing all his reserves into the balance at Rheims and about the river, and has no thought of attacking hereabouts: then vigilance becomes slack . . . and the troops are lulled into a sense of false security — they feel almost as if they were in Rest-Quarters.

". . . But suddenly this idyll is broken in upon by a surprise attack. . . . It falls like lightning — striking through the morning mists. I have been informed that when it took place numbers of the fighting men had just gone out to the harvest fields.

". . . The attack was made with an advance-guard of many hundreds of tanks, and — apparently — with tanks of a new design, small, and capable of great mobility; these, having advanced, were able to establish themselves as cover for the machine-guns, and thus the picture gained is that after a minimum of time, the front line had been penetrated at numberless points and our men were simply fighting for their skins, while their rear was at the same time exposed to further fire from the enemy's machine-guns. What actually took place at the time, and amid all this confusion, no one quite knows . . . but the troops became aware that they were surrounded — and lost their heads . . . such a thing is catching. Wherever the enemy advanced, he outflanked the neighbouring sections still fighting, widening to either side the gaps he had already made in our line. Side by side, in an uninterrupted storm of attack, came French and Americans . . . and the situation became more and more serious."

The French thrust gravely menaced the German forces in the Marne salient, and after some fierce fighting, Luden-

[1] Karl Rosner: "The King", *passim*.

dorff was forced to withdraw from it to the line of the Vesle. Indeed, it was with the greatest difficulty that he managed to rescue the bulk of his troops congested in the salient, leaving behind 25,000 prisoners and large numbers of guns and other war material.

It is interesting to note that General von Kuhl, in summing up the story of the last German offensive and Foch's counter-stroke, attributed the German failure to the lack of surprise in their attack, combined with the unity of command achieved on the Allied side. He points out that: —

"Foch had brought down the French troops, about eight divisions, from the Flanders sector to the French Front. Admittedly Haig had his worries, because he knew of the reserves standing behind the Crown Prince Rupprecht's Army group. But for all that he had to give up four English divisions to the French Front, and send four more to the neighbourhood of Amiens on the Somme. Foch was thereby enabled to move four French divisions from there to further on the right. These movements were completed in good time before the 15th. This showed clearly the importance of the unity of command which had been entrusted to General Foch. Without that it would hardly have been possible to unite the divergent interests of the English and the French." [1]

The victory of Villers-Cotterets had a much more far-reaching effect than the defeat of the Crown Prince's attempt to capture the mountain of Rheims. It was the turn of the tide. To quote Hindenburg: [2] —

"Although the fighting in the Marne salient had saved us from the annihilation our enemy had intended, we could have no illusion about the far-reaching effects of this battle and our retreat.

"From the purely military point of view it was of the greatest and most fateful importance that we had lost the initiative to the

---

[1] "Die Ursachen des Deutschen Zusammenbruchs im Jahre 1918", Vol. III, pp. 177 and 178.
[2] Von Hindenburg: "Out of My Life", pp. 385 and 386.

enemy, and were at first not strong enough to recover it ourselves. We had been compelled to draw upon a large part of the reserves which we intended to use for the attack in Flanders. *This meant the end of our hopes of dealing our long-planned decisive blow at the English Army.* The enemy High Command was thus relieved of the influence which this threatened offensive had had on their dispositions. Moreover, the English Armies, thanks to the battle in the Marne salient, were relieved from the moral spell which we had woven about them for months. It was to be expected that resolute generalship on the part of the enemy would exploit this change in the situation, which they could not fail to realise, to the full extent of their available forces. Their prospects were very favourable, as, generally speaking, our defensive fronts were not strong and had to be held by troops which were not fully effective. Moreover these fronts had been considerably extended since the spring and were thus strategically more sensitive."

It is very interesting to note the impression made by the Americans upon the old Prussian veteran.

"Of course, it was to be assumed that the enemy also had suffered very heavily in the recent fighting. Between 15th July and 4th August, 74 hostile divisions, including 60 French, had been suffering losses while the English Armies had been practically spared for months. In these circumstances the steady arrival of American reinforcements must be particularly valuable for the enemy. Even if these reinforcements were not yet quite up to the level of modern requirements in a purely military sense, mere numerical superiority had a far greater effect at this stage when our units had suffered so heavily.

"The effect of our failure on the country and our allies was even greater, judging by our first impressions. How many hopes, cherished during the last few months, had probably collapsed at one blow! How many calculations had been scattered to the winds!"

Ludendorff confirms the impression recorded by his Chief: —

"The attempt to make the nations of the Entente inclined to peace before the arrival of the American reinforcements by means of German victories had failed. The impetus of the Army had not sufficed to deal the enemy a decisive blow before the Americans were on the spot in considerable force. It was quite clear to me that our general situation had thus become very serious.

"By the beginning of August we had suspended our attack and reverted to the defensive on the whole front." [1]

Hindenburg and Ludendorff realised that this defeat was the loss not of a battle but of the War. It was the beginning of the end. Once more to quote from Rosner's vivid and picturesque description of this battle — one of the great decisive battles of history — it was: —

"The end . . . the dark, abysmal giant-maw, from facing which he (the Kaiser) has so persistently averted his eyes all this day, now suddenly confronts him. One single horror looms in sight: that of disbanded armies, hurrying homewards: then the terrible disillusionment of the masses, harried by privation . . . the Un-chained Horror . . . the Red Ruin of millions now roused to fury — cheated of their hour of triumph . . . the hour for which they had so long been waiting." [2]

The German Army had exhausted its reserves. The losses were so heavy that ten divisions had to be broken up in order to use their infantry for others. What was left was no longer strong enough either in numbers or in quality to enable Ludendorff to renew the offensive at any part of the front. It turned out to be quite unequal to the task of defending its lines against the reinforced and reinvigorated armies of the Alliance. The Germans knew that the game was up. It is a tribute to the moral supremacy which their armies had imposed upon the Allies that, with the exception of Foch, none of the Allied Commanders or their Staffs seem

[1] Ludendorff: "My War Memoirs", p. 677.
[2] Karl Rosner: "The King", p. 215.

to have realised the favourable actualities of the situation.

It is difficult to overestimate and it would be ungenerous and unjust to underestimate the part which the American Army played in this dramatic change in the fortunes of the Entente. They had eight divisions (the equivalent of twenty French divisions) in this fateful battle. These fought with reckless dash and courage and contributed substantially to the victory of the Marne salient. There were other divisions holding other parts of the Allied Front and several in reserve. New divisions were in course of formation from scores of thousands of men already landed in France; there were scores of thousands of men on the high seas and myriads training in America with millions in reserve. The Germans, whilst depreciating their efficiency in action owing to lack of training in officers and men, paid a warm tribute to their courage and fearlessness. They knew too well that material of that kind would improve by experience in actual fighting. The Germans had observed and suffered from the same process with the raw levies Britain flung so prodigally into the battlefields of France and Flanders. On the other hand there were no fresh sources of man power that the exhausted armies of the Central Powers could draw upon. In such circumstances the moral effect on the combatants on both sides of such a reinforcement for one of them must necessarily determine the issue. Here were brave duellists who had been for a long time inflicting angry wounds upon each other from which their strength was gradually ebbing. One of them decides to fling the last remnants of his power at the other in a desperate effort to rush a decision before he drops. The other — equally drained of blood — is reinvigorated by a transfusion from the veins of a virile and vigorous youth who comes to his timely aid. The result was inevitable. From the date of this battle the spirit of the German Army sagged. There were units amongst them which fought with desperate

Commandement en Chef
des Armées Alliées

Etat Major General

1° Section

3° Bureau

2374

G.Q.G.A. le __ 24 Juillet 1918

148

PERSONNEL ET SECRET

Le-Général F O C H

COMMANDANT EN CHEF LES ARMEES ALLIEES

à Monsieur le MARECHAL COMMANDANT EN CHEF

LES ARMEES BRITANNIQUES EN FRANCE.

Monsieur le Maréchal,

J'ai l'honneur de vous adresser le mémoire sur la situation militaire actuelle et les opérations prochaines à prévoir.dont il vous a été donné connaissance à la réunion des Commandants en Chef du 24 Juillet et sur le programme duquel vous avez bien voulu vous déclarer d'accord avec moi.

Je vous demande de vouloir bien me faire connaître sans retard les observations qu'après examen plus approfondi.ce programme aura pu vous suggérer.

Ci-joint également le questionnaire dont il vous a été donné lecture; il serait avantageux que les renseignements demandés me parviennent avant la prochaine conférence,à laquelle je me propose de vous demander de prendre part,dans un mois environ.

Bien sincèrement à vous

F.Foch

valour up to the end and the tenacity of their resistance is proved by the terrible losses they inflicted on their British, French and American assailants. But after the Battle of Rheims the German Army as a whole never put up the fight to which their foes had been accustomed during four years of incessant combat. Even the bravest men do not fight as well when they know in their hearts that no effort or sacrifice on their part will prevent them from being beaten in the end. If, in addition to this depressing knowledge, they are tired and worn out by constant fighting, then the stoutest heart begins to fail.

Foch's counter-stroke of July 18th put a definite end to all prospect of any further great German offensives. It was the turn of the tide. On July 22nd Rupprecht's Army group, opposite the British Front, was told that it must stand on the defensive, and give up its reserve divisions which had been prepared for the Hagen attack, partly to reinforce the German Crown Prince's Army group, partly to replace divisions in the line which were exhausted.

Most of the fighting since April had been done by the French Army. It needed some time to recuperate and to refill its depleted divisions before it was in a position to resume the offensive. But it was Foch's policy to give the Germans no time to recover from the blow they had sustained. Above all, he was insistent that no time should be given them to dig and wire new defences for the lines to which their advance in salients had carried them. The policy which he had so histrionically expounded to Mr. Balfour at Versailles in June was now to be put into operation.

Ever since his appointment as supreme commander, Foch had been thinking of and planning for an Allied offensive campaign; mishaps and defeats postponed the execution of his plan, but never altered his resolve to see it through. It was the plan of campaign sketched by him in his celebrated

Memorandum of the 1st of January, 1918, which was turned down temporarily by the opposition of the two Commanders-in-Chief. As soon as he saw that his counter-attack at Villers-Cotterets had succeeded, he drew up a Memorandum outlining his proposals, which he laid before the Allied commanders at a Council of War on July 24th. The photostat of this critically important document is before me as I write, and I reproduce as an illustration (p. 101) Foch's autographed covering letter to Haig, in which he enclosed his statement.

Foch's Memorandum started by pointing out that his counter-stroke had not only stopped the fifth German offensive but had turned it into defeat. This defeat must be exploited, not only in Champagne, but on a much wider scale. The Allies were now fully equal to the enemy in number of battalions and combatants, and held a superiority of reserves.

"Moreover, all the information tallies in revealing to us an enemy reduced to having two armies: an army of occupation, sacrificed, without effectives, held for long time in the line; and manœuvring in the rear of this fragile façade, an army of assault, upon which the German High Command lavishes all its attention, but which has already been badly knocked about."

The Allies also held an undoubted superiority in aeroplanes, tanks and artillery; the Americans, pouring in at the rate of 250,000 men a month, would steadily increase their preponderance; while the fact that the Germans had been stopped and defeated gave us now a moral superiority.

"The time has come to abandon the general defensive attitude hitherto necessitated by numerical inferiority, and to go over to the offensive."

In his Memorandum, Foch envisaged two stages for this offensive. The first was a series of attacks upon different important sectors of the front, swiftly executed one after the other, with such forces as the Allies for the moment could rally for the purpose, preparatory for a further stage when we should have secured a good position for manœuvre and the balance of strength had shifted still further in our favour.

For the initial stage, Foch proposed two series of operations. The former series was designed to free the lateral railway communications along the Allied Front, and consisted of three offensives: —

"(a) Freeing the Paris-Avricourt line in the Marne district. This constitutes the minimum result to be obtained from the present offensive.

"(b) Freeing the Paris-Amiens line, by a joint action on the part of the British and French Armies.

"(c) Freeing the Paris-Avricourt line in the Commercy district, by reducing the St. Mihiel salient — an operation to be prepared without delay and to be undertaken by the American Armies as soon as they have the necessary resources at their disposal."

The St. Mihiel operation, as he pointed out in a footnote, would enable the Allies to act on a large scale between Meuse and Moselle — "which may become necessary one day." Clearly Foch was not taking shortsighted views of the ultimate scope of his offensive.

The other series of these preliminary operations was an attack in the southern part of the Flanders Front, to free the mining districts of Bethune from enemy threats, and an attack farther north in Flanders for finally removing the enemy from the region of Dunkirk and Calais.

"As has been said above, these actions are to be carried out at brief intervals, in such a way as to disturb the enemy in the movement of his reserves and to deprive him of the time necessary for reconstituting his units.

"They must be heavily equipped with all the necessary resources so as to ensure unerring success.

"Finally, they must at all costs use surprise. Recent operations prove that it constitutes an indispensable condition of success."

Foch could not so early lay down with precision a term within which this first stage of his offensive would be completed: but in his Memorandum he indicated that there was —

". . . ground for anticipating an important offensive at the end of the summer or in the autumn of such a kind as to add to our advantages and to leave no respite to the enemy."

The scheme was not acceptable to the French and British Commanders-in-Chief. To quote a French military writer who was fully informed as to what occurred at the Conference: [1] "This Memorandum by the scope and number of the attacks contemplated, at once called forth objections from its audience. *Haig and Pétain plead the fatigue of their armies: Pershing, the inexperience of his.* Not one of the three Commanders-in-Chief frames a formal refusal, however, being convinced that events will be responsible for bringing the plan of the General-in-Chief of the Allied Armies back within the bounds of their own conceptions." Pétain, in particular, in a written reply forwarded on July 26th, states that the offensive directed at the St. Mihiel salient, together with that of the Armentières pocket, will constitute, in his opinion, *the offensive of importance* contemplated for the end of the summer or the beginning of the autumn and that it will exhaust *"in all probability the French resources for the year 1918, but for a useful and comprehensive result."* This last sentence is ambiguous. Foch records in his Memoirs that at the Council of War on July 24th both Haig and Pétain were greatly surprised at the ambitious nature and

[1] General René Tournès: "Histoire de la guerre mondiale", Vol. IV, p. 193.

magnitude of Foch's plan and the number of operations it contemplated.

Even Foch did not in July foresee that we should be able to finish off the War in 1918, and he thought the concluding blow would have to be struck in the following year. So far as the military situation on the Western Front was concerned, that was probably the sound view. But our victories in the Balkans and Palestine, which drove Bulgaria and Turkey out of the War, and the shattering effect of our blockade upon the morale of Germany and Austria, were to combine with Foch's strategy in the West to bring about an earlier conclusion.

2. THE WILSON MEMORANDUM

Wilson's report to the Cabinet — Consults Haig — Memorandum represents military beliefs — Haig dislikes its verbiage — Cautious view of effect of Foch's counter-stroke — Ludendorff's admissions — Five alternative prospects — No Allied advance anticipated — Stabilisation probable — Offensive in July, 1919 — My contemporary comments — Fantastic fears of German operations in the East — No hope in the Balkans — Nor in Palestine — Mesopotamia our only hope — Preparations for July, 1919 — Post-War problems — Quality of our military advice — Smuts corroborates Wilson's report — Unreliability of judgment of High Commands.

The British military view was communicated to the Cabinet by Sir Henry Wilson, first in a verbal report on the effect of the German defeat, and subsequently in an "appreciation" of the situation dated July 25th.

First as to his Report to the Cabinet:

When on July 19th, a report of the German advance and of the complete success of Foch's counter-offensive had been given to the War Cabinet, I at once felt the significance of the event. The Chief of the Imperial General Staff, however, was by no means so optimistic. He recognised that the sole object of the German offensive at Rheims had been to draw Allied reserves from the north and he quoted a telegram from Pétain's Headquarters confirming that opinion. Knowing Wilson's habit of putting himself in the place of the enemy and speaking from his standpoint, I asked him to furnish the Cabinet with an appreciation of the situation as viewed through German spectacles. He replied that the enemy might argue as follows: —

"I made an attack on a big front with a few divisions so as to draw down to Rheims the bulk of the French reserves. This I have done, and I am therefore not dissatisfied with the results. As regards the French counterattack, I am pleased with it, and I am quite prepared to give up ground, provided at the same time I draw into action the Allied reserves, and I am prepared to fight a rear-guard action and then attack further north when it suits me. Of course, I should not like it if I was liable to be cut off, but the Crown Prince's reserves should be sufficient to prevent any such success on the part of the enemy."

I was nevertheless convinced that we had reached a new and more promising stage in the progress of the campaign. For this reason I invited Sir Henry Wilson to prepare a thorough study of the military position for the enlightenment of the Cabinet as to the effect of the second victory of the Marne on the military situation. Before preparing it he wished to consult Sir Douglas Haig. He visited him at his Headquarters on July 21st, to consult him as to his opinions on the military situation. As a result of this consultation, I received a remarkable document from him entitled "British Military Policy, 1918–1919." In it he set out at length his appreciation of the military situation and outlook for the guidance of the British Government, whose principal military adviser he now was. He gave us his estimate of the prospects on the Western Front, and of what could be achieved on the subsidiary fronts, and his advice as to the aims we should pursue, and the distribution of available forces we should adopt during the coming twelve months. He submitted his forecast of when we should be able to re-

sume the offensive against the Germans, and an indication
of what he thought we might hope to achieve against them.
He had not only gone over to France and talked over the
situation with the Commander-in-Chief, Field-Marshal Haig:
he also knew Pétain's views about the possibilities of 1918;
and the communication he had received from Pétain's Headquarters as to the effect of the battle at Rheims showed that
this eminent French General had seen in that event no reason
for any change of opinion. At Versailles, Wilson was moreover
able to draw upon the information collected by the military
experts stationed there, and in the War Office he had at his
disposal all the military information which it was the business
of the Staff to acquire from every field and through our
highly efficient Secret Service. Bearing this in mind, one is
driven to judge his Appreciation, in so far as it bears on the
prospects on the Western Front, not as a mere personal
opinion of a very clever but somewhat erratic officer, but as
representing the sum of the military wisdom and foresight
available to him either at the War Office, at the British
G.H.Q. in France or at the French G.H.Q.

Judged from that standpoint, the document is an astound-
ing production, and to read it now in retrospect leaves one
gasping at its wild irrelevancies to the reality of the position.
Alike in fact and forecast it was wrong, grotesquely wrong.

Although the C.I.G.S. had been in communication with
Sir Douglas Haig and had visited him at his Headquarters
and had interchanged opinions with him as to the military
situation and prospect, Haig was contemptuous of the actual
draughtmanship of Wilson's Memorandum; he disliked its
verbiage and its ramblings into far-fetched speculations in
the Far East. But there is no doubt that it represented the
British Commander's view of the outlook so far as the
Western Front was concerned after the German defeat in
July. The quotation I have given from General René

Tournès' book bears out that interpretation of his attitude.

Wilson's Memorandum bears the date July 25th. It was, therefore, written *after* the last German offensive round Rheims of July 15th to 17th, and *after* Foch's great counter-attack of July 18th which smashed the German salient and compelled them to withdraw from the Marne. The Germans had been so weakened by war wastage and so disheartened by their defeat in their Champagne offensive that they had been compelled to abandon all hope of carrying out further major offensives in the West, and were busy organising the whole front for defensive warfare. It was written when Austria was falling to pieces, when the Bulgarian Army was disintegrating, and the Turkish Army had been reduced to a ragged remnant.

Bearing these facts of the situation in mind, let us see what information and advice our chief military adviser has to offer the Government as the result of his consultations with G.H.Q. Wilson's Memorandum starts with a review of the outcome of the Champagne battle. He correctly notes that the German offensive has been neutralised, and that —

"As the result of these operations the Germans may be said to have lost the initiative *in that particular* part of the field, and *the threat to Paris has been greatly lessened. . . .*"[1]

Wilson then asserted that Prince Rupprecht, on the Flanders Front, still had his reserves intact, and it remained to be seen whether that offensive would materialise at once, or be delayed a while, till the enemy had gathered and re-constituted as many divisions as possible after his reverse in the south. Indications obtained in the fighting showed that the German companies were in many cases under strength.

As a matter of fact, the Champagne reverse had done a great deal more. Ludendorff[2] says of it: —

[1] My italics.
[2] "My War Memories", Vol. II, p. 674.

"The serious weakening of the 18th Army and of the right wing of the 9th . . . had to be made good by reinforcements. These could only be drawn from the Army Group of Crown Prince Rupprecht. G.H.Q. therefore decided to abandon this (Flanders) offensive. The Rupprecht Army Group was to stand on the defensive and to surrender reserves to reinforce the 18th, 9th and 7th Armies. . . ."

In other words, the Champagne battle had for its immediate result that the long-projected Flanders offensive was abandoned, and Prince Rupprecht's reserves, instead of remaining intact, were used up in reinforcing the shattered armies further south.

Wilson's statement that the enemy formations were under strength was certainly not exaggerated. I have quoted in another chapter General von Kuhl's evidence as to the state of their battalion strength at this time, which shows that they were far weaker than Wilson estimated. The real combatant strength of the German battalions and companies at this time was less than half its proper figure. It is easy to understand, therefore, now that the Americans were pouring in on a great scale, and the Germans were utterly unable to keep up the combatant strength of their units, that the flow of the tide was strongly on the Allied side, and the battle front was set for a victorious advance.

With these facts in mind, let us see how Wilson views the prospects for the remainder of the 1918 campaign.

He sums up all the alternative possibilities which he considers might eventuate under five heads. The most favourable he can imagine comes first, and the others are in descending order of calamity for the Allies. These five possibilities are: —

"1. The German offensive may be fought to a standstill before any strategical decision has been obtained, leaving the Allied Armies in effective touch with each other, holding a line from the

North Sea to Switzerland, covering the Channel Ports and Paris.

"2. The British Army may be forced to abandon the Channel Ports either —

"(a) As the result of a successful attack on the British Front, or —

"(b) In order to keep in touch with the French and Americans south of the Somme.

"3. The enemy may capture Paris, or bring it under such effective fire as will deny the use of the railway communications through it and stop the working of the extensive munition works which are concentrated in its vicinity.

"4. The enemy may effect the complete separation of the British and French Armies, the former being driven back to positions covering the Channel Ports, the latter falling back to the south.

"5. The enemy may effect a breach in the line on some part of the front east of Paris, cutting the French Army in two and entailing a return to the conditions of open warfare."

It is worthy of note that an Allied advance does not figure at all as one of the possibilities! It is clear that the "moral spell" of which Hindenburg speaks had not yet been lifted from the minds of our high Commanders.

Wilson then goes on to discuss what would happen in the event of one or other of these possibilities being realised. Either of the last two would mean the decisive defeat of the French and serious loss to the British and Americans: —

". . . Alternative (3) would probably have such serious political and industrial results as to cripple the French powers of resistance. But, even should the French be compelled to make peace, the British Empire and America could still carry on effective maritime and economic war, though the withdrawal of their troops from France would be a delicate matter and might entail considerable sacrifices. Our military effort would then have to be exerted on the Eastern Front as well as in Mesopotamia and Palestine. The results to be obtained by this would almost entirely depend on the extent to which Allied intervention through Siberia had previously materialised.

". . . In the case of alternative (2), *i.e.*, the loss of the Channel Ports, the Allies could still continue operations in France though at a great disadvantage owing to the unfavourable naval situation thereby created. Our position would be prejudiced not only by the insecurity of our cross-Channel communications and the practical cessation of traffic to the Port of London, but by the adverse effect on the submarine situation in the Atlantic, which would probably reduce to a considerable extent the forces that America would maintain in France. So much so that there would probably be a substantial surplus of American troops over and above what could be transported to or maintained in France which could then be profitably employed on the Far Eastern Front, provided the latter had been reconstituted."

Americans will be interested to learn that it was contemplated in July, 1918, that their troops, if they were cut off by disaster from France, should be transported to the Far East to safeguard the Siberian Front. This is probably one of the flights of Wilsonian fancy which Haig characterised in his Diary as nonsense. On the whole, however, Wilson prefers to assume that the first alternative may be realised, and that —

". . . If the German advance is stayed without achieving any far-reaching strategical results, the immediate preoccupation of the Allies must be to secure such a margin of safety for our line in France as will remove all anxiety as to our position. This will enable us to devote our efforts uninterruptedly during the ensuing period to preparation for the decisive phase and, if necessary, to detach troops to other theatres without misgivings."

In this, the most favourable event, the utmost he hopes might be achieved in 1918 is a series of small local actions to improve our line by pushing the Germans rather farther from the Channel Ports, the Bruary coal mines, Amiens and Paris. That would require "the active coöperation of every man and gun that we can keep in the field until late in the autumn." In that event there could, of course, be no question of reinforcing any other front, with a view to launching offensives outside France.

Having thus in his vision led us safely through to the autumn with at least a chance of escaping one of the four disasters sketched in his possibilities (2) to (5), Wilson proceeds in the second part of his Memorandum to discuss the "period of preparation" which he presumes will supervene.

His hopes run high for a culminating military effort by the Allies. As to this, he asks: —

"The first question that arises is — when is this decisive effort to be made? That is to say, will it be possible to accomplish it in 1919, or must we wait until 1920?"

He proceeds to consider how the comparative man power of the Allies and the enemy will stand. Assuming that the Germans are already 200,000 under strength, that they do not enlist large numbers of Russians in their forces, and that the Americans keep their promises, he hopes that the present Allied inferiority of numbers (which he puts at 30,000 rifles) may have changed by July, 1919, to a superiority of 400,000 or more. He accordingly concludes that it will be possible for the Allies to take the offensive in *July, 1919*. He considers the case for postponing such an effort until 1920, but turns it down on the grounds that Britain is war-weary, France and Italy are exhausted, and America is impatient. He is afraid that there may even be some difficulty in lasting out until his chosen date, because "All enthusiasm for the war is dead", and to defer it longer would give the Germans time to exploit Russia. So he writes: —

"I have no hesitation in saying, therefore, that as a basis of calculation, we should fix the culminating period for our supreme military effort on the Western Front not later than 1st July, 1919."

As for what it may be possible to achieve by that offensive, he cautiously says that then our numerical superiority —

". . . if properly supported by the fullest equipment of every mechanical auxiliary, and efficiently directed under one supreme command, *will give us a fair chance of achieving substantial military success.*"

I see that when this document came before me in July, 1918, I noted against that statement the marginal comment: —

"What does this mean?"

On reading the Memorandum to-day I still wonder.

I see, too, that against his statement that the Allies were at this time inferior in numbers by some 30,000 rifles, I wrote the comment: —

"(?) Don't believe it. Based on some old fallacious assumptions that German divisions full up."

At this time the Allies had secured a definite numerical superiority owing to the arrival of the Americans. But our High Command had swung over from the reckless optimism of the autumn of 1917, when it exaggerated the losses and weakness of the enemy, to an equally mistaken pessimism, which made them exaggerate the enemy strength.

Having postponed the Allied offensive until July, 1919, Wilson proceeds pertinently to observe that the enemy in the meantime may be doing something, and asks what we can do to counter them.

He says that *"during this period the Germans need have no immediate anxiety as to their military position in France, although they will have lost their numerical superiority, and they can if they so desire detach considerable forces for operations in other theatres."* He then rambles into the most amazing fantasies. No one who knows Haig would hold him responsible for these vaticinations. They are purely Wilsonian.

He estimates that the Germans can concentrate 14 divisions a month on the Italian Front, up to a maximum of 93 divisions. They could also send 12 divisions to the Salonika Front. It would be less easy for them to despatch considerable reinforcements to the Palestine and Mesopotamia Fronts, but they might establish a force at Baku and command the Trans-Caspian railway up to the borders of Afghanistan, thus threatening the North-West Frontier of India.

All these adventures in distant lands were to be undertaken by a country which could no longer find enough men to maintain an army for the defence of its own frontiers. Wilson's recommendations are framed to cover these fantastic nightmares. During the autumn and winter of 1918 he thinks we should send a number of our divisions to winter on the Italian Front, in readiness to repel the probable German assault upon it; and for this purpose, we should improve the railway connections between France and Italy. An attack at Salonika is somewhat less probable, but he thinks our situation there very weak, and contemplates that we may be forced to abandon the port of Salonika with heavy loss. He debates the possibility of an offensive there by the Allies in the spring of 1919, but his conclusion is: —

"On the whole, I am averse to undertaking an offensive at present in the Balkans, and recommend that we economise British troops to the utmost in this theatre by the gradual substitution of Indian units as fast as they can be made available. The troops thus released will want a considerable period in which to recuperate and recover from the effects of their long sojourn in that fever-stricken district before they are fit for the arduous demands of the coming campaign in France."

The note betrays no realisation of the powerful reinforcement which the Allies had on this front through the addition of the Greek Army; no hint of a suspicion that it
would be on this front that the Allies would within two
months score the first of their final triumphs, defeating the
Bulgarians in a fashion that drove them out of the War and
compelled Ludendorff to appeal for an armistice.

As for the Palestine Front, where eventually the second
of those final victories was to be scored, Wilson bases upon
reports received from Allenby the conclusion that the furthest
advance to be expected there would be to the line Tiberias-
Acre, and that this would be of little strategical importance.
If the Germans reinforced the Turks in the spring of 1919
on the Palestine Front we should have to waste reinforcements there which would be wanted in France. How the
Germans with a grave inferiority on the Western Front would
be able to spare some of their attenuated forces for Palestine,
he did not explain. Anyhow, he thought the strategic importance of Aleppo, even if we took it, was much smaller
now, since the enemy could advance through the Caucasus
against Persia and India!

This brought him to the one field where he thought
significant operations should be undertaken in the winter
of 1918–1919 — Mesopotamia! True to the old Army obsession with the North-West Frontier of India, Wilson had
visions of the Germans working their way past the Caspian,
exploiting Persia and traversing Afghanistan to work their
wicked will in India. Not in the remote future, but in 1919!
Accordingly, here he saw prospects of a British offensive;
and, characteristically, here also he was prepared to admit
our superiority in numbers — a superiority so considerable
as to be excessive. It is noteworthy how steadily the Staff
view as to our inferiority or superiority varied with their
desire to launch or continue an offensive, or their disinclina-

tion for a proposed operation. In Mesopotamia, Wilson declared: —

"Our military situation gives no grounds for anxiety as regards direct attack in the immediate future, for we have a large superiority in strength over the Turkish forces in that theatre, in fact, too large to be strategically sound, *viz.:* 73,000 rifles or 115,000 combatants."

So he recommended a thrust up into Northern Persia, giving us a belt across to the Caspian, which would stop the Germans from advancing on India. This was the one operation on any front except the Western which Wilson advised as desirable between July, 1918, and the following summer.

The third part of the report deals with the great battle of July, 1919, which was to be the supreme Allied effort. Clearly it was too early to lay the tactical plans for it, so Wilson confines his proposals to schemes for cutting down our divisions during the winter to a number we can maintain at full strength, increasing their equipment of artillery, machine-guns and tanks — this last at the expense of the cavalry — and bringing back as many British troops as possible to Europe from the "out-theatres." All the white troops in Salonika and the 54th Division in Palestine, he proposes, shall be thus brought back. As we have seen, the victory he hoped for as a result of all this was very vaguely defined.

In the final section of the Memorandum, the C.I.G.S. stretches his wings for a survey of the situation of the British Empire after the War.

He expresses no opinion whether we should return her colonies to Germany, but is definite that we must maintain our railheads in Palestine and Mesopotamia; and we must hold a railway line from Baghdad to the Caspian. In consequence: —

"The end of the War will leave us with a much more formidable enemy on our distant marches than we had to encounter before, and it will tax our resources to the utmost to preserve our frontiers inviolate."

Wilson cannot get his mind away from the Khyber Pass. He warns us: —

"We have to remember that in the next war we may be fighting Germany alone and unaided, while she will have Turkey and perhaps part of Russia, if not on her side, at least under her thumb. In such circumstances Germany, with no preoccupation in Europe, could concentrate great armies against Egypt or India by her overland routes, which are beyond the reach of our sea power."

I have every reason to believe that Haig's mind did not accompany that of Wilson in his Far Eastern flights. But there is ample evidence that the C.I.G.S.'s estimate of the prospects of an Allied victory in France during 1918 coincided with those expressed by the two Commanders-in-Chief, Pétain and Haig.

There can be no better illustration of the difficulty of weighing the various factors that go to the making of a reliable estimate of the military prospects in a great war. At a moment when the German offensives in the West had finally collapsed, when we had secured a superiority of Allied man power and recovered the initiative in operations, when the Bulgarians could hardly be held in their trenches before Salonika, and the Turks were melting away in Palestine, when the Austrians had been repulsed on the Piave and their people were clamouring for bread and peace, our principal military advisers had come to the conclusion that the best prospect in front of the Allies was security on the Western Front for the rest of 1918, and a probable though not a certain victory in 1919.

That this extraordinary and pessimistic document from the pen of General Wilson did in fact faithfully represent the outlook of military leaders at that time finds striking corroboration from no less an authority than General Smuts. Smuts also had paid visits at various times to France, including one in mid-July, 1918, and had gathered an impression as to the military outlook from his consultations with Haig and his Staff. At a discussion in the War Cabinet on August 14th, he poured out the doubts and fears with which he had been filled from this source. Mr. Balfour had been expounding our war aims, and General Smuts felt constrained by the gloomy estimates imparted to him to sound a note of warning — all the more remarkable when we remember that this was after the successful blow of August 8th which Ludendorff described as the black day of the German Army, on which they suffered a defeat which robbed him of his last hope of maintaining a successful resistance to the Allied forces. On the heels of that victory, General Smuts, in making some observations on Mr. Balfour's Memorandum on War Aims, communicated his views as to the military situation at the end of August: —

"Mr. Balfour had stated our peace aims from the Foreign Office point of view and on the assumption of the complete defeat of the enemy. He [Smuts] could not see that the programme based on that assumption was justified by the present military situation. He did not suppose that anything would happen materially to affect that situation during the present year. . . . He feared that the enemy, giving ground slowly in the West, would concentrate a considerable effort, mainly carried out by Turkish troops, in the East. . . . What he feared was the campaign of 1919 ending inconclusively in the West and leaving our whole position in the East damaged and in danger. He was very loth to look forward to 1920. Undoubtedly, Germany would be lost if the War continued long enough. But was that worth while? . . ."

It reproduces the very tones of General Wilson's Memorandum, and obviously drew its inspiration from the same source. What gloomy infection must have permeated our

G.H.Q. to have an effect such as this upon a clever and courageous thinker like General Smuts! And how fortunate it was that the Government did not take too seriously the opinions and advice tendered to it by its military experts! Had we really believed their morbid prognostications at that time, we might well have felt bound, in the interests of the country, to bring the War to a hasty and abortive end rather than prolong the devastation and suffering by a continuance of it, dragging on into 1920.

The judgment of the High Commands on military prospects was never reliable. Our military leaders swung from the extreme of optimism to the opposite extreme of pessimism. Neither of those two moods had any justification in the actualities of the situation. In 1917 Haig was convinced that even if Russia withdrew from the Alliance, even if France had not completely recovered and the Americans were too untrained to fight, the British Army alone under his command could beat the Germans in 1918. A few weeks after this radiant forecast he plunged into a mood of inert and sulky gloom. Joffre and Foch were always optimistic, often without reason. On the other hand, Pétain was invariably timid and inclined to dejection. What power is there so absolute as that of the Commander of a great army? Great power is like alcohol. It exhilarates most men beyond the bounds of reality. In others it has the effect of depressing their spirits. But in all cases it poisons judgment.

3. The German Retreat

British to launch next attack — French to coöperate — A striking success — Success not exploited — Death blow to German hopes — German forces exhausted — Boys and Bolsheviks — German morale breaking down — Allied propaganda — Potency of the tanks — Germans admit their effectiveness — But fail to produce them — Allies hammer the German line — Successive offensives — Foch plans final advance to victory — Collapse of Germany's allies — First Austrian peace note — The general offensive starts — British overrun Siegfried line — Ludendorff in despair — Heroic resistance of German Army — Wilson's report on situation in mid-October — Haig's confirmation — The last victories.

As the British Army had on the whole enjoyed a quiet time for the better part of three months and had during that period repaired its losses and actually strengthened its equipment, Foch decided that it was their turn to make the next attack on the German positions. There were two or three alternative suggestions. Foch at first proposed that Haig should begin with the long-planned operation in Southern Flanders to free the area in front of the Bethune coal mines. But Haig had by this time abandoned his passion for a Flanders offensive and favoured Amiens as the best starting point for victory. Rawlinson had been urging that the prospects of a successful attack by his army in this area were excellent. In this Foch concurred. Haig's first idea was to attack on a front of eight miles. He was now a convert to the Pétain strategy expounded by Sir Henry Wilson's appreciation as "a series of operations with limited objectives designed to push the Germans back." Foch demurred to this proposal and advised an attack on a much wider front. It was to be one of a series of hammer strokes designed to smash up the German Army. When Haig objected that he could not muster the necessary reserves for an offensive on such a scale, Foch asked him whether there were no troops actually occupying the trenches to the right and left of his proposed front of attack. Haig thus brought into his scheme of the offensive the British divisions on the left, and the French Army to the immediate right was also placed under Haig's command for the assault. The Generalissimo had by this time come to the conclusion that the German Army was no longer in a condition to resist any resolute attack made upon it by the now victorious Allies. Their last defeat had wasted some of their best divisions and the heart had been taken out of the rest by the feeling which had spread throughout the German Army that victory was no longer within its reach.

Of the five major operations which Foch proposed in his memorandum for the first stage of his 1918 offensive, the first, in Champagne, was already in progress, and the second, on the Amiens Front, was thus agreed with Haig. Its details were fixed at a conference which Foch held on July 26th with Haig and Rawlinson and the French General Debeney, commanding the French First Army, which was to coöperate in the offensive. Foch followed up this discussion by sending Haig, on July 28th, two memoranda, one containing instructions for the operation, the other putting Haig in sole command over both the British and the French forces taking part in the contemplated attack, and asking him to expedite the attack for as early a date as possible.

The result of this offensive completely justified Foch's insight into the state of the German troops. Once more the Allies benefited by the new method of attack first attempted but bungled at Cambrai — a short bombardment followed by the advance of a large force of tanks. Foch had employed these tactics in his Villers-Cotterets attack. The utmost secrecy was observed in the preparations for the Amiens offensive, and when on August 8th it was launched, it took the Germans completely unawares. Six to eight miles of ground were won by the evening of the first day. The French extended the attack to the south, and two days later they recaptured Montdidier. In a week's fighting, 30,000 prisoners were taken — the British Fourth Army took 21,000 prisoners at a cost of only 20,000 casualties. German reinforcements were hurried up. Had Haig flung his army into the gap created and pursued the broken and demoralised Germans without respite an even greater victory was within his grasp. When the enemy was scattered and unnerved, and their reserves were not yet up, Haig did not press forward with relentless drive and the Germans were given time to recover and reform their lines. Both Hindenburg and Ludendorff dwell with gratitude and surprise on this welcome respite. Hindenburg writes of Haig's tactics: —

". . . As luck would have it he did not realise the scale of his initial tactical success. He did not thrust forward to the Somme this day, although we should not have been able to put any troops worth mentioning in his way.

"A relatively quiet afternoon and an even more quiet night followed the fateful morning of 8th August. During these hours our first reinforcements were on their way." [1]

Ludendorff says: —

"The situation was uncommonly serious. If the enemy continued to attack with even ordinary vigour, we should no longer be able to maintain ourselves west of the Somme."

He had made preparations for a further considerable retirement, but, as he puts it, the enemy attack on the 9th "fortunately for us, was not pressed with sufficient vigour." [2] The fact of the matter was that the British Army itself did not realise the extent and effect of the triumph they had won that day. They were thinking in the terms of past offensives when a gain of a few kilometres in an attack was as much as they could hope to accomplish, and experience had taught them the dangers of advancing too far because the Germans invariably rallied, brought up their reserves and counter-attacked with verve and skill. They had not yet understood that they were confronted to-day with an enemy who had lost much of his dash and combative strength. The reports of the battle received by the Cabinet from the front showed how little even the victors understood the immense effect of the triumph they had won. The actual ground captured was not extensive. The effect of the victory was moral and not territorial. It revealed to friend and foe alike the break-

[1] Von Hindenburg: "Out of My Life", p. 393.
[2] Ludendorff: "My War Memories, 1914–1918", p. 682.

down of the German power of resistance. More finally even
than by the French counter-offensive of July 18th were
the Germans driven by the British stroke of August 8th to
realise that all hope of victory had passed. After the July
defeat, whilst they came to the conclusion that their offensive
had finally failed they still hoped to reorganise their army
effectively for an impenetrable defence. After the Amiens
battle even this seemed impossible. Ludendorff admits: —

"The 8th August demonstrated the collapse of our fighting
strength, and in the light of our recruiting situation it took from
me any hope of discovering some strategic measure which would
reëstablish the position in our favour. . . . An end must be
put to the War."

And he published startling incidents during this fight which
were responsible for the gloomy conclusion at which he
arrived: —

"The report of the Staff Officer I had sent to the battlefield as
to the condition of those divisions which had met the first shock
of the attack on the 8th perturbed me deeply. I summoned divisional commanders and officers from the line to Avesnes to
discuss events with them in detail. I was told of deeds of glorious
valour but also of behaviour which, I openly confess, I should not
have thought possible in the German Army; whole bodies of our
men had surrendered to single troopers, or isolated squadrons.
Retiring troops, meeting a fresh division going bravely into action,
had shouted out things like 'Blackleg', and 'You're prolonging the
War', expressions that were to be heard again later. The officers
in many places had lost their influence and allowed themselves to
be swept along with the rest. At a meeting of Prince Max's War
Cabinet in October, Secretary Scheidemann called my attention
to a Divisional Report on the occurrences of 8th August which
contained similar unhappy stories. I was not acquainted with this
report, but was able to verify it from my own knowledge. A battalion commander from the front, who came out with a draft

from home shortly before 8th August, attributed this to the spirit of insubordination and the atmosphere which the men brought back with them from home. Everything I had feared, and of which I had so often given warning, had here, in one place, become a reality. Our war machine was no longer efficient. Our fighting power had suffered, even though the great majority of divisions still fought heroically.

"The 8th August put the decline of that fighting power beyond all doubt and in such a situation as regards reserves, I had no hope of finding a strategic expedient whereby to turn the situation to our advantage. On the contrary, I became convinced that we were now without that safe foundation for the plans of G.H.Q. on which I had hitherto been able to build, at least so far as this is possible in war. Leadership now assumed, as I then stated, the character of an irresponsible game of chance, a thing I have always considered fatal. The fate of the German people was for me too high a stake. The War must be ended." [1]

The Kaiser reached the same conclusion. In a conversation at Avesnes of August 8th, whilst the battle was in progress, he declared: —

"I see that we must strike the balance. We are at the limits of our endurance. The War must be brought to an end." [2]

Thereafter the German High Command devoted itself to the attempt to fight a rearguard action in the hope that they could drag on the conflict until the Allies would be sufficiently weary of it to agree to terms which would not be too disastrous for the Central Powers.

The Reichstag Committee of Enquiry, after reviewing the full evidence, came to the conclusion that —

"Up to 15th July, 1918, the Supreme Army Command rejected the view that victory was no longer possible of attainment by force

[1] Ludendorff: "My War Memories, 1914–1918", pp. 683 and 684.
[2] Alfred Niemann: "Kaiser und Revolution", p. 43.

of arms, and gave no support to peace negotiations upon the basis of a military stalemate. . . .

"The collapse of the whole offensive, which became evident after the defeat of 8th August, is explained by the fact that as a result of continuous fighting of incredible severity, the bodily and mental capacity for endurance of the troops had become exhausted, and that at the front reinforcements and supplies of war material were no longer adequate." [1]

General von Kuhl described in his evidence before this Committee the way in which the German forces were dwindling towards the end. He said that —

"The heavy losses could no longer be replaced. *Our reinforcements were exhausted*. In August, 1918, we had to break up ten, and in October, twenty-two divisions. . . .

"The Supreme Army Command found itself at the end of July compelled to reduce the establishment field strength of the battalions on the Western Front from 850 men to 700 men. It was soon evident, however, that even this strength of 700 men could not be maintained. . . . In August, the battalions of the [German Crown Prince's] Army Group maintained an average field strength of only 660 to 665 men. But the real combatant strength . . . was a long way below this figure. In reckoning the field strength we included not only those sick in hospitals or billets, those on leave and on the details, but those who had been missing up to three months, a number which steadily grew all through the summer. . . ." [2]

On August 17th, Ludendorff wrote to demand that the 1900 class of recruits — *i.e.* lads in their eighteenth year — should be placed at his disposal in the field depots of the Western Front, for him to transfer into the line at his discretion. The more mature of this class had already passed into the fighting line. His letter concluded: —

[1] "Die Ursachen des Deutschen Zusammenbruchs im Jahre 1918", Vol. I, p. 23.
[2] *Ibid.*, Vol. III, pp. 208 and 209.

"I know all the objections that can be raised to this early application of the juvenile class. But I see no other way to keep the army in the field at a sufficient fighting strength to face its tasks." [1]

The German Army was thus melting away, while the Allies were being reinforced by the steadily rising flood of American troops. Nor was the difference between the two forces confined to the growing disparity of their numerical strength. The collapse of morale on the German side was yet more disastrous. Von Kuhl complains that the new recruits forthcoming in the closing stages of the War were a source of weakness rather than of strength; for they had been dragged unwillingly from safe, well-paid work in munition factories, and many of them were imbued with Bolshevism. Whenever possible, they went sick. At the first opportunity, they ran away. They were insubordinate and mutinous. He speaks of the number of shirkers that were lost to the battle line: —

"Behind the front, hundreds of thousands of shirkers crowded up at the railway stations and the larger centres. Men who had been worked on by agitators when on leave moved about in masses behind the front, without seeking out their own units. So at the decisive moment, hundreds of thousands were lost from the front. . . ." [2]

The knowledge was slowly permeating all ranks of the army that the War was lost. Towards the end this sense of overwhelming defeat swept like a wave over the population in the Fatherland. For four years they had believed themselves invincible, and as recently as midsummer of 1918 they had been promised a final victory and a triumphant peace. The brilliant and easy victory of June over the French, following the tremendous victories of March and April over the British Army, seemed conclusively to demonstrate that the

[1] *Ibid.*, Vol. III, pp. 67 and 68.
[2] *Ibid.*, Vol. III, p. 212.

promises of the military leaders were not vain boasts. And now came these incomprehensible set-backs. It is idle for von Kuhl to lay the blame for the revulsion of feeling that ensued amongst the German people at the doors of pacifist agitators and Bolshevik emissaries. We had these in our country. But the conditions under which they operated were more favourable in Germany than they were in Britain. The bulk of the German population — especially the workmen, the professional classes and the small *rentiers,* were suffering privation as the result of the blockade. Men and women will endure a great deal if they can see a glimmer of hope at the end of the journey. The disintegration of the home front in Germany is attributed largely to the "lying propaganda" which the Allies organised. But the deadliest quality in the propaganda was its truth. Facts such as those relating to the numbers of American troops now in France, or the progress of our campaigns against Germany's allies, or the failure of the submarine campaign and the numbers of submarines we had sunk, were not made public in Germany by the authorities, for obvious reasons; but they formed highly useful information for us to drop from the air in the German ranks or behind their lines. And their great virtue was that they were correct. Our Ministry of Information arranged for a good deal of propaganda of this order to be disseminated across the frontiers. It was done with great skill and subtlety. The credit for its success is due to Lord Beaverbrook and Lord Northcliffe. A favourite method was to attach supplies of leaflets to little balloons, which could be released when a strong west wind was blowing, and in favourable circumstances would carry, not only into the back areas of Belgium and the occupied parts of France, but across the frontier into Germany. By this and by other channels we did a great deal to enlighten the troops and civilian population of the enemy as to the failure of their leaders to avert defeat. But such propaganda would have been a vain flutter in the air if the blockade were broken through in the east or were transferred to the Allies by the action of the submarines, or if Germans continued to smash into one Allied Army after another and drive them out of their entrenchments. In these operations there would be a certainty of approaching triumph to sustain the hearts of the German people.

In another important respect the Entente had a great superiority to aid their march to victory. This was the tank, the newest and most potent weapon yet devised for assault and advance. The Somme, Passchendaele and Cambrai had between them taught us the supreme lesson that tanks might prove irresistible provided they operated in large numbers and on suitable ground. Had our original programme been carried out and had G.H.Q. realised the importance of this weapon, we should have had an adequate supply which would have saved life. But the casualties amongst them were heavy and not enough allowance had been made for that fact. The Germans surprisingly neglected to develop this new device, even after they had witnessed its effectiveness. Its failure through stupid use at the Somme and Passchendaele and through ineffective exploitation of its success at Cambrai had misled the Germans as to its possibilities. Ludendorff was not greatly impressed by the tank in its early days. In the winter of 1916–1917 he held that the time had not yet come for them to go in for tanks, and in 1918 he declared that his assaults would succeed without them. A few German tanks were built, but they were clumsy and of low efficiency. But the tactics of the massed tank attack, which proved so successful in breaking the German line at Cambrai in November, 1917, were adopted by the Allies repeatedly in 1918. As we have seen, they were the spearpoint of the French thrust on July 18th which was the turn of the tide. Their nimble little tanks dashed through the German lines and created confusion and dismay. They similarly opened the British attack of August 8th and were largely responsible for that notable victory and still more for its depressing effect on the German Army. Four hundred and fifteen fighting tanks went over the top at zero hour that morning, and in all the engagements of the succeeding days, tanks played their part in smashing a way for the infantry, crashing through entanglements, sweeping across trenches, everywhere scattering and stampeding the enemy forces, circumnavigating machine-gun nests and receiving as little hurt from their sting as from ant-heaps in the path of a rhinoceros.

General von Kuhl admits that our tanks in the summer and autumn of 1918 achieved decisive results against "the thin lines of the worn-out German troops." A representative of the German G.H.Q., explaining the situation to party leaders of the Reichstag on October 2nd, 1918, said: —

"The enemy employed them in unexpectedly large numbers. Where, after a very thorough-going blanketing of our positions with smoke-clouds, they made surprise assaults, the nerves of our fellows frequently could not stand the strain. In such cases, they broke through our forward lines, cleared the way for their infantry, appeared at our rear, produced local panics, and broke up in confusion the arrangements for directing the battle. . . ."

The speaker went on to say: —

"We were not in a position to bring against the enemy a corresponding number of German tanks. To produce them was beyond the power of our industry, strained as it was to the uttermost, unless other important affairs had been let slide." [1]

The reasons given by the apologists of the German Army Command for their failure to develop tanks are in themselves a condemnation of the Staff policy in Britain and

[1] *Ibid.,* Vol. III, p. 211.

Germany of combing out all able-bodied men from industry and thrusting them into the trenches. Von Kuhl admits: —

"Without a doubt, German industry would have achieved the production of tanks, if that task had in good time been definitely and insistently set before it."

But Ludendorff suffered, as did our own Generals, from the obsession that all he needed to ensure victory was to have masses and masses of men with rifles. A few battalions more or less would not in fact have turned the scale between defeat and victory, whereas if they had been employed in manufacturing tanks, the effectiveness of the remaining battalions would have been multiplied manifold, and might have proved decisive. As our own official "History of the Ministry of Munitions" remarks, in the production of tanks, "the amount of labour required was small in relation to the tonnage involved, and the demands of the contractors were met by the Labour Supply Department." Indeed, in the autumn of 1918, when their man power was at its lowest ebb, the Germans for the first time began seriously to attempt to produce tanks on a large scale — forced thereto by a belated recognition of their decisive importance. The issue was one of the optimum distribution of the man power available. In the matter of tanks as well as in that of machine-guns and heavy guns, the common sense of the civilian, informed by intelligent advice from officers who were too independent to win high promotion, had saved the Allies from the narrowness and rigidity of Generals at the top. In this country, we insisted, in the teeth of a furious outcry from Staff officers and their friends, on retaining in the industrial side of warfare the men needful for equipping our forces with those mechanical aids and armaments which would avail to save their lives and ease their task. In Germany the military had become altogether supreme over the civil authorities, and in consequence Ludendorff got his men for the trenches, but without supporting them by some of the deadliest machinery with which his foemen were so lavishly equipped. And in the summer and autumn of 1918 he paid dearly for it. There were some shrewd observations made by Sir Austen Chamberlain in the course of a discussion on man power, when the military authorities were pressing hard for more men for the trenches at the expense of other essential national services: —

". . . The question which had in the past been put to the Army Council had never been answered — namely, assuming that a choice had to be made between a considerable reduction of men in the Army and a proportionate reduction in munitions and supplies, including those to our Allies, which would the War Office prefer? The Adjutant-General of the day had always answered that they must have the men, while the Master-General of Ordnance and the Quartermaster-General had said that they must have the supplies."

The French military authorities were also pressing us to comb out more men. At the same time they were urging us to supply them with more steel, food and other commodities. Sir Austen Chamberlain thought they also ought to be asked to choose.

After the British victory of August 8th, the story of the further fighting in the summer and autumn of 1918 becomes one of a series of hammer strokes by the Allies against their dwindling and disheartened foes, first here, then there, generally simultaneously on left, centre and right. They gave the enemy no rest and sent him staggering back from even his strongest positions. In these operations Haig earned high credit. He was fulfilling a rôle for which he was admirably adapted: that of a second in command to a strategist of unchallenged genius. Foch was responsible for the general plan of attack on the whole front. Haig, Pétain and Pershing worked out the details of the attack in their respective sectors and directed the onset with expert intelligence and resolution. The losses of Haig's expeditionary force in the spring battles had been made good to such an extent that its combatant strength in France in spite of its hideous losses was not reduced when in August the general offensive began. As a striking force it was far more powerful than it was in March, on account of the steady growth of its special mechanised units, worth many times their man-power total in effectiveness. Owing to the energy which Mr. Winston Churchill threw into the production of munitions, between March 1st and August 1st the strength of the Tank Corps increased by 27 per cent., and that of the Machine-Gun Corps by 41 per cent., while the number of aeroplanes in France rose by 40 per cent. In view of the pessimistic forebodings of both Pétain and Haig during the Versailles discussions as to the probable condition of the Allied Armies by the summer and early autumn of 1918, it would be well to give here the French estimate prepared in August, 1918, of the actual Allied and German strength at that date. The Allies' "combatant effectives" are placed at 4,002,104; the Germans at 3,576,900. The Allied artillery is placed at 21,843 pieces; the Germans at 18,100. The Allies had 5,646 aeroplanes; the Germans 4,000. The Allies had 1,572 tanks; the Germans practically none. This decisive superiority in men and machinery was increasing week by week. Americans were pouring in at the rate of 50,000 to 60,000 per week and Allied workshops were turning out an increasing output of guns, tanks and aeroplanes. This official calculation was not revealed at the time. An essential part of the Staff strategy at this stage was to underestimate Allied numbers and to exaggerate those of the enemy, in order to keep politicians up to the mark in the supply of men and material. As a temporary device this method may have been justifiable but as a historical record it is misleading.

On August 21st the Third British Army struck at the German salient in Flanders, and a week later the First Army extended this thrust northwards. These attacks drew the German reserves up to Flanders, and the Fourth Army was able then to renew its advance on the Amiens Front. By the 26th we had regained Albert and a considerable stretch to the north, and during the following week we broke across the Hindenburg line in front of Arras, captured Mount St. Quentin and Péronne further south, and turned the line of the Upper Somme. The French were making corresponding advances to the south of us, by means of the same tactics of successive, related strokes. By the latter part of August we were back on or beyond the front we had held at the beginning of the year along almost the whole line. In one part of the line the Allies recovered territory which had been in possession of the enemy since September, 1916. The Americans had in a brilliant action pinched out the St. Mihiel salient, south of Verdun, and once more taught the enemy an uncomfortable respect for their fighting quality.

By the latter part of August almost the whole of the operations which Foch had envisaged in his Memorandum of July 24th as constituting the first stage of his offensive had been completed — indeed, along most of the front the advances achieved were well in advance of what he had laid down as the necessary minimum — and the stage was now set for the second part of the offensive, a general assault along the whole line with the object of hurling back the enemy forces in defeat towards their own frontier.

That this phase of the battle was in sight had been clearly forecast by Foch as early as the end of August, and on the 30th of that month he had drawn up a scheme and communicated it to the Commanders-in-Chief, outlining a general assault by the Allied Armies. He proposed that the Americans, after reducing the St. Mihiel salient, which was one of the preliminary operations noted by him on July 24th, should attack northward, west of the Meuse. The French should press forward in the centre, the British on their left, and the Belgians and British in Flanders. He followed this up on September 3rd by a written General Instruction to the Commanders-in-Chief, outlining the different operations to be undertaken along the whole front; and on September 8th he wrote asking Sir Douglas Haig to prepare and launch without delay an offensive to capture the Hindenburg line and to advance beyond it towards Valenciennes, Solesmes, Le Cateau and Wassigny. Next day he arranged personally with the King of the Belgians for the Flanders advance, and proceeded to confirm the arrangements with Haig and Plumer. As ultimately fixed his schedule was:

September 26th: A Franco-American attack between the Suippe and the Meuse.

September 27th: An attack by the British First and Third Armies in the general direction of Cambrai.

September 28th: An attack by the Flanders Group of Armies between the sea and the Lys, under the command of the King of the Belgians.

September 29th: An attack by the British Fourth Army, supported by the French First Army, in the direction of Busigny.

Finally, he ordered the French Tenth Army to prepare for an attack across the Chemin des Dames, which could be launched the moment the enemy was shaken and in the toils of these successive offensives.

Before these attacks materialised events had occurred in other theatres which made the German position hopeless and convinced the most stout-hearted amongst their leaders that the cause of the Central Powers was irretrievably doomed. All the allies of Germany were beaten and acknowledged that they could no longer keep up the fight.

The Austrians had been sagging right through the year. They were on the point of abandoning the struggle in January and February, but Germany pulled them back, partly by a feed of corn, partly by implicit threats. The victories of the spring and the early summer kept them steady so long as they were allowed to lean on the parapet of their trenches. But when under German prodding they got over the top and assayed a feeble offensive they were easily beaten and driven back into their mountain fastnesses, and they waited in their dug-outs for news of a German victory. This crumbling conglomerate of Southern Germans, Magyars, Yugo- and Czecho-Slavs and Roumanians all belonged to brave races which have always shown fearless courage in the multitude of wars that, for unknown centuries, they have fought against others and each other. But the heart was out of them by 1918. Hunger and privation had depressed their vitality. They had no cause which inspired and maintained them to endure years of hardship. They had no purpose that united them in common sacrifices. Their rulers were persuaded in February to postpone negotiations for peace in order to give the Germans their chance of making a final dash for victory. The second great defeat of the Marne convinced them that the game was up and that Germany could not win. This decided them to make peace without delay. Every effort was made to dissuade them from peace overtures to the Allies. But in the first week in September, Burian issued the note which definitely started Austria on the glissade of surrender. Then followed on September 15th the defeat and collapse of Bulgaria. The Allies on that date broke through the German-Bulgarian line. The barrier of the Balkans was penetrated. The Bulgarians retreated and would listen to no appeal from the Germans to continue the fight. They sought an armistice. The South-Eastern Front of the Central Empires was uncovered and the road to Constantinople was also opened. The Allied Army of Salonika made preparations for advancing to and afterwards across the Danube and another Allied contingent was to march on Constantinople. In Mesopotamia the Turkish Army was annihilated and by the 20th of September Allenby had destroyed the last army of the Turks in Palestine. Germany, before the combined assault in the West was launched by the Allies, had already been abandoned by all her allies and we took the necessary measures to acquaint her soldiers and her people with the facts. The Germans were in the position Napoleon was in when he was deserted by his allies; when he was being driven out of Germany by an overwhelming allied force, while the British Army was advancing from the south, and French politicians and Generals alike were clamouring for a speedy peace in order to avert utter disaster to their country. In such circumstances the spirit of the bravest army quails. The despised side-shows made their contribution towards the Allied triumph on the Western Front. Had Germany's allies stood firm, the loss of morale amongst the German troops which weakened their resistance and gradually disintegrated the Army would not have occurred. The certainty of disaster and the sense of impending encirclement were largely responsible for the rapidity with which the Germans were driven out of formidable entrenchments which had defied the most tremendous Allied onslaughts for years.

While Germany's allies were thus deserting her, Foch set his programme in operation, and the whole Western Front burst into flames, from the North Sea to Lorraine. Never in the history of human rage has there been such a vast eruption of destructive fury. The operations on each sector were in the hands of the Commander-in-Chief of the particular group of Allied forces — Belgian, British, French, American — responsible for the attack; but behind them all the master-mind of Foch was at work, planning his successive hammer-strokes, and organising the distribution of forces and reserves so as to secure the maximum effect. And on the battlefield the Allied troops pressed forward with a new confidence, born of the well-grounded certainty that they were now superior in men, material and leadership, that a complete victory had already been achieved on other fronts and that final triumph on the most formidable front of resistance was in sight. The enemy could no longer stand up against the impact of the impending assault.

Beyond a doubt, one of the most brilliant performances and decisive strokes of this succession of colossal battles was the smashing blow delivered by Haig and his dauntless Army of British and Dominion troops at the Siegfried line between Marcoing and St. Quentin. The Germans, not without reason, thought they had made that line impregnable, and the very troops who overran it could hardly understand their own achievement when they examined afterwards in cold blood the defences they had stormed: immense tank-proof trenches, sunken fields filled with barbed-wire entanglements, strong points and machine-gun nests, and vast shell-proof dug-outs and underground chambers, where whole battalions could shelter from a barrage — and the highly fortified line of the Canal du Nord adding a natural and seemingly impassable obstacle in the heart of this network of massive and ingenious defences. It was strongly held, too, for the American attack in the Argonne which was to have diverted the German forces southwards did not in fact succeed in doing so in time to affect this struggle. Ludendorff records in his Memoirs that the effect of this blow was such as to compel him to order a general retirement of his whole front from the Scarpe to the Vesle, and to evacuate the salient on the Lys in Flanders. By September 28th, the British had smashed through the incredible defences of the Siegfried line in front of Cambrai and crossed the Canal du Nord, while in combination with the Belgians they had launched a thrust in Flanders which carried them well beyond the farthest limit of the Passchendaele offensive of evil memory. As an illustration of the unsuitability of this ground for a crucial campaign, it has to be noted that although this attack in Flanders met little opposition, it had to be suspended for a fortnight because the transport was bogged. The French had also made considerable progress on their front. On September 28th, as Ludendorff records in his book, "The General Staff and its Problems", he and Hindenburg came to the conclusion that the only course left for them was to demand an immediate armistice, and to offer to conclude peace in terms of President Wilson's Fourteen Points.

The outlook for Germany was summed up by Ludendorff in a Report of September 30th, in which he reviewed the situation on the various fronts, the collapse of Bulgaria and threatened collapse of Turkey and Austria, and the weakness in the West. Of this last he said: [1] —

"The position on the Western Front is well known. Twenty-two German divisions must be broken up. The numerical superiority of the Entente thus increases to 30 or 40 divisions. The 38 American divisions have a particularly high establishment. On the other hand, the strengths of our divisions are progressively dwindling. Several divisions only exist on paper.

"It is not, however, the low strengths of our divisions which make our position serious but rather the tanks which appear by surprise in ever increasing numbers. . . . Owing to the effect of the tanks our operations on the Western Front have now practically assumed the character of a game of chance. The General Staff can no longer work with definite factors. . . ."

Between mid-March and October 1st the strength of the German Armies had been reduced by more than one and a

[1] "The General Staff and its Problems", Vol. II, p. 164.

half million men. General von Kuhl describes its further wastage in the following terms: —

"During the heavy defensive battles of October, the average field strength of the battalions fell, at the beginning of the month to 545, at the middle of the month to 508, and at the end of the month to 450 men. If you deduct from these the non-combatants, these numbers corresponded to a combatant strength of 250, 208, and 142 men. In the end the divisions mostly counted only 800 to 1,200 rifles." [1]

The smashing through the rear of the Siegfried line, followed a few days later by the fall of Cambrai, simultaneously with a powerful thrust towards Lille in the north, sent the whole German Front reeling backwards. Ludendorff had confidently expected to be able to stand on his great fortress line, and let the Allies weary and waste themselves against it until they were willing to come to terms. The ceaseless body blows delivered with increasing power by the Allied forces left the German Army breathless and helpless. But it is fair to acknowledge that they retreated fighting for every kilometre they had ultimately to concede.

It was not a chase and hardly a pursuit. Starved, decimated, despairing, the German soldiers fought on, making us pay a heavy price for every mile we wrested from them. Throughout the whole War the Germans had shown themselves doughty fighters, but there was nothing finer in their record than the pluck with which they continued to withstand us in the hour of their defeat. They could not but know that they were beaten. At home their families were starving. Yet in the month of October, the last whole month of the War, the British forces in France suffered over 120,000 battle casualties as evidence of the resistance they encountered. Between July 1st and the conclusion of hostilities

[1] "Die Ursachen des Deutschen Zusammenbruchs im Jahre 1918", Vol. III, p. 210.

the British battle casualties in fighting a beaten foe and a foe that knew he was beaten on every Front totalled 430,000 in killed, wounded, prisoners and missing. During practically the same period the French lost 531,000 men and the Americans over 200,000. Let us do honour to a brave people with whom we have had but one deadly quarrel. They fought to the end with desperate valour. The heroic fight put up by some of the German units to the very last probably accounts for the fact that almost to the end our military leaders had no real understanding of the actual situation on the German side, and did not comprehend the extent to which the break-up of Germany's allies in other theatres was affecting the German military situation. On the 16th of October the Chief of the Imperial General Staff gave to the Cabinet an appreciation of the military situation at that time on the Western Front.

He said: —

"The French Army was extremely fatigued, and the British Army was very tired, both Armies needing rest, whilst the American Army was hampered in its mobility by the inexperience of its Staff. The Germans, on the other hand, were the most fatigued of all the Armies fighting on the Western Front. In these conditions, and with the imminent approach of the mud rendering further movement very difficult, it was not easy to forecast what results it would be possible for the Allies to achieve before the approaching end of the fighting season."

In reply to the Chancellor of the Exchequer, General Wilson said that it was a legitimate deduction from his remarks that there was nothing to warrant the assumption that the present military situation justified the Germans in giving in. In answer to a question as to what would be the position if no decisive result was obtained in the next three weeks, the Chief of the Imperial General Staff said that the enemy would, in the north, probably take up his position behind the Scheldt to Valenciennes, with his right on Ghent, and that south of Valenciennes the enemy would have to remain on the uplands as far as the Aisne. The Chief of the Imperial General Staff gave a sketch of the forthcoming military operations in the Western theatre.

This view of the military situation on the Western Front was confirmed in every particular two days later by Sir Douglas Haig in the statement he made to the Cabinet. His appreciation of the situation is given in a subsequent chapter ("How Peace Came").

Both Sir Henry Wilson and Sir Douglas Haig had underrated the general demoralisation that had set in amongst the German people and had extended to their Army. Even on the Somme, on the Scarpe and at Passchendaele, when after months of hard fighting we only won a few kilometres, our soldiers never faltered. Now that they were driving the foe before them mile after mile and capturing one town after another there was a stimulant to valour which they had hitherto never tasted. By October 19th, Ostend and Zeebrugge had been regained and the Belgian coast at last cleared of the enemy. Courtrai, Roubaix, Lille, Le Cateau, were in our hands. The Americans were butting their way stubbornly in the Argonne, and between them and us the French were marching forward across departments that had been in German hands since the first year of the War. On October 26th Ludendorff resigned. On November 1st the Canadians entered Valenciennes. On the 4th, Haig launched a great attack before which the German forces in that area finally crumbled and broke. The French were advancing steadily further still pressing the Germany Army back to the frontier. The Americans were fighting a terrible battle in the Argonne. A mutiny broke out at Kiel where the sailors of the German Navy, ordered to sea to strike a last despairing blow, refused to obey, and hoisted the red flag.

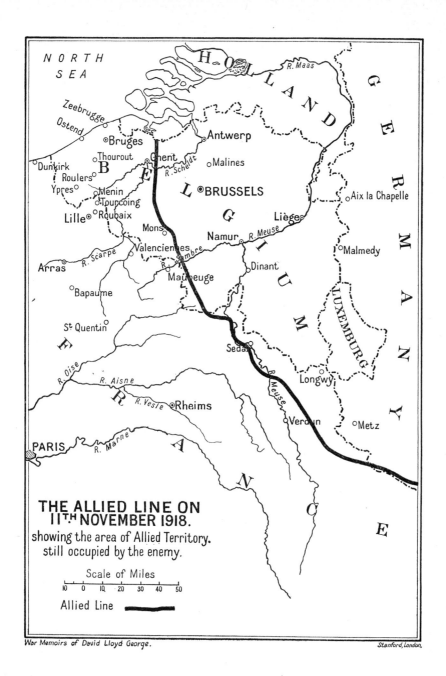

NORTH
SEA

HOLLAND

GERMANY

BELGIUM

FRANCE

LUXEMBURG

R. Maas

Zeebrugge
Ostend
○Bruges
Thourout
Dunkirk
Roulers
Ypres○
Menin
Tourcoing
Lille○ ○Roubaix

Ghent
R. Scheldt
Malines
○BRUSSELS
Liège○
Mons○
Valenciennes
R. Scarpe
R. Sambre
Maubeuge
Arras○
Bapaume
Antwerp

Namur
R. Meuse
Dinant
○Malmedy
Aix la Chapelle○

St Quentin○

R. Oise
R. Aisne
R. Vesle ○Rheims
PARIS
R. Marne

Sedan○

Longwy○

Verdun○ ○Metz

R. Meuse

THE ALLIED LINE ON
11TH NOVEMBER 1918.
showing the area of Allied Territory.
still occupied by the enemy.

Scale of Miles
10 0   10 20 30 40 50

Allied Line ▬▬▬

War Memoirs of David Lloyd George.   Stanford, London.

On the 9th of November the Kaiser abdicated. Two days before, the German delegates coming to negotiate an armistice had crossed the French lines. On November 10th, the British entered Mons. The Germans fought desperately to the last hour of the War. At 5.0 A.M. on the 11th of November, the Armistice was signed, and at 11 o'clock hostilities ceased along the whole front, from Holland to Switzerland.

CHAPTER IV

AFTERMATH IN RUSSIA

1. GENERAL

Russia after Brest-Litovsk — Insecurity of Bolshevik Government — Lenin the strong man — How Russia broke up — Confusion and conflict — Germany's prospects — Russian supplies for Germany — Allied military stores — Allied attitude to Bolsheviks — Germany's need of Russia — Starvation in Austria — Army without food — Germany distrusts Russia — Aims of Allied intervention in Russia — Russia's rival governments.

THE condition of Eastern Europe after the signing of the Brest-Litovsk treaties was one of extraordinary confusion. The Bolshevik authorities had agreed to the severing from the territory of the former Russian Empire of Finland, the Aaland Islands, Esthonia, Livonia, Courland, Lithuania and Poland; of the Ukraine and the Caucasus; they had undertaken to demobilise all their military forces and intern their fleets; and they had pledged themselves to pay a tribute to the Central Powers and permit them to penetrate the country economically and exploit its resources. But the authority of the Bolshevik rulers over the territory they represented at Brest-Litovsk was a most uncertain quantity. They had only recently seized power by means of a *coup d'état*. They maintained it by methods of ruthlessness and terrorism. How far their dictatorship rested on popular consent it was hard to say, for the first Russian Constituent Assembly, which met on December 11th, 1917, a month after the Bolshevik revolution, was forcibly dispersed by Lenin's orders two days later. On January 18th, 1918, it met again, and on the following day it was once more forcibly dissolved. Lenin was not concerned about democratic government. His main purpose was the social and economic emancipation of the worker under any form of government that would be most suited to achieve that end. The Bolsheviks were numerically a small party, drawn almost entirely from amongst the town workers, and their grip on power was not based on any principle of majority rule, gauged by the counting of heads, but on the right of the strongest, measured in terms of firm will, clear purpose and armed force. The peasants acquiesced with the patient docility of a people accustomed for generations to autocratic rule.

Since they made no pretence of consulting the chosen representatives of Russian opinion, it was obviously very hard for observers outside Russia to be sure whether their government had come to stay or whether it was only a brief interlude of despotic authority by a group of sectarians, which before long would give place to a more conventional rule. Quite certainly there were very large sections of the population in Russia that bore no love for the Bolshevik masters established in Moscow and Petrograd. Indeed, the whole country appeared to be disintegrating. Province after province of the former Empire was breaking off and declaring its independence, and the areas which were not definitely organising themselves on separatist lines were derelict and chaotic, without any stable government of their own or any coherent, systematic affiliation to the Central Government. They formed their local committees or Soviets, but these were not necessarily in sympathy with Lenin.

Democratic self-government is an art which it takes a nation long years to learn. Russia was far from having acquired it. Kerensky had for some months deceived himself and us into imagining that the Russian Socialists could at a bound pass from abject subservience to Czarist autocracy into a steady and responsible self-control and orderly administration. Actually the Russians had been accustomed to the rule of the strong hand; and for good or evil the strongest hand on the board was that of Lenin. But no one could at that time say whether a stronger than he would arise. He was a Communist; but whilst fanaticism does not always endow its possessor with great administrative ability, it is not incompatible with a genius for government, and no one can doubt that Lenin was one of the greatest leaders of men ever thrown up in any epoch. Only a few months earlier he had reached Russia in a sealed carriage, in which the Germans had passed him across Central Europe, as they would some plague bacillus they wanted to loose upon their enemies. One small, solitary figure, he had now risen to supreme power. But he was balanced there precariously. He and his Bolshevik colleagues depended on their hastily organised formations of Red troops drawn from the ranks of the Communist workmen of the towns and of police drawn partly from the Czarist police service. Their army had one of the qualities which made the Ironsides such a formidable fighting force. Their fanaticism partook of the fierce religious zeal which inspired the Cromwellians. Until the Communist recruits had been fully trained and equipped and the Red Army was efficient, it could put up no fight against the German invaders. Much of the strength of the Bolsheviks lay in the inertia of public opinion, its disintegration and the lack of unity among possible opponents. They rested mainly for support on industrial workers in the towns — who themselves formed but a small minority among the overwhelmingly agricultural population of Russia. Outside the towns there was no firm support of the Bolshevik Government. The Cossacks who dominated in the east and southeast were openly hostile.

The way in which the Russian Empire had broken up can be shown by the following dates: —

12th September, 1917. — Poland's independence of Russia was recognised by the Central Powers, which granted her a temporary constitution.

20th September, 1917. — A Council of the Transcaucasian peoples, Armenia, Georgia, Azerbaijan and Daghestan, proclaimed Transcaucasia a Federal Republic.

20th November, 1917. — The Ukraine proclaimed itself an independent Republic.

28th November, 1917. — Esthonia declared its independence.

6th December, 1917. — Finland declared its independence.

23rd December, 1917. — Bessarabia formed independent Moldavian Republic.

4th January, 1918. — Finland's independence was recognised by Russia, France and Sweden.

12th January, 1918. — Latvia declared its independence.

9th February, 1918. — Ukraine made a separate peace with the Central Powers.

By the time the Russians had signed the peace treaty of Brest-Litovsk with the Central Powers, German forces had captured the Russian islands in the Baltic, had pushed up through the Baltic provinces to within 150 miles of Petrograd, and were steadily pressing forward across the Ukraine in South Russia. From the south-east, the Cossacks of the Don under General Alexeieff had risen against the Bolsheviks and marched on Moscow, but had been defeated in February. Eastward, the whole of Russia-in-Asia was a disorganised confusion, where the conflicting motives of Bolshevism, Nationalism, Pan-Turanianism, and Pan-Islamism rallied groups to rival standards in one district and another. Where bands of former German and Austrian prisoners drew together they sought to get control of affairs in the interests of the Central Powers; and where compact forces of Czecho-Slovaks had prior to the Bolshevik ascendancy been fighting on the Russian side, they strove to continue their struggle against the advancing forces of the Germans. With the collapse of the Russian offensive in Asia Minor, the Turks had again plucked up courage to push up towards Transcaucasia. In all these areas, Bolshevism was working locally like a ferment. But while it was breaking down the old social and administrative structure, it was as yet far from supplying an organised and connected alternative system of government. That it might in time do so appeared for the moment scarcely probable. A still victorious Germany had already obtained a measure of control over Finland and the Baltic provinces, Poland and the Ukraine. She was pressing eastwards along the north of the Black Sea, while her ally, Turkey, was once more advancing along the south, towards the Caucasus and Caspian. If Germany could escape defeat in the World War, it seemed likely that she would emerge with a great extension of her power in the east; with at least a suzerainty over the ring of puppet states she had erected between the Baltic and the Black Sea; with a wide band of controlled territory running to the Caspian, and possibly across Siberia to the Pacific. It was apprehended that the destructive working of Bolshevism might in fact prove merely to have broken up and ploughed a field in readiness for planting with Prussianism.

Although the Bolshevik Government of Russia had deserted the Entente and signed a separate peace with Germany, it was obvious in these circumstances that the Entente could not afford to abandon Russia to the domination of Germany. We could not acquiesce in the vast accession of strength which Prussian Imperialism stood to gain from its treaty spoils, especially from its dominance over the Ukraine, which gave it access to great stores of wheat and cattle, to the coal of the Donetz basin, and ultimately, by way of the Black Sea and the Caucasus, to the vast oil deposits of the Caspian. If Germany succeeded in provisioning itself freely from these sources, the whole effect of our blockade would be lost.

There can be no question that throughout 1918, the Germans looked to Russia, not merely to supply them with substantial territorial gains to reward them for their war effort, but still more as a vitally important source of food-stuffs and fodder, of oil and minerals. By controlling the Ukraine and the Black Sea, the Caucasus and the Caspian, and penetrating into Siberia, they hoped to escape from the stranglehold of the Allied blockade. In those regions, rich in natural resources, they expected to secure immense stocks of cereals and meat, draught animals for their army transport, leather, petroleum, copper and iron. Had their hopes been fully realised, the War might have had a different outcome.

Further, there were very considerable military stores, warehoused or stacked at the ports of Archangel, Murmansk and Vladivostok, which we had sent to Russia for use in her conflict with the Central Powers. Now that she had signed a peace treaty, the danger was that these would fall into the hands of Germany and be used against us. It was unlikely that the Bolshevik Government would hand them over to Germany out of good will, but it might be forced to do so under pressure. German forces were pressing into Finland, and could easily advance thence to the Murman coast and the White Sea. In Siberia there were Austrian and German troops at large, formed of released prisoners. And German agents were active everywhere.

I have decribed in a previous chapter[1] the attitude which we and our Allies had decided to adopt in regard to Russia's new rulers. It was not our duty to settle the political order of Russia. We did our best to maintain friendly diplomatic relations with the Bolsheviks, and we recognised

[1] Vol. V, Chap. III: "Bolshevism Conquers Russia."

that they were *de facto* rulers of the region of old Great Russia. But there were now wide areas in which the *de facto* rule was in other hands. There were nationalist movements dominating the Volga and the Don; Georgians and Armenians forming independent governments in the Caucasus; and in the vast, confused area of Siberia there were local autonomies, Bolshevik and non-Bolshevik, Cossacks, and compact formations of Czecho-Slovaks, organised out of Czechs and Slovaks resident in Russia at the outbreak of the War, and of companies and regiments of those nationalities that had given themselves up *en masse* in the course of the War, rather than fight for Austria. They had fought alongside the Russians for the Allies, and when Bolshevik Russia laid down her arms, they continued to stand for the Allied cause, from the victory of which alone they could hope to see Czecho-Slovakia gain her independence, and return to their home-country without being arrested as traitors. The Bolsheviks, while not willing allies of Germany, were in a military sense at her mercy. But the various Russian nationalist movements were strongly opposed to Germany's progressive invasion of their country. And while we did not desire to take sides as between Nationalist and Bolshevik in their struggle for the control of Russia's government, we were interested parties in regard to their respective resistance to German penetration.

General von Kuhl, in his evidence before the German Reichstag Committe after the War, devotes very considerable space to an examination of the question whether more forces could have been brought over from the Eastern Fronts to the West in 1918, to reinforce their dwindling effectives against the Anglo-French onset. His conclusion is that it could not have been done. Had the Germans abandoned their project of forcing a decision in France and remained on the defensive there, they might have overrun Russia and temporarily conquered it. But once they decided on a great offensive in the West, it was imperative that they should withdraw their best troops from the East. Their forces in Russia had, in fact, been reduced to the lowest point consistent with maintenance of the policy of exploiting the Ukraine and Southern Russia for supplies. Von Kuhl's account of the food shortage in Germany and Austria and of the vital need of drawing supplies from Russian sources, is very revealing. As early as December 15th, 1917, he says, a letter from the Secretary of the War Food Ministry was forwarded to Ludendorff which stated that —

"The state of our food supplies of breadstuffs and provisions makes it a matter of extreme urgency to give first place to the possibility of bringing corn from Russia. . . . Quite apart from the position of Austria, it is for us ourselves of decisive importance for carrying on the War that the possibility of bringing in corn should be realised." [1]

He cites the evidence of Count Czernin as to the still more desperate state of Austria. In January, 1918, when the Brest-Litovsk negotiations were in progress, the Count noted that —

". . . a catastrophe resulting from lack of food was actually knocking at the door. Total collapse could hardly be averted; the situation was terrible. . . . The outbreak of revolution would be unavoidable if they could not succeed in securing help in the shape of corn. At the same time, Count Czernin cast his eyes on the Ukraine. 'I have hopes of securing supplies from the Ukraine, if we are only successful in maintaining ourselves without disturbance for the next few weeks.' " [2]

Von Kuhl cites evidence from General von Arz that at the end of December, 1917, a number of armies had not even

[1] "Die Ursachen des Deutschen Zusammenbruchs im Jahre 1918", Vol. III, p. 16.
　[2] *Ibid.*, pp. 16 and 17.

a single day's ration of flour in their possession; and on January 5th, 1918, he informed the German Quarter-master-General that —

". . . The Austro-Hungarian Army has for a number of weeks past been in such a critical state with regard to provisions that there are absolutely no reserve rations of flour or fodder-grain in hand, and we have had to reduce the daily bread ration to 280 grammes (10 oz.) and the daily ration of fodder-grain to 1½ kilogrammes." [1]

Much more evidence of the same kind is given by von Kuhl. As a result, the Germans and the Austro-Hungarian forces invaded the Ukraine, and advanced to the Crimea, to get food. They obtained a certain amount, though nothing like as much as they had hoped. There was no ordered government, and the peasants burnt or buried their surplus rather than see it requisitioned by the foreigner. What they got was secured only by military force. Pleading with the German Government to send more soldiers to the Ukraine to secure their harvest, the Secretary of the War Food Ministry wrote on August 7th, 1918: —

"In the new economic year there is a peril of complete collapse if we are unsuccessful in securing from the Ukraine those supplies for the final two months which cannot be obtained from home sources. . . ." [2]

Statements such as these demonstrate that the enemy powers regarded their exploitation of Russian territory as vitally necessary to the maintenance of their war effort. Nor was the importance of the food and other supplies they were extracting thence the only issue for them. In addition, they felt they dare not leave Russia free to reorganise herself against them. As General von Kuhl says: —

[1] *Ibid.*, p. 17.
[2] *Ibid.*, p. 30.

"A peace could only be relied on with Soviet Russia if we were able to hold it in bounds and could protect our Eastern Front. The peace was in truth nothing but an armistice. The Soviet Government was our enemy for good and all. Besides, we had always still to reckon with an attempt on the part of the Entente to establish once again a front against us in Russia." [1]

Ludendorff declares in his Memoirs that it would have been absurd to evacuate Russia, as they needed it for their own existence, and they had to prevent it from being reinforced by the Entente. They also felt it necessary to establish a cordon along the border of their occupation, with the aim of damming back the Bolshevik propaganda that was flooding across into Germany. Ludendorff even had hopes of raising troops among the Russians of the west and south. He remarks pathetically that he had hoped —

". . . we should at least obtain some assistance from the sons of the land we had liberated from Bolshevik dominion." [2]

But the ungrateful Russians did not rush forward to fight his battles for him. Two divisions were formed in Germany of selected prisoners of war of Ukrainian origin. But "unfortunately they did not turn out well."

But if the Germans failed in the event to make quite so good a use as they hoped, and as we feared they would be able to do of their success against Russia, clearly we should have been extremely foolish to leave them a free hand there in view of the possibilities that existed, alike of war-time exploitation, and of permanent penetration and domination of Russia and Siberia. During the summer and autumn of 1918 we made a number of moves of which the main objects in the East were: —

[1] *Ibid.*, p. 39.
[2] Ludendorff: "My War Memories", Vol. II, p. 566.

To prevent Germany and Turkey from gaining access to the
oilfields of the Caspian;

To prevent the military stores at Murmansk, Archangel and
Vladivostok falling into enemy hands;

To succour the Czecho-Slovak troops in the Urals and
Vladivostok, and enable them either to reconstitute an anti-
German front in combination with the pro-Ally Cossacks and
other Nationalist forces in Russia, or to withdraw safely and join
the Allied forces in the West.

A constant preoccupation of the British War Cabinet
and of the Inter-Allied Supreme War Council was to devise
means whereby these objects could be secured. It was a com-
plex and difficult task. The Czarist Russian Empire had been
under one ultimate control. So is the U.S.S.R. to-day. But
from the autumn of 1917 onward, during the rest of the War
period and for some time afterwards, the territory which had
been the Russian Empire was broken up into regional organisations, independent governments, rival and warring
political combinations. And the conflicting efforts of the
Central Powers and of the Entente criss-crossed through
this medley in a bewildering tangle. Thus in Finland, Germany was supporting the White Guards against the Red or
Bolshevik elements, and encouraging the Whites to advance
across North Russia towards the Murmansk coast. In Siberia,
German troops and agents were making common cause with
the Bolsheviks against the pro-Ally Czecho-Slovaks and the
nationalist Cossacks. In the Ukraine, the Bolshevik Government was destroying or removing the peasants' hoards of
food, to prevent them from falling into German hands. In
Baku, the Entente were supporting an anti-Soviet Government, since Lenin had conceded to the Germans the exploitation of the Caspian oil resources. The Bolsheviks
would on principle keep no faith with either Germany or
the Entente, save under compulsion, for their avowed aim

was to bring to the ground every capitalist government, so that fundamental antipathy was the only policy we could expect from them. In that respect they treated both the belligerent coalitions with impartial suspicion and dislike; not that the Soviet Government were averse, as I shall point out, to seeking Allied assistance in an emergency. But we were fighting our last desperate battle in a Great War and we had to take our own measures to protect our vital interests in the East.

2. Murmansk and Archangel

Guarding military stores — Trotsky's appeal — Allied cruisers for Murmansk — Difficulties at Archangel — Threat from Finland — Situation of Czecho-Slovaks — Archangel occupied.

There were two lines of approach for the Allies to Russia: one via the Arctic, through Murmansk and Archangel; and one via Siberia, through Vladivostok. Our major concern was to keep these lines open.

During 1917, upwards of two million tons of military stores had been delivered by us at these ports. There were immense dumps of cannon, shells, clothing, etc., at Archangel and Murmansk, which owing to the wretched transport facilities of Russia had never been cleared to be used by the Russian Armies. During the summer there had been a small squadron of the British Navy operating there to convoy supply vessels and repel submarine attacks. A few of these vessels still remained in the Kola inlet at Murmansk during the winter of 1917–1918.

When, after the refusal of the Soviet authorities to sign the Treaty of Brest-Litovsk, the Germans proceeded to advance on Petrograd, Trotsky grew terrified that they might now refuse to accept the Russian signature. On March 2nd, he telegraphed to the local Soviet government at Murmansk: —

"Peace negotiations apparently broken off. Danger threatens Petrograd. Measures are being taken to defend it to last drop of blood. It is your duty to do everything for defence of Murman line. Germans are advancing in small bodies. Opposition is possible and compulsory. Nothing must be left to the foe.

"*You are ordered to coöperate with Allied Missions in everything and to put all obstacles in way of advance of Germans. The robbers are attacking us.* We are obliged to save the country and the revolution." [1]

The local authorities on this applied to Admiral Kemp for his help, and put forward their suggestions for united action to resist any advance by the Germans.

We were not at the moment able to spare troops for Murmansk, but we at once dispatched a cruiser, the *Cochrane,* to reinforce our squadron, and asked the French and the Americans to do the same. The French sent the *Amiral Aube,* which arrived there on the 19th of March. Later on the United States sent the *Olympia.* It is worth noting that our expedition to Murmansk was undertaken at the invitation of the Russian Government and of the local Soviet. When, later on, the central authorities ceased to welcome our presence there, the local government continued to coöperate with us and supported us against Bolshevik attacks.

The signing of the Brest-Litovsk treaty barred the Russians from any further naval activity. But sea transport to Murmansk and Archangel was still being threatened by German submarines, which also sank several Russian steamers and bombarded a Russian signal station. So the Murmansk Soviet turned over their local naval force — three destroyers — to the Allies, the British, French and Americans each taking one, to defend the coast and Russian shipping against U-boat attacks.

But while the problem of maintaining a foothold at Mur-

[1] "Official History: Naval Operations", Vol. V., p. 311.

mansk was thus fairly simple to handle, the Archangel situation was far more difficult. Archangel was impossible to approach by water until the summer should thaw the ice. It was, however, important to secure control of it for a number of reasons. A large body of Allied refugees had assembled there, unable to get through to Murmansk because Bolshevik troops had broken the line. There were a million tons of Allied stores there, including a large quantity of manganese, and these would probably be taken by the Germans, or sold to them by the Bolshevik Government, if left unguarded by us. At an Allied Diplomatic Conference held in London on March 16th, a report was considered from General Knox, which recommended that we should send a force of 5,000 men to Archangel; and annexed to this report was a message from Captain Proctor, the British Military Representative at Archangel, suggesting a joint Allied force of 15,000 troops. The matter was remitted for study to the Allied Naval Council and the Permanent Military Representatives at Versailles. But by the time these two bodies met in joint conference on March 23rd, the German offensive on the Western Front had broken out, and it was for the moment impossible to consider a military expedition to North Russia.

As the spring advanced, the German threat to North Russia grew more serious. Finland was at this time virtually a German protectorate, with 20,000 German troops in it, and we gathered that they purposed to extend Finnish territory up to the Arctic, giving the Germans submarine bases on the Murmansk coast. Early in May, Finnish troops advanced on Pechenga, a harbour to the west of the Kola inlet. But Admiral Kemp sent a force of Russians, at the request of the Murmansk Soviet, along with a detachment of Royal Marines, which met and drove back this attack.

By this time the Czecho-Slovak troops which had rallied

together in Siberia were estimated at about 70,000, of which some 20,000 had moved off east to Vladivostok, while the remaining 50,000 were in Western Siberia. The Allies were of opinion that if these could be encouraged to make their way to North Russia, they would be able there to join hands with our forces and assist in re-forming an anti-German Front in the East. For this purpose it was necessary to go further with the organisation of pro-Ally forces there, and on May 17th, we dispatched General Poole to Murmansk with a Military Mission of 500 officers and men, for organising the Czech troops it was hoped to rally there. He travelled on the American cruiser *Olympia,* which was proceeding to reinforce the British and French vessels at Murmansk, and on arrival was placed in command of all forces on shore.

The scheme of effecting a connection with the Czecho-Slovaks in North Russia made it imperative to occupy Archangel. But, outside the jurisdiction of the Murmansk Soviet, the Bolsheviks were now growing hostile to the Allies, and toward the end of June a force was dispatched from Petrograd for the purpose of ejecting us from Murmansk. At this the Murmansk Soviet decided by a resolution of a mass meeting of the local inhabitants to break off relations with Petrograd and Moscow, and thereafter we found ourselves in North Russia supported by the local people but in a state of war with the Bolsheviks.

Further British and French troops arrived in June and July, and on August 2nd, after some fighting, an Allied expedition occupied Archangel. In the following weeks it pressed some way up the Dvina, but the water-logged, fog-bound tundras were difficult country for operations. Some American reinforcements for the North Russian troops arrived in North Russia in September, but long before this, all hope of making a junction with the Czecho-Slovak troops in

Western Siberia had proved vain, and these had been reduced to fighting their way out eastwards to Vladivostok.

When the Armistice was signed in November, the Archangel forces were securely frozen in at that port and along the lower Dvina. They had succeeded in the immediate objective of preventing the Germans from gaining a footing in the Arctic; and they had opened the road for escape to the considerable numbers of Allied refugees who had made their way northwards after the Bolshevik revolution. They had also prevented the military stores which were piled up at Archangel and Murmansk from slipping into enemy hands and being used against us in the War. But the expedition had not attained the full strategic value which had at one time been hoped. It had failed to connect with the Czecho-Slovaks or to rally the general body of the Russian people to form an anti-German Front. The presence of German forces in Finland made it difficult for any bold move southwards from our North Russian bases, and the Bolsheviks themselves were far from desiring to coöperate with us. They were at enmity with Entente and Germans alike.

3. SIBERIA

The long way round — Recommendation of Versailles experts — Reasons for action in Siberia — A move by Japan — Peril of German penetration of Russia — Pros and Cons of Japanese intervention — Mr. Balfour's despatch to U.S.A. — Allied intervention necessary — Suspicion of Japan unwarranted — A joint expedition suggested — President Wilson's uncertainty — The Czech Legion — Ludendorff's protest — Czechs resist Bolshevik treachery — Ludendorff's tribute to their services — Allies support non-Bolshevik movements — Advice from Japan — Wilson fears Czarist restoration — Problem of transporting the Czechs to Europe — Troops sent to Vladivostok — My interview with Kerensky — Optimism without action — Kerr's report of further interview — Kerensky wants Allied recognition — Wilson objects to General Knox — Mr. Balfour's note — My message to Wilson — Versailles Council appeals to Wilson — He agrees to joint intervention — A valuable insurance.

An intervention on a much larger scale, and one which achieved far greater success in hampering the enemy, was that which we eventually carried out across Siberia from Vladivostok. It was an extreme example of the fact that the long way round may be the quickest in matters of strategy. Here we had to operate from the most distant of all bases, a port on the Pacific coast of Asia, across the whole desolate expanse of Siberia. Yet by this roundabout route we were in fact able to exert considerable pressure on the Germans in Russia, and render support to those forces which were opposing their penetration into the oil and corn areas.

The Allied policy in Russia after her military collapse is explained in the decisions taken at Versailles after the Bolshevik Government had entered into negotiations with Germany.

In December, 1917, the Military Representatives at Versailles brought under review the Russian situation. At that time the Bolshevik Government had ceased hostilities with the Central Powers, though neither Russia nor Roumania had yet made peace. In their Joint Note No. 5, dated the 24th of December, 1917, the Military Representatives pointed out the danger of Germany getting foodstuffs from South Russia, and by securing command of the Black Sea, gaining a footing in the Caucasus. For such reasons they urged that —

". . . without being able to guarantee that the troops of Southern Russia and Roumania are or are not able to resist the Bolsheviks helped by the Germans, the Military Representatives are of opinion that all national groups who are determined to continue the War must be supported by all the means in our power.

"The Military Representatives realise that this resistance could not be sustained for an indefinite time unless it should prove possible to open a more direct communication between the Allies and our friends in Russia either by way of Vladivostok and the

Siberian railway, or by operations in Turkey which might open a direct route to Tiflis, or lead to a separate peace and the opening of the Dardanelles."

As I relate elsewhere, we did not succeed in the earlier part of 1918 in crushing Turkey so as to open the Dardanelles or gain possession of Tiflis. But the route *via* Vladivostok was, after some delay, exploited by us.

Among the various considerations which eventually led to our intervention there may be mentioned, first, the fact that there was at Vladivostok a big accumulation of military stores intended for use by our Russian allies against the Central Powers. We did not want these to be used by the hostile Bolsheviks for exterminating those non-Bolshevik movements in Russia which were still opposing the Germans; still less did we want them to be seized by Austro-German forces in Russia, or surrendered by the Bolsheviks to the enemy as a condition of peace. In the second place, Vladivostok remained our one channel of communication with the anti-German forces operating in Russia — the Cossacks of the Don and the Kuban, the non-Bolshevik governments of the Caucasus. Thirdly, it was imperative to prevent the Germans from penetrating into Siberia and securing a hold upon it and its great natural resources. There were considerable numbers of former enemy prisoners there — Germans and Austro-Hungarians who had been captured by Russia in the course of the War — who were now holding together in the midst of the general chaos and were likely either to seize and garrison the important points of the country for the enemy, or to get back to Central Europe and reinforce the enemy armies against us. Fourthly, we were compelled to take note of the fact that our ally, Japan, was favourably placed for intervention on land across Siberia, and was showing a very lively interest in the situation there. It was difficult to refuse her proffered help. On

the other hand, it was highly desirable that Britain and the
United States should also be represented in any action taken.
If Japan were allowed to operate independently, the Russians
in Siberia would certainly suspect her, rightly or wrongly,
of cherishing designs on their territory; and that might
throw them straight into the arms of the Central Powers.

As early as December, 1917, we had inquired of Japan
and the United States their views as to the desirability of
occupying Vladivostok and controlling the Trans-Siberian
railway, which in the chaotic state of the country had ceased
to function. At the beginning of January we learned that
the Japanese had sent a warship to Vladivostok, so we
promptly ordered the H.M.S. *Suffolk* to proceed thither.
Her captain reported on his arrival that this action had dis-
pelled the local suspicion aroused by the advent of the
Japanese vessel, but that the Russian garrison and navy there
were in a state of anarchy. In February he further reported
that the Cossacks of Eastern Siberia had held a conference at
Iman, where they had condemned Bolshevik policy and all
attempts to make a separate peace, and had appealed to the
Allies for financial and material assistance. At the beginning
of March, when the conclusion of the Brest-Litovsk treaty
was imminent, we received a further appeal from the Cossacks, who were ready, if supplied with food and arms, to
take possession of the railway and establish an authority for
the eastern half of Siberia which would be anti-German.
We were told they could probably be induced to accept
Japanese help if the other Allied Governments were co-
operating with the Japanese.

This question of a possible Japanese intervention in
Russian *via* Siberia became an acute preoccupation of the
Allied Governments. It was at this stage impossible to foresee just how far the Germans would press their domination
of Russian territory and resources, if left undisturbed by

us. There was not merely the certainty that Germany would make effective use of the vast resources of foodstuffs, coal and oil which Russia was capable of yielding. We could not rule out the possibility that the Germans might start to enrol and train Russian man power for use in the War. Such a development seemed well within the bounds of possibility. Napoleon had enrolled conquered races in his *Grande Armée*. The Germans themselves had it in mind to do the same. They had several Polish divisions in their Army. Why not Russians too? Here were one hundred and eighty millions of people, disorganised, without a settled Government, largely illiterate and so, presumably, easy victims of suitable propaganda, of whom large numbers were trained to arms and first-class fighting material, but now disbanded and out of work. The danger that Germany might establish a grip on this country and utilise its resources for supplying her deficiencies in food and material and its masses for her campaigns looked very formidable, and amply justified the efforts the Allies made to intervene in Russia and organise whatever elements they could influence to resist that peril.

Japan was one of our Allies in the War, but although she had formidable military forces, their remoteness from any of the War theatres had prevented any considerable use being made of them. Now, however, it seemed possible that the Russian situation might provide them with an opening. They were for entering Russia via Vladivostok and Siberia and rallying the Cossacks, Czechs and other pro-Ally elements there to resist the Germans. Against such a move had to be weighed the considerations that a Japanese invasion would irritate the Soviet Government, and excite the hostility of the Russian people, and thus drive them into the arms of Germany; that it was no part of our policy to risk any permanent establishment of Japan in Siberia; and that the good will and coöperation of the United States in any arrangement was essential.

At the Allied Diplomatic Conference held in London on March 16th, 1918, it was decided to send to the United States Government a despatch which had been prepared by Mr. Balfour, setting out the views of the British, French and Italian Governments upon the Russian situation and the possibility of Japanese intervention via Siberia. This despatch ran as follows: —

"At a Conference of the Prime Ministers and Foreign Ministers of France, Italy and Great Britain held on the 15th of this month in London, I was deputed to lay before the President of the United States of America their views on the expediency of Allied intervention in Eastern Russia for the purpose of checking the complete penetration of that country by enemy influences.

"The danger, in the opinion of the Conference, is both great and imminent. Russia has utterly destroyed both her Army and her Navy; and she will never be permitted by Germany to reconstitute them. Her territory swarms with hostile agencies; such energies as she still possesses are expended in internal conflicts; and no power of resistance is left her against German domination. Her sole protection is to be found in the vast distances which the invader must traverse before obtaining complete military occupation of her Empire.

"Unfortunately, however, complete military occupation is quite unnecessary. What Germany desires is that Russia should be impotent during the War, subservient after it, and in the meanwhile should supply food and raw material to the Central Powers. All this can be effectually accomplished in the present helpless condition of the country, without transferring great bodies of troops from West to East.

"Such is the disease. What is the remedy? To the Conference it seemed that none is possible except through Allied intervention. Since Russia cannot help herself she must be helped by her friends. But there are only two approaches through which such help can be supplied; the northern ports of Russia in Europe, and the eastern frontiers of Siberia. Of these, Siberia is perhaps the most important, and is certainly the most accessible to the available forces of the Entente Powers. Both from the point of view of man-power and of tonnage, Japan is in a position to do much more in Siberia than France, Italy, America and Britain can possibly do in Murmansk or Archangel. It is therefore to Japan that, in the opinion of the Conference, appeal should be made to aid Russia in her present helpless condition.

"The Conference was well aware that there are weighty objections to this course. Though Russia has gladly availed herself of Japanese assistance during the whole course of the War, there are many observers who think that, if that assistance now took the form of a Japanese Army operating on Russian soil, it would be regarded with distrust, and even aversion. If this be so, it is doubtless due in the main to the fear that Japan would treat Russia in the east as Germany is treating her in the west, would rob her of her territory, and cover her with humiliation. No such suspicion can be entertained by those associated with Japan in the present War. If she intervenes at the present juncture, it will be as the friend of Russia and the mandatory of Russia's other Allies. Her object would not be to copy the Germans, but to resist them; and without doubt this would be made abundantly clear to all the world before any overt action was undertaken by Japan.

"This, in brief, is the argument for Japanese intervention which the Conference desired me to lay before the President. I have only to add that, in its view, no steps could usefully be taken to carry out this policy which had not the active support of the United States. Without that support it would be useless to approach the Japanese Government, and even if the Japanese Government consented to act on the representations of France, Italy and Great Britain, such action, without the approval of the United States Government, would lose half its moral authority.

"I earnestly trust, therefore, that favourable consideration will be given to a policy which, with all its admitted difficulty, seems required by the dangerous situation which has recently arisen in Eastern Europe.

A. J. BALFOUR.

"Foreign Office,
    16th March, 1918."

The sending of this despatch to President Wilson was the result of strong pressure by the French, who were anxious to secure immediate intervention by Japan. I was, however, dubious as to the wisdom of such a step if it were likely to be strongly resented by the Russian Government, and felt it essential that any such action must be supported by the United States. When we learned that Wilson was opposed to Japanese intervention unless it were asked for by the Russians, we suggested that the problem might be solved by proposing a joint expeditionary force of Americans, British and Japanese, to which some of our advisers thought the Russians might agree.

On April 5th the Japanese landed some marines at Vladivostok to protect their nationals, as there was no proper government there, and three Japanese had been shot by robbers on the previous day. The British promptly landed a similar contingent, to ensure that any move made would be an Allied one, not an independent Japanese venture.

During the next three months there was continual discussion as to what course to pursue in Siberia. President Wilson was very unwilling to intervene there. It was admittedly difficult to foresee any very large positive result that might be attained thereby in Russia. On the other hand, unless the Germans collapsed completely in the West, we foresaw that they could at need withdraw from France and Belgium and establish an almost impregnable front based on the Rhine, carrying out meanwhile a process of penetration and expansion in shattered Russia and Siberia which would leave them far bigger and stronger than ever when the War ended. It seemed worth while to make some effort to prevent this. And in any case, there were the Czecho-Slovaks. At the meeting of the Supreme War Council on May 2nd, it was reported that between 40,000 and 50,000 of these were making their way to Vladivostok in the teeth of Bolshevik efforts to stop them. They were a very fine force, and worth using either in the East or the West against the enemy.

I have already referred to these Czecho-Slovak troops. Imperial Russia had been loth to use these potential allies, who were rebelling against the dominion of a sister Empire, even though she was momentarily an enemy. But after the revolution they were formed into the Czech Legion, and in 1917 it fought valiantly in the Russian Army on the Allied side. When Bolshevism overthrew the provisional revolutionary Government, the Czechs were in the Ukraine, where Ludendorff bears witness that they were the only serious opponents of his penetration of that region: —

"The Bolshevik troops offered very little resistance but the Czecho-Slovak troops — composed of Austro-Hungarian prisoners of war — fought much better, and fierce engagements with them took place. Operations and actual fighting continued into May." [1]

Their subsequent activities also caused him grave annoyance, and called forth an indignant, if rather inaccurate, protest from him. Further on in his Memoirs he remarks: —

"In Russia events had developed along lines of their own, illustrative of the lying propensities of the Soviet Government. With the consent of this Government, the Entente had formed Czecho-Slovak units out of Austro-Hungarian prisoners. These were intended to be used against us, and were therefore to be conveyed to France by the Siberian railway. All this was sanctioned by a Government with whom we were at peace, and we actually took it lying down!" [2]

Actually, the Czech Legion was formed before ever the Soviet Government took office. And although that Government, which was at peace with us as well as with the Ger-

[1] Ludendorff: "My War Memories", Vol. II, p. 566.
[2] *Ibid.*, p. 564.

mans, nominally was willing that the prisoners of war of both sides should go home to their own countries, and accordingly gave the Czechs permission to proceed to Vladivostok for this purpose, it viewed these movements with increasing suspicion. The Soviet Government disarmed the Czechs and started to dispatch them across Siberia in detachments. The Czechs regarded these Bolshevik attentions with distrust and were not sure that the Soviet authorities had not a sinister purpose. But they were an athletic, disciplined, purposeful body of men, and tactics which might be abundantly successful against the disorganised and bewildered and terrified *bourgeoisie* were not adapted for dealing with such men as these. They disarmed the troops sent to attack them, and seized the Trans-Siberian railway. Thenceforward they were in a strong strategic position, both for securing their safe journey to Vladivostok, and for resisting Bolsheviks and Germans alike in Southern and Eastern Russia. It is not too much to say that the presence of the Czech Legion was the determining factor in our Siberian expedition. Not only were we bound to take the necessary steps to protect and succour them, but we were able by means of them to establish something like an anti-German front in South-East Russia and along the Urals. Ludendorff, though again inaccurate in stating that our object was to overthrow the Moscow Government, correctly summarises the importance of the part played by these troops when he says that: —

"The Entente, realising that they could not work with a Government which looked for support to Germany, took action against Bolshevism, and instead of sending these troops to France, held them up along the Siberian railway on the frontier between Russia and Siberia, in order to fight against the Government in Moscow. They gradually pushed forward to the middle Volga, in the direction of Kazan and Samara. In addition to this, by garrisoning the railway, the Entente prevented the return of our prisoners of war from Siberia. This was unquestionably a serious loss for us. . . .

"The new Entente front in Russia began with the Czecho-Slovaks on the middle Volga." [1]

The Germans here acknowledge that the measures we adopted inside Russia deprived them of a formidable re-inforcement on the Eastern Front, and contributed ma-terially to their failure to exploit the resources of Russia.

We were not concerned to overthrow the Bolshevik Government in Moscow. But we were concerned to keep them, so long as war with Germany was afoot, from over-throwing those non-Bolshevik administrations and move-ments outside of Moscow which were prepared to work with us against the enemy. And it was inevitable that before long our coöperation with these allies should give our Russian activities an appearance of being aimed at overthrowing the Bolshevik Government. That was certainly not their original intention.

For a time we hoped that the Soviet Government, which obviously could not wish to see the Germans penetrating into Siberia, might extend to us an invitation to send an Inter-Allied force through Vladivostok to hold them back. For this reason we decided, in April, to give instructions that Ataman Semenoff, an anti-Bolshevik leader in Eastern Si-beria, who had been encouraged by the Japanese to campaign against the Bolshevik movement there, should be told to hold his hand, and we persuaded the Japanese to adopt the same course. But the Bolsheviks did not invite us to help them, and Semenoff continued his progress. A despatch from the Japanese Government dated May 19th, 1918, outlined the situation there as follows: —

"Some time ago the British Government made a proposal to the Imperial Government looking to an intervention in Siberia,

[1] *Ibid.*, pp. 654 and 655.

which they deemed necessary in order to check the penetration of German influence. Subsequently, however, having regard to the attitude of the American Government in the matter, the British Government are understood to have found it advisable to induce, if possible, the Soviet Government to invite the Allied intervention, and instructed Mr. Lockhart to enter upon the negotiations with the Soviet Government on these lines. The recent course of these negotiations is unknown to the Imperial Government, but it is presumed that no concrete result has yet been obtained. On the other hand, the British Government, fearing that the continued support on the part of the Allies of the Semenoff detachment whose avowed object is to crush the Bolsheviks, might hinder the progress of the negotiations above referred to, requested the Japanese Government to give also an advice to Semenoff, with a view to restraining for the time being the advance of his detachment. The desired advice was given to Semenoff through a Japanese in touch with him, but it is found impossible to dissuade him from his determination. On the contrary, he is continuing his advance encouraged by the success he has so far achieved over the Bolsheviks, and, thanks to the continuous enlistment of the Cossacks in his detachment, its strength has already reached 5,000 and is growing stronger every day. He is now menacing Kalimuskaya. . . ."

The despatch proceeded to hint that there was little prospect of the Allies being invited by the Soviet Government to aid it against the Germans; that indeed intervention in coöperation with the Soviet would only alienate the anti-German elements in Russia; and that we were morally bound to support Semenoff.

Our difficulty still was the negative attitude of President Wilson. His view was that any move to intervene in Russia otherwise than with the approval of the Soviet Government would develop into a move to displace the Soviet Government in favour of an Imperialist restoration. None of us had the least wish to restore Russian Czardom. We did however think it essential to re-create an anti-German front in Russia whilst the War lasted. But as regards the question of intervention in Siberia, we were confronted with the American suspicion of Japan, and the distrust of her intentions on the mainland of Asia, which was not exactly without foundation, as later events have shown. Semenoff came later to be known as the "Japanese Puppet", and it is possible that the discouragement which they asserted they had given him on the strength of our request was not a very emphatic one.

At an Anglo-French Conference held in London on May 28th, M. Pichon pressed strongly on behalf of the French that steps should be taken to transport the Czechs forthwith to France. At that time the French were desperately anxious to get every man they could to France to aid their defence against the German offensive. But the difficulty was that there was no shipping available for such an operation. We could only move the Czechs by asking the Japanese to bring them across the Pacific, and then we could only get them to Europe at the cost of an equivalent number of American troops. Even by such means we could not hold out any hope of moving more than 4,500 to 5,000 Czechs to France by mid-September, and there was a possibility that the transfer would interfere with Japan's sending of troops to Siberia. However, the issue was thrashed out at the meeting of the Supreme War Council at Versailles on June 1st to 3rd, and decided in favour of the French proposal. We agreed to ask the Japanese to assist with tonnage in moving the Czechs unless and until their shipping was required for an expedition to Vladivostok. We further agreed as regards Japanese intervention in Siberia, that if they were willing to promise to respect the territorial integrity of Russia, to abstain from taking sides in her internal politics, and to advance as far west as possible for the purpose of encountering the Germans, we should make an effort to secure the approval of President Wilson for Japanese intervention.

During May and June it had become increasingly clear that there was no hope of getting the Bolsheviks to coöperate with us in putting up a resistance to German penetration of Russia. For that purpose, our only potential allies were the anti-Bolshevik groups which controlled various parts of the dislocated empire. A party of the Czechs fought their way through to Vladivostok, which they captured on June 29th, after a three hours' battle with the Bolsheviks. They occupied the town, and a pro-Ally Coalition Government was set up there under their protection. Among the prisoners taken by the Czechs were 600 Magyars, a proof that Bolshevik opposition to us was being stiffened by the presence among them of subjects of the Central Powers. On July 10th we decided to send a battalion from Hongkong to Vladivostok to support them, and we urged the French to move troops there if possible.

Events were thus compelling us to take action on Russian soil, and in coöperation with organisations there other than those who were associated with the Soviet authorities of Moscow and Petrograd, and without their concurrence. But it was not our business to determine whether the Bolshevik or the anti-Bolshevik sections of the Russian peoples would ultimately dominate the whole Empire. On June 24th, M. Kerensky came to interview me at Downing Street, with a view to securing the support of the Allies for the relics of the old Socialist parties which had formed the Provisional Government before their overthrow by Lenin. He claimed that he was speaking "for the whole of Russia except the reactionaries and the Bolsheviks", and said he was supported by the Executive Committee of the Constituent Assembly, which the Bolsheviks had dissolved; the Conference of the Party Leaders of the Socialist Revolutionaries; the Popular Socialist Party; the Social Democrats (except Bolsheviks); and the Cadet Party, the party of propertied middle-class reformers. These various parties disagreed with one another, but he asserted that they all agreed in wanting Allied intervention to oust the Germans and the Bolsheviks.

Kerensky was very anxious for an Allied expedition *via* Siberia. A purely Japanese one would be unwelcome, but if all the Allies took part, the Japanese contingent might be as big as it liked. The difficulty I found in discussing the situation with him was that I could get no clear assurance that he represented any organised force, apart from resolutions passed in secret by disgruntled Socialists. Resolutions on paper are of little value against machine-guns, and in the heart of Russia it was the Bolsheviks who had the machine-guns. Kerensky was vague as to how many of his friends and Committees had been left at large in Soviet Russia; he had held no communication with them recently. He expressed the opinion that the Bolsheviks could not deal a heavy blow at these organisations.

Their power in a military sense was negligible, but they were powerful enough as a police force to deal with a powerless and unorganised population. Large play had been made in the west with the Bolshevik experiments in the creation of the Red Guards, compulsory military service and so forth, but in practice these measures produced no results. He said that the influence of the Bolsheviks was waning. . . .

It seemed to me that Kerensky was underestimating the strength of the Bolsheviks, and overestimating that of the chattering conventicles he represented. I told him: —

If there were any elements in Russia which were prepared to fight Germany, the Allies would give them all the help in their power.

M. Kerensky said that he had come to say that in the event of Allied intervention there would be no opposition. It was essential, however, that he should know what were the intentions

KERENSKY

of the Allies and what he and his friends could expect. If the Allies were willing to help it would be necessary for further conversations to take place in regard to military, economic and other preparations in Russia itself.

The proposal for "further conversation" sounded rather ominous to me. I saw a prospect of any practical measures in Russia being postponed to the end of a far vista of negotiations and discussions. So I passed my visitor over to Mr. Philip Kerr (now Lord Lothian) for a further examination of his proposals. Kerr's report of this further interview showed that Kerensky's real object was to get the Allies to recognise him and his exiled friends as the real Government of Russia, and to guarantee to put them in the saddle again. The bait was the fact that they were willing to approve Allied intervention on Russian territory against Germany.

M. Kerensky said that the essential point he wanted to clear up was as to the attitude which the Allies took towards Russia. The Coalition, which he represented, regarded itself as being the legitimate authority in Russia. The Bolshevik régime was a usurpation which destroyed the Constituent Assembly, partitioned and ruined Russia, and based its authority not on representative institutions, but on autocratic principles. When he and the people for whom he spoke talked about Russia still being in the Alliance, they were not using mere words or indulging in ideals, they were expressing their profoundest convictions. They believed that the continuance of the Alliance between Russia and the Western Allies was essential just as much to the Allies as to Russia itself, because they believed that the reconstruction of Russia as an independent power politically, militarily and economically, was essential to any lasting peace. The Allies must look for their friends among the Liberal parties for whom he spoke. They would get no real support either from the Bolsheviks or the reactionaries. The only real policy was to continue on the lines of the old alliance.

It was evident that Kerensky's purpose and that of the Allies were not identical. Our one concern was to prevent the vast and productive area of the Russian Empire from becoming subject to the Central Powers, and a source of supply for them in the War. It was not our business to decide whether the Russians preferred to be ruled by Lenin or by Kerensky. Kerensky, on the other hand, was chiefly concerned to secure our undertaking to regard him and his friends as "the legitimate Government of Russia." About the extent to which, if at all, he and his friends could rally military forces to fight with the Allies against the Germans, he was extremely vague and non-committal. On the whole, I gathered that there was little of a practical and material nature which he and his Socialist colleagues were in a position to achieve at that stage, either to establish their own authority in Russia or to resist the Germans. So far as the latter object was concerned, our best hope lay in the warlike Cossacks, reinforced by the Czech Legion and such forces as the Japanese and ourselves could throw into Siberia.

We had for some time been considering the advisability of sending General Knox out to Siberia to examine the situation on the spot and take counsel with the pro-Ally Russians. On May 30 we had decided to sound Lord Reading as to whether it would be desirable for the General to travel *via* Washington and talk over the Russian situation with President Wilson. But Wilson had got it into his head that Knox, being strongly anti-Bolshevik, would work for the restoration of Czardom, and he not only did not want to see him; he disliked the idea of Knox travelling across the United States upon such a mission!

In mid-July, when we had definitely decided to send General Knox to Vladivostok, we received a message from Lord Reading, strongly deprecating the idea of Knox going *via* America, on account of the state of opinion there. We discussed the matter in the War Cabinet on July 16th, and decided that the General should proceed forthwith to Vladivostok, but should be told not to go to Washington nor grant any interviews on the way. Lord Reading should be informed that Knox was being sent to act as head of a British Military Mission coöperating with the Allied Headquarters which would be formed at Vladivostok — a post for which he possessed exceptional qualifications.

In a Memorandum which he gave me the same day, Mr. Balfour pointed out the absurdity of the American attitude.

"The fact is that an autocratic system is not only repulsive to Englishmen of all shades of opinion, but that reëstablishment of the Russian autocracy would, so far as I can judge, be a misfortune for the British Empire. Autocracy and militarism naturally go together; and it is almost inconceivable that, if the Czar could be reëstablished, Russia would not again become a purely military Empire. If so, she would inevitably be a danger to her neighbours; and to none of her neighbours so much as ourselves. . . .

"In my opinion, moreover, a restored Czardom would be more dangerous to British interests than the Czardom which has just vanished; for it would almost certainly be dependent upon Germany. . . . If I am right, Russian autocracy, always in danger at home, would have to look for support to its autocratic neighbour in Germany. If the German autocracy survives both the War and the political agitation which will succeed the War, it is very difficult to believe that it will not thus control the policy of the Russian Empire. . . .

"It is of course perfectly true that, however strong and genuine be our desire to keep out of Russian politics, it will probably be in practice almost impossible to prevent intervention having some (perhaps a great) effect on Russian Parties. The intervening Force must necessarily work with those who are prepared to work with it. Indirectly it will strengthen the Parties who are prepared to fight the Germans. It will directly injure the Parties which turn to Germany for assistance. We can do no more than attempt to the best of our ability to keep aloof from these internal divisions, and to give full opportunity to the Russian people to determine the future of their country."

I sent Mr. Balfour's minute to Lord Reading to help him to explain the situation to President Wilson. With it I sent him a private note pointing out that General Knox was not a politician, and had been very unpopular with the old régime in Russia because of his criticism of their methods; that he was wholly concerned with the military situation in the East, and was therefore the best man to deal with the military aspects of the Siberian question. We ourselves were far from sympathising with reaction in Russia, and had been careful from the beginning of the year to maintain relations with the Bolsheviks. I added that the real security against reaction in Russia was the President himself. If he joined in the intervention in Siberia, he could dominate its developments, for the rest of us, apart from Japan, were too much preoccupied in the West to give it much attention. If, finally, Wilson was ready to send an important political mission to Siberia, I would certainly see that a Liberal or Labour representative from this country accompanied it.

At a meeting of the Supreme War Council at Versailles, held on July 2nd, a long Memorandum to President Wilson had been adopted, setting out the situation in Siberia, and the reasons which led us to urge intervention there. It ended with an appeal to the President to approve the policy we were recommending and thus enable it to be carried into effect before it was too late.

It was not until the end of July that President Wilson finally decided to approve the scheme for joint intervention in Siberia. Even then he seems to have quite misunderstood the scale of effort which would be necessary to achieve any result. The arrangement to which he gave his consent was that the British and Americans should each send 7,000 troops, and that the Japanese, supported by the presence of these contingents, should furnish a force capable of advancing to rescue the Czecho-Slovaks who were still in Siberia, holding out near Lake Baikal; and while Wilson suggested that a Japanese contingent equal to the American in size would be enough, the French and ourselves recognised that a far larger force would be required. The difference of opinion was surmounted in a curious fashion. The American contingent turned out, with all its ample subsidiary services, to be nearer 9,000 than 7,000; and the Japanese promptly made this an excuse for increasing their own contingent. In the end, the troops landed by the Japanese at Vladivostok totalled over 70,000. Our combined forces, supported by a Russian Army gathered by General Knox, gave us a hold upon the whole of Siberia. When the Armistice was signed on November 11th, 1918, a curious miscellany of troops was holding a picket line right across Siberia, along the route of the Trans-Siberian railway, up to the Ural Mountains. It included White Russians, Czechs, British naval and military units, Japanese, Americans, and small bodies of French and Italians. Its positive value was that it prevented any German penetration of Siberia, and served as a barrier against their establishing any predominance there which they might utilise after the War. As events turned out, the final collapse of the Central Powers was so complete that the Treaty of Brest-Litovsk became scrap-paper, and the ambitious programme of expansion eastwards which Germany had envisaged came to nothing. No claim materialised under the insurance policy, and critics could assert, wise after the event, that it was a needless expense. That is true of most insurances. But in the spring of 1918, when the issue of the War was in doubt, it was eminently prudent to do everything

possible to prevent German exploitation of the immense resources of Russia and Siberia, and her imperial expansion
over their territories.

4. THE CASPIAN

Enemy race for Caspian oil-fields — Dunsterville's expedition — Baku occupied —
Results of Allied intervention.

There was a third area of Russian territory where, after
the collapse of Russia and the Treaty of Brest-Litovsk, we
found it necessary to intervene in order to hold the Central
Powers in check and prevent them from securing valuable
supplies. This was in the south, around the Caspian, where
were the oil-wells of Baku.

When the Russian Army under Judenitch disintegrated,
and the road to that valuable region lay open, both the Germans and the Turks began to race for it. Our concern was
to prevent either of them from winning. During April, May
and June, 1918, the Turks were thrusting up through Armenia and North-Western Persia into Georgia, while the
Germans were pushing eastwards across the Ukraine in the
same direction. In April, the Turks occupied Batum, and on
June 8th the independent government of Georgia signed
peace with Germany and Turkey. Thereupon the Germans
sent a force across the Black Sea, which on June 12th occupied Tiflis.

Meantime we had not been idle. On January 27th, 1918,
a Mission had been dispatched from Baghdad, from our
army in Mesopotamia, to carry out famine relief in North
Persia and keep open the route between Baghdad and the
Caspian. It was in charge of General Dunsterville — the erst-
while "Stalky" of Kipling's schoolboy tales. On February
17th, Dunsterville's Mission reached Enzeli, on the southern
shore of the Caspian. In the following months he carried on
relief work in North Persia, making his headquarters at

Kasvin, and holding the region against Turkish and Bolshevik agents.

The German and Turkish invasion of Georgia roused nationalist sentiment there, and on July 26th the Bolshevik Government at Baku was overthrown by a *coup d'état* and the new administration appealed to Dunsterville for aid, sending transports to ship them up the Caspian. Dunsterville set to work to organise the local levies, but they proved to be poor material. The Turks launched an attack on Baku on August 26th, which was beaten off by our troops. They then invested the town, and eventually, on the night of September 14th–15th, Dunsterville and his forces evacuated Baku and retired to Enzeli. The expedition had served the purpose of keeping the oil wells of Baku out of reach of the Central Powers at a critical period of the War, and it was now too late for the enemy to make any use of them. Six weeks later, Turkey was out of the War.

The concluding chapters of the story of the Allied intervention in Russian territory belong to the post-War period of history. The peril against which they were originally directed vanished with the total collapse of all the enemy powers on all fronts, East and West, before the end of 1918. Thereafter it became only a question of how far we should continue to give help to those allies in Russia whose co-operation with us against Germany had lately been so welcome. When it became clear that their bid for power was doomed to failure, and that the choice of the Russian people was definitely swinging across to support a Bolshevik régime, our withdrawal was inevitable.

That, however, is another story. As parts of the military effort of the Allies during the Great War, the expeditions to Murmansk and Archangel, to Siberia, and to the Caucasus, played their part in maintaining opposition to what at one time appeared to be a very real and terrible danger of Prussian imperial expansion in Russia and across Asia. They barred the road to the Arctic and the Pacific Oceans, to the cornfields of Southern Russia, to the minerals of Siberia and the oil of the Caspian. They enabled us to bring to safety scores of thousands of Czecho-Slovaks and Serbians, and a large number of refugees stranded in a country where law and order had temporarily vanished.

CHAPTER V

DAWN BREAKS IN THE EAST

Importance of minor war theatres — Weakness of Germany's allies — Successes in the East ignored — German verdict.

DURING the spring and summer months of 1918 such a colossal struggle for final mastery was raging on the Western Front in France and Flanders that other theatres of war were almost completely overlooked by the principals in this tremendous conflict, being only considered as a source of reinforcement for the great battles in the West. Every great Entente general had predicted a continuation of the War into 1919 and the Governments were all enjoined to prepare a sufficiency of men and mechanism lest it continue into 1920. Nevertheless the events in those forgotten and despised theatres in the East brought the War to an end in 1918; but for them it might have dragged its bloody course into the spring and summer of 1919.

In all these theatres the situation was favourable for a decisive blow by the Allies, and had it been delivered earlier the collapse would have come all the sooner.

The Turks were tired, disheartened and disorganised. Desertions had thinned down their forces almost to vanishing point. There were no units of any consequence threatening General Marshall in Mesopotamia, although the collapse of the Russian Armies on his right, the general unrest in Persia and the length of his communications limited his power of pressing an offensive with the forces at his disposal. In Palestine, although the Turkish troops still put up a resistance to us in various minor frays and skirmishes, they had dwindled to a miserable remnant, scourged by disease, "hungry, ragged, verminous, comfortless, hopeless, outnumbered." [1] On the Salonika Front the Bulgarians had lost interest in the War and were longing to get back to their fields. In Italy the Austrian forces were dispirited by the hunger and war-weariness that ravaged their home front. They launched one flaccid offensive, in June, on the Piave, but when it failed the front relapsed into quiescence until the final Italian offensive in October.

I have elsewhere indicated how the Bulgarian collapse precipitated the German surrender and made unnecessary another year's campaign, though this had been anticipated by all the great leaders of the Allied Armies, by Pétain throughout, by Foch in July after the great German defeat in Champagne, by Haig as late as October.

All Westerners closed their minds to the possibilities of the Eastern theatres. One can understand the French taking that view. The enemy was within cannon fire of their capital. But it is less comprehensible that our own military leaders and advisers should have succeeded in maintaining so limited and short-sighted an outlook. It was quite contrary to all the great military and naval traditions that built up our Empire. But we all remember how every little success in France or Belgium was magnified and how real great victories won by the Allies elsewhere were relegated to smaller print and less conspicuous headlines. The smallest advance on the West was blazoned forth as a great victory. The striking victories won by the Serbians in 1914 were barely recorded. The battles won by Brusiloff with hundreds of thousands of prisoners did not attract the same notice as a kilometre's advance with a few thousands of prisoners in the West.

The Reichstag Commission of Enquiry, set up after the

[1] "Official History: Military Operations, Egypt and Palestine", Vol. II, p. 446.

War to investigate the causes of the military collapse of Germany in 1918, came, after exhaustive researches, to the conclusion that: —

"The War was lost in a military sense when, during the retirement of the German Western Front in September, 1918, the collapse of Bulgaria, which was followed by that of Austria-Hungary, completely changed the situation of the German Army in the field. From then on, every attempt to obtain peace by purely military means was obviously vain." [1]

I have already quoted Ludendorff's statement that when he and Hindenburg heard of the Bulgarian débâcle they came to the conclusion that they also must apply for an armistice. They knew then that the game was up.

1. Salonika

Muddle of Allied Balkan policy — Sarrail recalled — My letter to Ribot — No prospect of offensive at Salonika — The Cinderella of the Allied Armies — Short of supplies — Malaria — French troops withdrawn — Lack of plans — Command again changed — Good prospects for offensive — Guillaumat's report on Salonika prospects — Military pessimism unjustified — Sir H. Wilson's comments — My approval of offensive — German efforts to reinforce Bulgaria — Allies' overwhelming success — Armistice signed — Reaction in Germany: decision to end the War — The oil sanction.

Of all the "side-shows", the most important turned out to be that of the despised Salonika Front. Here it was that the deadly thrust was delivered against the Central Powers which crumpled their resistance and finally compelled them to abandon hope of continuing the War. The Balkans are the back door of Central Europe, and when it had been forced, the end was in sight.

Allied policy in the Balkans throughout the earlier part of the War was marked by a singular lack of prevision or common sense. We refused Greek help when it was proffered

---

[1] "Die Ursachen des Deutschen Zusammenbruchs im Jahr 1918", Vol. I, p. 23.

to us at the beginning of the War and when Greek troops could have occupied and held the Gallipoli Peninsula and placed Constantinople at the mercy of our Fleet. They could also have held Bulgaria in check. We failed to support Serbia at the outset, when we could have saved that country from devastation and turned it into a corridor for Allied attacks upon Austria. Then, too late, we planted an expeditionary force at Salonika, too small to carry out serious offensives against the enemy, yet unduly large for mere garrison and defence purposes. We failed to keep Bulgaria from joining in with the enemy, and for a long time we so muddled our relations with Greece that instead of being our ally she was a peril in our rear. In June, 1917, we compelled King Constantine to abdicate, and thereupon Greece, under the rule of M. Venizelos, joined in on our side. This meant that the Greek Army was available to strengthen our forces in the Balkans, and Venizelos offered to contribute twelve divisions — nine of them by the end of 1917 — provided the Entente could supply the necessary equipment, heavy guns, etc. Unfortunately, General Sarrail, who was in charge of the Allied forces there, was by no means in favour with his authorities at home, and as a result his efforts to get material and food for the Greeks were muddled, neglected and brought to nought. At a conference of the Supreme War Council on December 1st, 1917, we learnt from M. Venizelos that his inability to redeem his promise of raising twelve divisions was due to the failure of the French to provide what had been promised. The result was that only three divisions had so far been mobilised, and even these were short of heavy guns and other equipment. It was not possible to call up more men until they could be fed and equipped. As soon as the attention of the Supreme Council was called to this stupid neglect, the Governments concerned put it right; but meanwhile six months had been lost.

The French Government recalled General Sarrail before

the end of December, replacing him by General Guillaumat. He was instructed to complete his defensive arrangements for the Balkan Front, and to study the possibility of an offensive. The change had long become inevitable, for General Sarrail, although a man of considerable ability and charm, had rather gone to pieces as a commander of an Inter-Allied force. He was more interested in politics than in his own business, which he completely neglected. His passion for political intrigue led him to meddle in Near East politics and provoked continual trouble with the Greeks. It had been largely responsible for creating the unsatisfactory tangle which we ultimately cut by deposing King Constantine. A more tactful General might have handled the situation without driving the King into open hostility. Reports on the situation which were demanded from him were not forthcoming. As far back as June 6th, 1917, I had reluctantly found it necessary to write to M. Ribot begging him to appoint another General in place of Sarrail and to supersede him without delay. The letter was as follows: —

"6th June, 1917.

"My dear M. Ribot,

"The War Cabinet have been deeply concerned by a number of serious reports which they have received about the recent offensive operations on the Salonika Front — reports which reflect very gravely on the fitness of General Sarrail for the command-in-chief of the great force which is there.

"It has been part of the Allied strategy that early this spring offensive operations should be undertaken upon the Salonika Front, and so far as we can ascertain it was generally agreed among all competent judges upon the spot that with proper leadership there was an excellent opportunity of dealing a heavy blow at the enemy. Yet the operations appear to have been a complete fiasco.

"According to the reports which we have received from our representatives, the result was due to no want of courage or determination on the part of the troops engaged, but entirely to failure on the part of the higher command. There does not appear to have been any properly concerted plan of campaign, or any proper contact between General Sarrail and the armies under his command; the offensive seems to have consisted of a number of isolated operations, neither properly coördinated nor adequately supported, and to have been conducted without any attempt to press home the advantages gained.

"The War Cabinet finds that these reports are fully borne out by the information which they have received from the Italians, the Russians, and the Serbs. It would further seem from these reports that General Sarrail, after more than a year and a half in command, has entirely lost the confidence of the Allied troops entrusted to his care.

"In these circumstances, the War Cabinet have come to the conclusion that they are not justified in continuing to leave the very large British forces in the Balkans under General Sarrail's command.

Speaking for myself, I must say that it is with the deepest regret I write in this sense. As you know, I have by no means been an opponent of General Sarrail. I was favourably impressed by him when we met in Rome, and I have on more than one occasion defended him in order that he might have every chance of carrying out the policy which was then agreed upon. And I wish to recognise without reserve the loyalty with which he has observed the pledges which he gave. But after reading the reports we have received, and making full further inquiries, I entirely concur with the War Cabinet that we should not be justified in leaving the British forces in the Balkans under the supreme command of General Sarrail.

"We sincerely hope that the French Government will recognise the necessity for the appointment of another General in place of General Sarrail, and will issue immediate instructions to some competent officer on the spot to take over the command until the new Commander-in-Chief can arrive.

Yours sincerely,

D. LLOYD GEORGE."

Soon after the receipt of this letter Ribot resigned and was followed by Painlevé, who was deeply attached to General Sarrail, and was convinced that the opposition to him in French military circles was purely political in its origin.

But when Clemenceau took office our request was renewed and he promptly acted upon it.

While the change in the command gave a prospect of greater harmony and efficiency in the Salonika expeditionary forces, it did not carry with it any prospect of renewed offensive activities there. On the contrary, the position in Macedonia in December, 1917, and for the first half of 1918, so far as it was known to the Supreme War Council, seemed to put any serious offensive out of the question. We had taken advantage of the entry of the Greeks into the War on our side to withdraw two of our divisions for use in Egypt and Palestine. According to a statement made by the D.M.O. to the War Cabinet on December 12th, 1917, the total rifle strength of the Allies in Macedonia, including British, French, Serbians and Greeks, was 160,000, while that of the Bulgarians and Germans opposed to us was 203,000 rifles. This meant that we were compelled to stand carefully on the defensive.

The fact was that our Balkan force, which eventually was destined to give a dramatic *coup de grâce* to the enemy, remained until the second half of 1918 a miserable Cinderella among the Allied Armies. The British War Office never loved it. The British Official History retails a wretched story of neglect, delay and official bungling in relation to its essential supplies, which quite unnecessarily aggravated its sufferings from malaria and impeded effective action. As I have elsewhere related, it owed its existence more to diplomatic necessities than to the foresight of the military. The expedition was launched not to defeat the enemy, but to rescue the remains of the Serbian Army, and prevent the whole of the Balkans, including Greece, from becoming an Austro-German province. The French Government were the prime movers, with the more hesitant agreement of our Government, and the recurrent ill will of our military authorities, who again and again urged our complete withdrawal from Salonika to concentrate all our troops on the Western Front on elaborate offensives which brought us nothing but immense casualties.

M. Clemenceau, who became French Premier on November 16th, 1917, was also unsympathetic to the Salonika expedition, and in the following months the French troops there had their share of neglect. On January 25th, 1918, it was reported to us by the D.M.O. that the French forces in Salonika were short of supplies and suffering from hunger — a condition which did not apply to the Italian or British troops. They were also 28,000 men below strength. Another weakness to the force was occasioned by the fact that it included a Russian division, and by February, 1918, this unit could no longer be trusted to hold its part of the line, and had to be withdrawn, its front being taken over by the British. The Russians were used for non-combatant work behind the line, but on March 12th it was reported to the War Cabinet that they would have to be withdrawn altogether, as they were attempting to corrupt the Serbians, and there was a danger that they might also demoralise the Greeks.

When the Germans broke through the Western Front in March, and we were scraping together all the reserves we could muster to reinforce our line, the idea of bringing back men from Salonika was considered. However, it was decided that —

None of the four British divisions (with one brigade) in the Salonika theatre, should be brought to France, since, although up to strength numerically, they were weakened by malaria.

The further German offensive on the Lys caused this question to be reopened, and the army authorities debated whether to bring back two divisions, but abandoned the idea in the face of French protests. Then, at the meeting of the Supreme War Council on May 2nd, I advanced the suggestion that as these divisions were still twelve battalions strong, we might reduce them to a nine-battalion basis, and bring the surplus battalions to France. Clemenceau was agreeable to our replacing British by Indian battalions, and substituting Greek for French troops at Salonika, provided General Guillaumat thought it could be done; and eventually we decided that a French and a British General Officer should be sent to examine the situation with Guillaumat. The War Office chose Lieutenant-General Sir C. L. Woolcombe for this task, and he was sent out on May 15th. On May 30th he reported that the French were withdrawing 12,000 troops from Salonika to France. It struck me as a rather curious proceeding to remove these troops without a word to us, when at the Supreme War Council at Abbeville they had strongly protested against our withdrawing troops. However, instead of urging a protest against this, the C.I.G.S. suggested that it would serve as an excuse for our replacing some of our battalions there with Indian troops, bringing the British units to the Western Front. There was not at this time any idea of passing over to the offensive on the Salonika Front.

Hitherto our safety in the Balkans depended less upon the efficiency with which the Allied forces there were maintained and commanded, than upon the reluctance of the Bulgarians to embark upon an offensive in which they were bound to suffer hard knocks, for the dubious privilege of overrunning territory which they had no prospect of being able to retain permanently. General Guillaumat, on replacing General Sarrail, had been specifically instructed to prepare and submit plans for the defence of the front, including the possible carrying out of a retirement if attacked in force. At the meeting of the Supreme War Council, on March 15th, I complained that these plans were not yet forthcoming. I was told they were then on their way, and would be communicated to the Military Representatives at Versailles on arrival. On June 12th, the War Cabinet was informed by our Military Representative, General Sackville-West, that no proper plans had been received, and his complaint that the situation in regard to Allied defensive policy in the Balkans was not on a satisfactory footing was strongly endorsed by the C.I.G.S. who said that —

General Guillaumat had been repeatedly asked for his plans in the event of a retirement, but so far they had not been obtained. If (as there was reason to believe) there were no proper plans, it was quite possible that there might be a bad disaster to our troops in that theatre of war.

The C.I.G.S. further informed us that Clemenceau was recalling Guillaumat, and sending out General Franchet d'Esperey in his place.

The change in the Balkan Command coincided with a considerable change in the military outlook. The Germans, exhausted by their repeated offensive in the West, were driven to withdraw the bulk of their forces from the Balkan Front, leaving it to be held by Bulgarians who had by now grown weary of a war to serve Austro-German ambitions in the Balkans. The Bulgarians were hungry, too, for Germany had stripped them of all the foodstuffs she could collect to feed her own starving people; their armies were running out of equipment, and Germany had stopped subsidising their treasury. On the Allied side, the flow of American reinforcements to France made it no longer necessary to contemplate withdrawing troops from Salonika. The Greek Armies had now been mobilised and equipped, and had tested their own prowess in a short but successful local offensive on a seven and a half mile front at the Skra di Legen, west of the Vardar, where on May 30th they pushed forward one and a quarter miles and took 2,000 prisoners. This victory opened the eyes of the Entente Governments to the possibilities of the Balkans. It proved that the Greek troops raised by Venizelos possessed a high fighting value and could be depended upon in the event of an offensive being undertaken. It also proved that the Bulgarians were not fighting with the spirit they displayed in 1915 and 1916. General Franchet d'Esperey — a very competent soldier — came to the conclusion that the situation was favourable for a great offensive on that front. The question was discussed at a meeting of the Supreme War Council in July and it was decided to refer the desirability of an offensive to the Military Representatives for their consideration and advice. By this date Clemenceau, who had been an opponent of the "side-shows", was converted to the idea of an offensive in the Balkans and was pressing for it. This was all the more remarkable because he had been a consistent opponent of the Salonika Expedition. As he himself put it during the discussions at this Council meeting: —

He, himself, from the commencement had been wholly against any Balkan expedition. He had never believed that an offensive would give satisfactory results. Could he then be accused of wishing to start a grand offensive in the Balkans? So utterly opposed was he to any such proposals that, at one time, he had suggested withdrawing the whole of the troops from Salonika.

For the moment, pending a report by the Military Representatives, the only operation conducted on the Balkan Front was an advance by the Italians in Albania.

On September 4th, General Guillaumat, who was now back in France after handing over the Balkan Command to General Franchet d'Esperey, came over to Downing Street for a Conference upon the matter of a Balkan offensive. He gave an account very much at variance with the reports we had received from the War Office as to the condition and outlook of the Allied Armies on the Macedonian Front: —

"When I took over the command at Salonika in December, 1917, I left Paris under the impression that I should realise great difficulties with an army which was inferior to that of our enemies. I was soon convinced that this impression was not correct. I was much struck to find at Salonika a force so strong and so well provided with equipment, and I was still more astonished that this force had been left for so long in idleness. The British troops, especially, were the finest I had ever seen in my life, better even than those I had met on the Somme. The French troops were good and complete in all respects. The Serbian Army had some very good soldiers, and the Italians were equally well supplied with men and material. The same holds good to-day, and I may say at once that I consider there is no serious danger to be incurred. What is now necessary is to consider how best to utilise these forces. The situation has been further improved by the mobilisation of the Greek Army. At the end of 1917 there were only three divisions of the National Defence, which were formed by the Provisional Government, but since that M. Venizelos, at the head of the Athens Government, has increased this force to nine divisions."

The contrast between this highly optimistic account of the efficiency of the Salonika Army and the statements made to the Cabinet as to divisions so weakened from malaria as to be unfit for transport is only one out of many illustrations afforded during the War of the difficulty of obtaining reliable information as to conditions which were easily ascertainable, whenever the War Office thought it desirable to withhold the truth from the Government.

General Guillaumat's description of the Salonika forces was completely justified by the smashing success of the Balkan offensive later in the month. We experienced the same methods of overestimating enemy prowess and understating Allied strength in the Turkish campaign. Our military advisers, in their dislike of "side-shows" and their eagerness to concentrate all efforts on the Western Front, misled their Governments as to the possibilities in these theatres. The nine Greek divisions could have been there by the end of 1917 if the War Office had provided equipment for them more promptly, as I have already noted in an earlier chapter. And thus reinforced, we might have been smashing up the enemy front from the south-east at a time when the only advice we received was to the effect that we must confine ourselves there to a timorous defence, and to making careful plans for a retreat and the possible abandonment of Salonika. Such a blow by us in the Balkans would have had a most disconcerting effect upon the German strategy in the West. To save their Bulgarian allies from disaster they would have been obliged to divert several divisions to the Balkans.

I questioned and cross-questioned Guillaumat very thoroughly on the situation with a view to elucidating the real facts as to the condition and equipment of the Coalition Armies and also as to the numbers and morale of the Bulgarians. I then withdrew into another room with Lord Robert Cecil and Sir Henry Wilson, the C.I.G.S., to consider our decision. Wilson was still doubtful. His comment on Guillaumat's proposition for an offensive was: —

"He makes this proposal for three reasons: namely, to give the Bulgars a good tap; to put the Greek Army on its feet, and thereby to release a certain number of French and English troops, all with the off-chance of something good. His scheme is somewhat sketchy; for instance, that of putting six Serbian and two French divisions on a front of 14 kilometres; but we shall not go in until after the Serbian success. If the Serbian attack is unsuccessful, there will be no attempt to recover on us."

Wilson was always an ultra-Westerner and this was the utterance of a man who frankly did not expect any good to come from Macedonia. That this was, even in September, 1918, the opinion of the Government's military advisers, explains why it was that despite my long-held belief in the desirability of attacking the enemy where he was weakest, I had been unable hitherto to secure their support for any operations on this front. Now, however, I had the evidence of a French General who was thoroughly acquainted with the facts, and I was determined to press for an attack. Coming back to the Conference, I gave the consent of the British Government for the offensive. I recommended that the Italians should be urged to launch a simultaneous attack on their front against Austria, but I said that the Macedonian attack must on no account be postponed whilst waiting to secure Italian coöperation. The plan communicated by General Guillaumat for a forward movement in the Balkans, starting on the 15th of September, was to be carried out by an attack all along the line.

When we launched our offensive Ludendorff diverted to Serbia the Alpine Corps from the Western Front, two divisions from the Italian Front, one from the Ukraine, and three German divisions from the East which had been released for service in the West and had already begun to move across. But though he thus depleted the actual or potential reinforcements of the Western Front by six or seven divisions, he was unable to save Bulgaria, for his help came too late. The Allied attack was opened on the 15th by the French and the Serbians, on the western sectors on the Salonika Front; and its success was immediate and overwhelming. If the long years of stationary warfare had worn out the Bulgarians and made them long to be getting back to their homes and farms, it had made the Serbians desperate and they were led by one of the ablest Generals of the War.

They were ravening to be up and at the foe, and at long last to hack their way back into their own land. Plucky fighters though the Bulgars were, they were in no mood to resist such an onset, and the Serbs went through with resistless valour. The front of attack, which was 7 miles long at the outset of the offensive, extended to 15 miles on the second day, and to 25 on the third, by which time the point of farthest advance by the Serbs was 20 miles ahead of the original front line. On September 18th there was a still further extension, when the British and the Greek Armies on the right of the front, east of the Vardar River, threw in their weight against the Doiran sector of the front, the most firmly held sector of the whole enemy line. It was fiercely contested, but collapsed after four days' fighting, as a result of the retreat of the Bulgars on the rest of the front. Meantime the Serbians had continued their victorious advance further west. Across broken, mountainous country which military opinion would have judged hopelessly difficult for rapid movement, they swept on as if it were an open plain. Their attack had started on September 15th. On September 23rd they had advanced 40 miles and split the Bulgarian Armies beyond repair. The Serbian onslaught on a foe entrenched in the fastnesses above them is one of the most brilliant feats in the War. By the 26th the Bulgarian Commander-in-Chief was appealing for a truce and peace terms. Three days later Bulgarian plenipotentiaries accepted drastic armistice terms dictated by Franchet d'Esperey at Salonika, and on the 30th these were ratified by the Allied Governments and hostilities ceased. During the first half of October, while the Italians pressed forward in Albania, the Serbs were racing back across their own country, clearing out any lingering pockets of Austrian and German troops still garrisoning it, and by the 19th they had reached the banks of the Danube. Therewith the Allies were on that great waterway by which

supplies were borne to them from Roumania and the Black
Sea. Had we gone there in 1914 or 1915 when the road
was still wide open to us, instead of in October, 1918,
the War would have been shortened by years. On November 1st the Serbians reëstablished themselves in Belgrade;
and on the same day Hungary revolted from her Austro-German allies and set up an independent Government at
Budapest.

Ludendorff records that on the evening of September
28th, the day that the Bulgarian envoys reached Salonika,
Hindenburg and he decided that immediate steps must be
taken to ask for an armistice and terms of peace. Next day
he instructed the German Foreign Secretary to take the
necessary steps to this end; and on the morning of September 30th he issued a *communiqué* to the German military representatives at Headquarters which began: —

"Events in Bulgaria have taken Main Headquarters by surprise. The Bulgarian Army has collapsed. Armistice concluded
to-day. . . .

"Events in Bulgaria and their consequences, the strain on the
Western Front with no prospect of any improvement, the impossibility of restoring the situation by an offensive have convinced the Field-Marshal and myself that in the interests of the
Army it is necessary that hostilities should end." [1]

Apart from the fact that the road to Vienna and the
Danube was now opened to the victorious Allies, there was
the certainty that Roumania would fall into Allied hands.
This would deprive Germany of her oil supplies and thus
completely cripple her military activities.

General von Kuhl, one of the ablest of the German Staff
Officers in the War, stated in the course of his evidence before the Reichstag Commission: —

[1] Ludendorff: "The General Staff and Its Problems", Vol. II, pp. 614 and 615.

"After the collapse of Bulgaria on 3rd October, 1918, the question was raised by the General Staff: 'If to-day Roumania falls away, how long can we last out with petrol? Will the collapse of Roumania compel us at once to abandon hostilities?' The outcome of the discussion was as follows: —

"Aircraft can maintain their full activity for roughly two months (one month's service at the front, one month's service at home). Then they will be completely immobilised.

"Motor vehicles can maintain their full activity for roughly two months (one month's service at the front, one month's service at home). Then they will have to cut down to half service.

"Lubricating oil is available for six months. Then all machines will be brought to a standstill. . . .

"The illuminating oil industry (*i.e.*, provision of petroleum for the civil population, agriculture which is very important) will collapse in one to two months. . . .

"In a session held under the presidency of the Reichs-Chancellor on October 17th, 1918, the Minister of War, Scheüch, explained that we could carry on the War for another month and a half, if Roumania were no longer at our disposal. . . ."[1]

One can understand why Hindenburg and Ludendorff regarded the defeat of Bulgaria as bringing all hope of further resistance to an end. Even with the help of Roumanian oil the Germans experienced great difficulties in the matter of transport. If we had taken steps to secure the Balkans in 1915 as we ought to have done, this failure of oil supplies would have shortened the War by at least two years.

Von Kuhl also cites evidence to show that the food supplies obtained from Roumania were of vital importance, and justified the retention there of German forces despite the shortage of man-power in the West. The same was true of

[1] "Die Ursachen des Deutschen Zusammenbruchs im Jahre 1918", Vol. III, pp. 12 and 13.

the Ukraine food supplies. These, after much difficulty and frequent setbacks, had just been organised satisfactorily when the collapse of Turkey, Bulgaria and Austria-Hungary severed the communications between Germany and that source of supply.

2. THE TURKISH COLLAPSE

Opportunities lost in Turkey — Smuts advises concentration on Palestine — Allenby's bracing influence — Brains and imagination — British forces depleted for Western Front — 1918 summer operation — Condition of Turkish forces — Weakness of divisions — Megiddo — Turkey collapses — Why not years before?

No less spectacular than the Balkan campaign, if perhaps less vital at this stage for bringing the War to an end, was the British victory over the Turks in Syria. Had it come three or even two years earlier, while Russia was still an active belligerent, its effect in opening the Dardanelles to the Allied Fleets would have enabled us not only to supply the Russian Armies on a scale impossible through her Arctic or Pacific ports, but to make full use of Roumania's adhesion to the Allied cause, eliminating Bulgaria and turning the whole of the Balkans into an Allied bastion. In the autumn of 1918 the collapse of Turkey was a part of the general débâcle of the Central Powers and their allies. It contributed to the general feeling in Germany and Austria that they were being isolated and would soon be encircled and invaded from the south.

Our twofold campaign against the Turk, in Palestine and in Mesopotamia, had reached a period by the end of 1917 with the capture of Jerusalem and Baghdad and the consolidation of our dominion over the regions around them. In Mesopotamia there was thereafter a practical cessation of active military operations, apart from the despatch of a force to the Caspian, until the latter part of October, when we advanced on Mosul. Local advances were made by the Mesopotamia force in the early summer of 1918, and some thousands of Turkish prisoners captured, but no attempt was then made to carry out a major advance.

This was in accordance with the plan for the war with Turkey recommended by General Smuts, whom the War Cabinet had deputed on January 28th, 1918, to proceed to Egypt, with full power on our behalf to confer with Generals Allenby and Marshall and other naval and political authorities there about the military situation in the Middle East, and advise us as to the best use and coördination of our resources in that quarter. Smuts telegraphed us on February 15th, giving his view that neither force was strong enough for an offensive campaign, and that as the Mesopotamian force was further from Aleppo, it had better stand on the defensive and hand over two divisions and a cavalry brigade to General Allenby to enable him to take the offensive in Palestine. Already the 7th Indian Division had been transferred, and by the beginning of April the 3rd Indian Division was also sent to Allenby; but the Government decided against Smuts' further suggestion of taking the 13th (Western) British Division from Marshall. The Palestine campaign, which had been conducted with a flabbiness and lack of nerve which presented a wretched contrast to the dash and resolution displayed by Maude in Mesopotamia, was now in the hands of a General whose courage, vigour and resolution had transformed the military situation in that theatre. The story is told by a vivid pen in the Official History of the campaign. When Allenby arrived the Army was depressed by a sense of futility. The attack of Dobell and Chetwode on Gaza had been the most perfect sample exhibited on either side in any theatre during this Great War of that combination of muddleheadedness, misunderstanding and sheer funk which converts an assured victory into a humiliating defeat. Gaza was "virtually captured" when the

order came to withdraw. We had in our possession at the
moment of the withdrawal intercepted wireless messages
which showed that the German Commander considered the
position hopeless. Dobell alleged that these messages only
reached him after the withdrawal had commenced! The
defences of Gaza when Chetwode attacked were merely
skeleton entrenchments and its garrison was heavily outnumbered by our Army in men and artillery. It may be said
that Allenby had received substantial reinforcements for
his troops before he succeeded in capturing Gaza. But so had
the Turks. When Allenby attacked in October the garrison
had been considerably reinforced in men and guns and the
defences had been strengthened by every device of which
German engineers were capable. The year 1917 up till the
summer was the best moment that could have been chosen
for sweeping the Turks out of Palestine. Their Army was
undermanned and ill-equipped. The Turkish leaders were
taking no interest in Palestine. Their hopes and ambitions
were turned in another direction. That opportunity we threw
away through lack of nerve. By July, 1917, Falkenhayn had
taken charge. He diverted some of the best divisions in the
Turkish Army to Palestine. He had a body of specially
picked men brought with him from Germany to strengthen
and stiffen the Army more specially on the mechanical side.
The artillery was improved and abundant ammunition provided. But there was also a change in the British Army. A
new Commander had been appointed and he a man of high
courage and resolution, and that made all the difference.
He raised the spirit of the Army by his presence and the inspiration of his personality. His plans were carefully and
skilfully thought out and perfectly carried into operation.
He introduced an element of imagination into his tactical
arrangements. There is the famous ruse by which he deceived the enemy into the belief that his first assault would

be on Gaza with a feint attack on Beersheba. This was suggested to him by a brilliant young officer called Meinertzhagen who subsequently, at the risk of his life, successfully carried it out. But Allenby had the intelligence to perceive the value of the plan. Great leadership does not consist merely in the invention of schemes but in the selection and execution of the best. Meinertzhagen's device won the battle. Needless to say he never rose in the War above the rank of Colonel. I met him during the Peace Conference and he struck me as being one of the ablest and most successful brains I had met in any army. That was quite sufficient to make him suspect and to hinder his promotion to the higher ranks of his profession.

The orders I gave to Allenby before he started — "Jerusalem by Christmas" — were faithfully carried out. The campaign was to be vigorously prosecuted in 1918.

But the plans for the renewal of the offensive in Palestine were frustrated by events on the Western Front. After the British defeat in March, Allenby was instructed to send back to France two of his divisions. He despatched the 52nd (Lowland) Division in April, and the 74th at the beginning of May. He was also called on to withdraw altogether 23 British battalions from his remaining divisions, which would in due course be replaced by Indian battalions, and to send them to France. This meant that for the moment his force was disorganised, and that he could not undertake a large-scale advance until the replacement troops had arrived and been incorporated in his formations.

In February, Jericho had been captured, and thereafter until early May a series of abortive efforts were made to advance into Transjordania. But from mid-May to early October the hot weather militated against active operations. Time, however, fought for us on this front, for the Turkish Armies were wasting away through desertions and disease.

This process had been going on for a long period.[1] Allenby used the interval to complete the reorganisation of his army with the new Indian units that had reached it, and to prepare his plans for a big offensive in mid-September. The War Office was unable to promise him any additional troops for this. But as regards comparative fighting strength, he already held a heavy superiority over the enemy in front of him. His difficulties were not so much those of combatant power as of carrying forward communications for the supplies and equipment of a modern army.

Some idea of the condition of the enemy can be gained from a telegram which General Liman von Sanders sent to Enver Pasha on June 16th, to protest against the withdrawal of the German troops for use in the Caucasus. He wrote: —

"After the continuous hard fighting of the last three months and the heavy losses, the strongest Turkish regiments[2] average 350–400 rifles in addition to machine-guns, and many Turkish regiments are weaker.

"On the side of the enemy the partial exchange of troops for Indian battalions 800–1,000 strong has increased his numbers, and the Indian troops so far engaged have fought well. In infantry the enemy is three or four times superior to us, and in artillery he is far superior. . . ."[3]

On June 20th, Liman von Sanders addressed to Count Bernstorff, the German Ambassador at Constantinople, a telegram in which he said: —

"The Turkish troops here cannot hold the front by themselves. Other events have sufficiently demonstrated what will happen when Turkish troops are retreating. Moreover the troops

---

[1] *Cf.* the Report of the Military Representatives to the Supreme War Council, January 1st, 1918, Joint Note No. 12 (Vol. V, Appendix A to Chapter VI: "The Military Position").
[2] These Turkish regiments each contained two battalions.
[3] Von Sanders: "Five Years in Turkey", p. 241.

to-day are undernourished, very poorly clothed and wretchedly shod. . . .

"The number of Turkish deserters is higher to-day than that of the men under arms. . . . The clothing of my army is so bad that many officers are wearing ragged uniforms and even battalion commanders have to wear tschariks [1] in lieu of boots. . . . According to reports of German Officers of the Sixth Army from Irak, which are on file in the Prussian War Ministry, 17,000 men of that army have died of hunger and its consequences, up to April, 1918. . . ." [2]

Later on, von Sanders states that in September, 1918, at the time when our offensive was launched in Palestine, there were some ten infantry divisions between the sea and the Jordan. Eight of these had been in the front line without relief for more than six months.

"Each Turkish division averaged about 1,300 rifles. The strength of the battalion, of which each division had nine, averaged 130–150 rifles. Some battalions had reached a strength of 180, others had been reduced to 100 by sickness and other losses.

"The number of desertions had increased alarmingly during the last few weeks. In the Eighth Army they amounted to 1,100 between 15th August and 14th September. The invariable excuse of the men when captured was that they did not get enough to eat, that they had no linen or foot-gear, and that their clothing was in rags." [3]

With the enemy forces in such a deplorable state, it is clear that Turkey was ripe for the Allied plucking. The remarkable victory which Allenby secured against them was distinguished, not so much as a feat of desperate valour against a redoubtable opponent, but rather as a well-designed and faultlessly executed manœuvre, yielding the maximum results at the minimum expense.

---

[1] Animal skins tied on with string.
[2] Von Sanders: "Five Years in Turkey", p. 243.
[3] *Ibid.*, p. 270.

Sir Edmund Allenby's own estimate of the comparative fighting strengths of the Allied and enemy forces when he launched his offensive was: —

British: 12,000 sabres, 57,000 rifles, 540 guns.
Turkish: 3,000 sabres, 26,000 rifles, 370 guns.

Other estimates give both larger and smaller figures for the Turkish strength. But in any case there was a clear preponderance on the British side, which Allenby skilfully increased still further on his actual front of attack by carefully camouflaged massing of his troops there, combined with a pretence of assembling troops for assault on another sector.

On September 19th, Allenby launched his great attack, planned with real military skill. His aim was not just to beat back but to encircle and wipe out the Turkish forces in Palestine. The Battle of Megiddo was a brilliant operation, of a kind supremely satisfactory to a military commander. The available weight was so crushingly applied at successive key points, and the blows so swiftly and adroitly followed up, that with a minimum of losses on our side the whole of the Turkish forces opposed to us were killed, captured or dispersed. Twelve days after the battle started, Damascus fell into Allenby's hands, and of all the Turkish forces in Palestine, with a ration strength of about 100,000, only a broken rabble of about 17,000 escaped his net and fled northwards. His tale of prisoners amounted to 75,000, while the total battle casualties of his forces were only 5,666.

The pursuit was hotly pressed, and by October 26th, Aleppo had been taken by the Allied forces. Since September 19th, our front had been moved forward 350 miles, and by the capture of Aleppo and the Muslimyia Junction to the north of it we straddled not only the railway running down through Syria and Palestine, but the line passing eastward to Mosul, and on to Baghdad. During the last stage of this ad-

vance our defensive force in Mesopotamia made its contribution to victory by starting to advance briskly towards
Mosul. But before it could get there the fight was over. On
October 30th, Turkey signed an armistice with the Allies,
and on October 31st, hostilities ceased. The Dardanelles
were at last open to us; but we no longer needed them, for
eleven days later Austria-Hungary laid down arms, to be
followed after another week by Germany.

In reviewing this ultimate dramatic success of our arms
against Turkey, it is very hard to escape the conclusion that,
granted good generalship, we might have attained a similar
victory years before. Granted that in 1918 the Turkish
Army was becoming very inferior in quality; but our own
force was a comparatively small one, of only seven infantry
and four cavalry divisions, from which many of the finest
units had been withdrawn to reinforce the Western Front
and replaced by raw Indian levies that had seen no service.
Twenty-two of the Indian battalions were in this condition,
as were some of their commanding officers, and the Official
History records that they were largely made up of recruits
who had done no musketry. When they landed in Egypt
they had hardly any signallers, few Lewis gunners, no
bombers, and were deficient in a number of other respects,
notably in officers who could speak Hindustani. Prior to the
substitution of these for the experienced troops which Allenby
sent to France in the spring of 1918 — upwards of 60,000
officers and men — our force in the Near East was far more
potent than that which ultimately gained so striking and
decisive a victory. Had we reinforced our Egyptian Army in
1916 with a few of the men we were wasting by the hundred
thousand on the Somme, at a time when the Allies outnumbered the Germans on the Western Front by more than
fifty per cent., we might have broken the Turkish power in
time to save Roumania, equip Russia, and end the War

two years before it finally dragged to its tragic close. In a Turkish campaign our sea communications gave us a decisive advantage over the Central Powers. The railway accommodation was so limited and so broken that Germany could not have reinforced the Turks, however desperate their plight might be. The military advisers who scorned the Palestine campaign as a futile and wasteful "sideshow" have a heavy reckoning to settle.

3. ITALY

Italian Front neglected — Allied superiority — Austria ordered to attack — Italian nervousness — Vittorio Veneto — Sideshows decide the World War.

The survey of those theatres of war which the British War Office regarded as subsidiary would not be complete without a swift glance at Italy. This was the front where, at the Rome Conference at the beginning of 1917, I had urged that a serious effort should be made to deal Austria a blow which would drive her out of the War. Our military leaders had preferred to plan for the Chemin des Dames and Passchendaele. In consequence, the Allies had suffered serious checks and losses in France and left the Italians to the catastrophic defeat of Caporetto. We had been forced to detach considerable forces to Italy, not to help in achieving a victory but in averting the consequences of a defeat. Even at that the French and ourselves utilised in Italy not a quarter as many men as we had lost as casualties in Passchendaele and on the Chemin Des Dames.

Thereafter, the Italian Front, seventy miles farther back than it had been in 1917, no longer offered so favourable a starting-point for a deadly thrust at the Central Powers, and the Italian Army had by no means recovered from the shattering blow inflicted upon it in November, 1917. Yet it was destined before the end to play its own decisive rôle in the achievement of the Allied triumph, by its ultimate defeat of the Austrian Army in the field, which precipitated a revolution in Vienna and the withdrawal of Austria from the War.

After the reëstablishment of the Italian Front on the line of the Piave at the end of 1917, the Entente had on this front a nominal superiority over the Central Powers. The revised figures supplied to the Man-power Committee showed that in December, 1917, the combined Italian, British and French forces there had a combatant strength of 1,324,000 as against a total Austro-Hungarian and German combatant strength of 915,000. But the Italian figures were admittedly approximate only, and the Italian Army needed a good deal of reorganisation after the débâcle of Caporetto. On December 1st, 1917, the Supreme War Council resolved that its Permanent Military advisers should study the immediate situation on the Italian Front from the offensive as well as the defensive point of view. However, winter had then closed down all possibilities of immediate action, and with the approach of the following spring came the menace of a German offensive in France. Two of the five British divisions in Italy were brought back to the Western Front, and eventually, in the latter part of April, the Second Italian Army Corps was sent to reinforce the French in the Argonne. The idea of an Italian offensive was abandoned for the time being, and all available resources were concentrated upon the Western Front. Foch, it is true, as soon as he became Commander-in-Chief on the West, had urged the Italians to attack. But the Italians were not willing at that time to embark upon an offensive. They did not feel even yet quite up to an attack and they were also in daily expectation of an Austrian attack which was then being prepared.

The Germans, indeed, demanded sternly of their exhausted and supine ally that she should help their offensive in France by one in Italy, and insisted the more on this when they found to their disgust that Italian troops had been brought to the Western Front to oppose them. The Austrian Army, where so many hostile races were held together in uneasy fellowship, largely by military domination, was at this time hopelessly riddled by sedition, disaffection and despair. Neither the Czechs, Croats and other Slav troops, nor those drawn from the Trentino, could be relied on not to desert their Imperial master on the battlefield; but the Austrians, the Germans, and the Hungarians, would have been still capable of putting up a stubborn fight had they been well fed. No soldiers can keep up their fighting spirit in cold and comfortless trenches on thin rations. Confident plans were laid by General von Arz for an attack on the Italians, of which he wrote to Hindenburg that he expected it to bring them to the Adige and achieve the military dissolution of Italy. At that time the Austrians had almost their whole army on the Italian Front, as only small forces were now in Russia, Roumania and the Balkans. The attack was launched on June 15th, but it was made without *élan* and after eight days of attack and counter-attack, it ended in complete failure for the Austrians. Lord Cavan urged that the Allied success should be at once followed up with a counter-offensive, but the Italians declared they were too much exhausted by the struggle to risk such a further stroke. The fighting spirit of the Italian Army had not yet been completely restored.

Thereafter the Italian Front remained quiescent until the autumn. An American regiment was sent to reinforce it, and at a meeting of the Supreme War Council on July 24th, 1918, when the tide had turned on the Western Front, it was suggested to the Italians that they should now take the offensive. But they argued that the Austrians were still too strong for them to do so. Haunted by the memory of Caporetto, they had lost their nerve so completely that despite the fact that they now held an impressive numerical superiority, they still feared the foe who had once struck them such a blow.

But by mid-October, the course of the War had so changed in favour of the Entente that the Italians could see their enemies tottering, and could pluck up courage to join in the attack. Bulgaria had fallen, and the Allied forces were sweeping towards the Danube. Damascus had fallen, and the British cavalry were racing for Aleppo. On the Western Front we had regained all the Belgian coast, and were thrusting the Germans far back behind the lines they had held since the first year of the War. The Italians agreed to make their contribution, and Foch was able to include an offensive by them in his scheme for the final general advance to victory. In the Battle of Vittorio Veneto they struck down and defeated the Austrian Army, the British contingent playing a valiant and vital part in the attack. Thereby they shattered the only remaining element in the Austrian Empire that possessed any vestige of coherence. Their victorious attack was launched on October 24th. After three days the Austrian Government was suing for an armistice. After three more a revolution broke out in Vienna. By November 3rd the Italian forces had occupied Trieste and an armistice was signed. It was a complete surrender, according to the Entente the right to make full use for military purposes of all the ways of communication of the Austrian Empire. By its terms we should have been able to take our armies to the southern frontiers of Germany — a move which would have turned the front of the Rhine, and made vain any attempt by Germany to stand upon it. But no such move by us was needed, for a week later Germany herself had laid down her arms.

This was the last of the "sideshows", apart from the strategically unimportant colonial affair of German East

Africa. And it is not without significance that all of them, contemned and neglected though they were by the pundits who dictated our military strategy, ended in victory before our triumph on the favoured Western Front. These victories, had they been achieved earlier in the conflict, would have had a critical influence on its further course and have hastened its end. Even as it was, they proved decisive in saving us from a further winter of war. Before the collapse of Bulgaria, Turkey and Austria-Hungary supervened, there was still a prospect that the Germans might hold out into 1919. After her allies had fallen, she had no choice but to surrender out of hand.

We had pledged France our support for her recovery of
Alsace-Lorraine; but had she wearied of the fight and
thought the price to pay too heavy, we would have left the
decision to her. But so long as we could maintain the struggle,
we were resolved not to abandon it without securing the full
restoration of Belgium's independence and integrity. And that
resolve was as firm among the common people who knew
little of high politics as it was among those, more deeply
versed in statecraft and history, who knew of the long effort
of Britain to keep the Flanders coast from falling into the
hands of any powerful, potential enemy.

The restoration of Belgium had become for us symbolic
of the insistence on just dealings between nations and the
suppressing of ruthless aggression by the strong against the
weak. If aggression had been allowed to profit, to hold and
keep its booty, it would have been an acknowledgment on the
part of Britain of either hopeless defeat or utter dishonour.

On the other hand, the German militarists saw in Belgium
a highly valuable trophy, and one which put them in a far
more favourable position for challenging Britain on the sea,
if we made difficulties for their ambitions as a World Power.
The German industrialists saw the advantage of commanding
so convenient an outlet to the sea. So until they had finally
abandoned all hope of either victory or stalemate, they clung
to their purpose of retaining a grip on Belgium after the
War. Although they were quite definitely informed that it
was the one matter on which we would consider no compromise, they were careful in all their peace feelers prior to
their collapse in the autumn of 1918 to make no unreserved
and unqualified promise for the restoration of Belgian independence.

During the latter part of the War, the German High
Command dictated Germany's policy. So long therefore as
they clung to their Belgian ambitions, the politicians could

not make any offer of peace which we would regard even as a basis for negotiation. The German High Command stepped into supreme authority when it successfully insisted on the dismissal of the Chancellor, Bethmann-Hollweg. Thereafter, all civilian statesmen were its creatures. In the summer of 1918, it secured the dismissal of the Foreign Secretary, von Kuhlmann, because he had dared to say publicly to the Reichstag that the War could not be settled by weapons alone, thus hinting at the need to compromise on the ambitions of the German military leaders — Belgium being in his mind. Expansion of the Eastern frontiers of Germany, especially on the Baltic, was also an essential objective of any acceptable peace.

A notorious Memorandum written by Colonel von Haeften on June 3rd, 1918, which Ludendorff forwarded to the Imperial Chancellor with "the strongest possible recommendation", advocated a "Peace Offensive" — not as a sincere effort to secure peace, but to delude the enemies of Germany into thinking she was ready to make peace. This, it was suggested, would rally pacifist sentiment, make war weariness more vocal, and rouse opinion in Britain against the Government — especially to the point of displacing its Prime Minister whom von Haeften honoured by regarding him as the main obstacle in the path of a peace that would fulfil the ambitions of the Prussian militarists. And "when the English home front breaks down, we should have to expect the moral collapse of France and Italy also." Germany would be left victorious, able to impose her terms on her enemies. That was as far as the "will to peace" of Germany's rulers had gone in June, 1918.

The Reichstag Committee after the War dug out a very interesting document summarising the conclusions reached at a Conference in Spa, on July 2nd and 3rd, 1918, between the Kaiser and his chief Ministers, military, naval and civilian.[1] The document summarised the peace terms which this Conference decided at that date it would be necessary to secure. The terms with Russia had already been settled at Brest-Litovsk. As regards Poland, it was decided that she must become a vassal state of Germany — not of Austria — and that Germany should control her economy and her railways, lay tribute on her to help pay the cost of the War, and annex further strips of Polish territory. As to Belgium, the Conference decided: —

"Belgium must come under German influence, so that it can never again come under Franco-British influence and serve as an area of deployment for the enemy.

"To this end we must insist on the division of Flanders and the Walloon provinces into two separate states, united only through a personal union and economic arrangements. Belgium will be brought into the closest relations with Germany through a Customs Union, Railway Company and so on. For the present no Belgian Army must be formed.

"Germany will protect itself by a long occupation, which will be gradually reduced, until finally the Flanders coast and Liège will be evacuated. Complete evacuation will depend upon Belgium allying herself as closely as possible to us. In particular, there must be a guarantee of unconditional reliability for the defence of the coast of Flanders."

And the Reichstag Committee declared in their findings that: —

"Up to 15th July, 1918, the Supreme Army Command rejected the view that victory was no longer possible of attainment by force of arms, and gave no support to peace negotiations upon the basis of a military stalemate. . . ."[2]

[1] "Die Ursachen des Deutschen Zusammenbruchs im Jahre 1918", Vol. II, p. 346.
[2] "Die Ursachen des Deutschen Zusammenbruchs im Jahre 1918", Vol. I, p. 23.

Evidence of such a kind, from German sources of undeniable authority, makes it clear that at no time prior to the autumn of 1918 could we have concluded a satisfactory peace with Germany. Ludendorff would have nothing to do with any terms which would involve complete restoration of Belgium, and as the Reichstag Committee point out in their findings: —

"The Government relied upon the judgment of the Supreme Army Command, until this body itself confessed to the impossibility of victory. The Government was devoid of any person who was capable of making a stand against the will of the Supreme Army Command." [1]

Nor, it may be added, was the Austrian Government able to stand up to Ludendorff and insist upon peace being negotiated, even although the Austrians were starving, Vienna was rioting, and only by means of military pressure in the Ukraine and by embezzlement of supplies of grain passing along the Danube for Germany was it possible for them to avert utter breakdown. For all her desperate plight, Austria did not dare to make peace until all hope of success was gone in the West, until her own armies had been routed on both the Italian and the Serbian Fronts, and a revolution had broken out in Vienna which displaced the Emperor and his officials, substituting for them men who were ready to disregard the fading authority of Germany.

It was not until the defeat of the German offensive at Rheims and the collapse of the German resistance on August 8th had shattered Ludendorff's last hope of putting up an effective defence that he began seriously to contemplate the possibility of having to seek peace on the best attainable terms. And even then he could not bring himself to recognise that it would have to be negotiated very quickly, if it were

[1] *Ibid.*, Vol. I, p. 24.

to find him still in a position to defend the Fatherland. On August 14, a conference was held at the General Headquarters at Spa, presided over by the Kaiser.[1] It was a gloomy gathering. Reports were received of food shortage, war weariness and political unrest at home, of failure of sympathy among the neutral nations, and despair among Germany's allies. Ludendorff had to cap this with the declaration that it had become hopeless to break the will of Germany's enemies by military operations, and all that could be done was to hold them up with a strategic defensive.

The Kaiser agreed, and admitted that Germany would have to find a suitable moment in which to come to an understanding with the enemy. This, he proposed, should be through the mediation of a neutral, and he mentioned the King of Spain and the Queen of Holland as suitable agents for such a procedure. But the view of the Conference was that "a suitable moment" was not yet come.[2] Hindenburg, like the stout old warrior he was, expressed his view of the military situation in the words: —

"I hope, for all that, that we may succeed in keeping our footing on French soil, and thereby in the end impose our will on the enemy!"

When the minute of the Conference came before him, Ludendorff took it upon himself to strike out the opening phrase of this pronouncement, and make it read that the General Field-Marshal "declared that we would succeed in keeping our footing, etc." [3] What had been an expression of courageous hope thereby became an explicit assurance. The result of this, and of the vagueness in which the Conference left the question of the "suitable moment", was that the old Chancellor, Count Hertling, was quite deceived as to the real

[1] *Ibid.*, Vol. III, pp. 195, *et seq.*
[2] *Ibid.*, Vol. II, pp. 229 *et seq.*
[3] *Ibid.*

gravity of the situation, and had no sense of urgency about the launching of peace negotiations. The fact was that neither soldiers nor civilians were ready to shoulder the responsibility for making peace on the assumption of an assured defeat. There was no man strong enough to admit that it was no longer possible for Germany to dominate the peace negotiations through the strength of her armies and the extent of her conquests. Two courses were at this moment open for such a man had he been at the top. Either he could have insisted on immediate negotiations being opened, while his armies were still capable of a dangerous resistance and the area they occupied was considerable; or, judging that a confident and advancing enemy would not be in a mood to make terms, he could have thrown all his energies into the development of formidable defence works along the German frontier, and have withdrawn his armies behind them as promptly as possible, abandoning Belgium before he was driven out, and massing his forces on a very greatly shortened line which he could hold against any attack with the troops he still possessed until peace terms had been agreed. The latter course would have had the moral advantage of an appeal to the German people to make a supreme effort to defend the Fatherland. It would also have had the practical advantage of delaying the Allied attack on the new line of defence until the spring. The necessary artillery and supplies to resume the offensive could not have been brought up before the winter closed.

The German leaders took neither course. They fell between the two stools. They delayed appealing for peace, and at the same time insisted on contesting every yard of ground in France and Flanders as long as possible. As a result, their forces were wasted away in futile struggles to hold back the Allies, and they were unable to spare the men to erect sound fortifications on the frontier. By the end,

they did not dispose of the strength among the beaten and
dispirited troops to make a successful stand on any line, and
Germany had to capitulate on most abject terms.

Ludendorff's misreading of the situation comes out clearly
in the fact that, when definitely interrogated by von Hintze,
the German Foreign Secretary, as to the peace terms he was
willing to consider in regard to Belgium,[1] he replied, on
August 21st, that he could not agree to a restoration of the
status quo ante. On the strength of his declarations, von
Hintze summoned that day a meeting of the party leaders,
and told them that: —

"In the view of the Supreme Army Command, the military
situation gives no occasion for depression. There is no reason to
doubt that we shall be victorious. We shall only be defeated if we
give up hope of victory. In the view of the Supreme Army Command, we are warranted in maintaining the hope that we shall
reach a military position which enables us to achieve a satisfactory peace."[2]

On August 24th, the Chancellor and Vice-Chancellor
prepared a statement to the effect that on the conclusion of
peace Germany would give up Belgium without imposing
an indemnity on her or any condition other than that Germany should enjoy as full political, military and economic
relations with her as any other country.[3] But when they submitted this to Ludendorff on the following day, he refused
to agree to it. He insisted that it should include mention of
the fact that Germany proposed special relations with the
Flemish, and also that in exchange Germany must have all
her colonies back. He ultimately agreed on a summary that
brought out these points, and also the freedom of the
seas and the insistence on continued territorial integrity

[1] *Ibid.*, Vol. II, p. 236.
[2] *Ibid.*
[3] *Ibid.*, p. 237.

of Germany and her allies. This statement was not to be published, but could set out the basis for any negotiations.

On August 30th, the Austrian Ambassador at Berlin informed the German Government [1] that Austria felt herself compelled to take independent steps to bring the War to an end. The German Foreign Secretary, von Hintze, was promptly despatched to Vienna to dissuade Austria from such a course. He took a message from Ludendorff to the effect that the Allies were about to launch a big offensive on the Western Front, and that he was anticipating its outcome with complete confidence, and therefore did not think the moment well-chosen for any peace move.

The confidence, however, turned out to be misplaced. Attacks had been launched along the whole Franco-British Front at the end of August which —

". . . press strenuously upon four retreating German Armies.

"On 26th August the English 1st Army captures the heights of Monchy-le-Preux, reaches Croisilles on the 28th on the tracks of the German 17th Army and comes into contact with the Hindenburg line. After having repulsed violent counterattacks on 29th August, it thrusts on 2nd September into the Hindenburg Line, goes several kilometres beyond it and compels the German 17th Army to withdraw over the canal in the north, from the Sensée to Péronne.

"In the south, beginning on 27th August, the English 3rd and 4th Armies, and the French 1st and 3rd Armies follow the German 2nd and 18th Armies which are fighting in retreat in accordance with Ludendorff's orders; they capture Bapaume, Combles, Chaulnes, Roye, Noyon. On the 30th and 31st, the English 4th Army conquers Péronne; thereby the line of the Somme has been turned.

"East of the Oise, during this same period, the 10th Army puts up a hard fight between the Aisne and the Ailette and on the

[1] *Ibid.*, Vol. II, p. 240.

plains north of Soissons; but the German 9th Army hangs on vigorously to the Saint-Gobain range, since its fall would involve the rupture of the Hindenburg Line at its most vulnerable spot, the hinge forming the junction of the north to south branch and the west to east branch. However, on 2nd September, south of the forest of Coucy, the 10th Army reaches and even in places goes beyond the Chauny–Soissons road — the last objective which Foch appointed for it in his General Directions of 11th August; it is thus in position for the attack on the Hindenburg Line." [1]

On September 2nd the British attacked along the line from Péronne to north of Arras, and in the centre they stormed the Drocourt-Quéant switch — the strongest point in the Hindenburg system and the key to the whole line. The Kaiser fell ill when he heard the news, and Hertling, the Chancellor, wrote urgently to Hindenburg for news as to the military outlook.[2] Hindenburg replied that he would tell him by word of mouth, but somehow managed to let the succeeding days pass without the interview. Meantime, von Hintze had a cheerless visit to Vienna. He got there on September 3rd, Ludendorff's confident message now merely a torn and crumpled piece of waste paper in his pocket. At a big conference on the 5th, Count Burian bluntly declared: "For us, it is the absolute finish!"[3] On September 6th, von Hintze came back to Berlin with tidings that Austria-Hungary was bent on immediate peace.

Next day, however, the Austrian Emperor offered to postpone his Peace Note, if he got satisfactory answers to the questions how the military situation now stood, on what line Hindenburg intended to take up his final stand during peace negotiations, when that line would be reached, and

---

[1] Général René Tournès: "Foch et la victoire des Alliés" (Vol. IV of "Histoire de la guerre mondiale", p. 210).

[2] "Die Ursachen des Deutschen Zusammenbruchs im Jahre 1918", Vol. II, p. 247.

[3] "Die Ursachen des Deutschen Zusammenbruchs im Jahre 1918", Vol. II, p. 243.

when the Supreme Army Command thought the time would be ripe for the negotiations to start.

Von Hintze went off to Spa to get the answers to these questions, alike for the benefit of Austria and for his own Chancellor. The information he collected was hardly satisfactory. It showed that: —

"The number of divisions available as reserves changed daily; some divisions were being broken up to complete others. The Supreme Army Command described major offensives as out of the question; counterattacks as possible. To the question about a line which could be held under all conditions, if necessary by counterattacks, the Supreme Army Command answered: 'Our basic intention is to stay where we are.' The question about reserves and war material was answered cautiously: 'we certainly were building hardly any tanks . . . the fighting value of the troops was suffering from insufficient food; potatoes were lacking. . . .' To the question whether an offensive against the Salonika Army was expected, the answer was: 'Yes, a little one.' "[1]

Hindenburg said he could not agree to the issue of the public appeal for peace which Austria-Hungary now contemplated. But he would be prepared forthwith to concur in an approach to the other side through a neutral Power to arrange for a conference on peace terms. His statement to this effect, dated September 10th, was the first explicit consent of the German Command to enter immediately on peace negotiations. It was followed next day by a message that the Kaiser and the Supreme Army Command were agreeable to such a *démarche* being made through the Queen of the Netherlands.

But the Emperor Karl could wait no longer. His Empire was crumbling around him. Not even a special telegram which Kaiser Wilhelm sent him on September 14th diverted his

[1] *Ibid*, Vol. II, p. 244.

purpose.[1] On that day he issued his appeal for peace, in the form of a public invitation to all the Governments of belligerent States to hold a confidential discussion in some neutral meeting-place with a view to agreeing on a basis for the speedy negotiation of peace.

The Austrian Note of September 14th was a long document, which began by referring to the pronouncement of the Central Powers in December, 1916 (described in an earlier volume of these Memoirs[2]), and asserted that they had never given up the conciliatory and basic ideas of that offer. But it went on to argue that there were signs of a growing unity of the ideas on both sides since then, and suggested that the agreement on general principles should be now transformed into concrete terms of peace: —

"The basic standpoint has changed under the influence of the military and political position, and hitherto, at any rate, it has not led to a tangible and practically utilisable general result. It is true that, independent of all these oscillations, it can be stated that the distance between the conceptions of the two sides has, on the whole, grown somewhat less, that, despite the indisputable continuance of decided and hitherto unbridged differences, a partial turning from many of the extremist concrete war aims is visible, and a certain agreement relative to the general basic principles of a world peace manifests itself.

"In both camps there is undoubtedly observable in broad classes of the population a growth of the will to peace and understanding. Moreover, a comparison of the reception of the peace proposal of the Powers of the Quadruple Alliance by their opponents with later utterances of responsible statesmen of the latter, as well as of non-responsible but in a political respect by no means uninfluential personalities, confirms this impression. . . .

"For an unprejudiced observer there can be no doubt that in

[1] *Ibid.*, Vol. II, p. 245.
[2] "War Memoirs", Vol. III, Chap. II: "The German and Wilson Peace Notes of December, 1916."

all belligerent States without exception the desire for a peace of understanding has been enormously strengthened, that the conviction is increasingly spreading that a further continuance of the sanguinary struggle must transform Europe into ruins and a state of exhaustion that will cripple its development for decades to come, and this without any guarantee of at the same time bringing about that decision by arms which has been vainly striven after by both sides in four years full of enormous sacrifices, sufferings, and exertions."

The difficulty was that no Government cared to risk its standing with its own people by a public offer of concessions. Accordingly, Austria-Hungary proposed that there should be a conference at which delegates of the warring powers should put forth in a confidential and non-binding discussion their terms — after which exchange of views the Governments would know just what hope there was of meeting to conclude peace.

"According to our conviction all the belligerents owe it to humanity jointly to examine whether now, after so many years of a costly but undecided struggle, the entire course of which points to an understanding, it is possible to make an end to the terrible struggle. The Royal and Imperial Government would like, therefore, to propose to the Governments of all belligerent States to send delegates to a confidential and non-binding discussion on basic principles for the conclusion of peace in a place in a neutral country and at a near date, which would have to be agreed on, the delegates who are appointed to make known to one another the conception of their Governments regarding those principles, to receive analogous communications, and to request and give frank and candid frank explanations on all those points which need to be precisely defined."

This offer was rejected by the Allied statesmen. This was hardly surprising, in view of the fact that two days before it was issued, Herr von Payer, the German Vice-

Chancellor, had delivered a speech in Stuttgart on Germany's war aims which gave little colour to the idea that our enemies were as yet prepared to make any terms which would satisfy us. It was a speech in a defiant vein. As regards the east of Europe, he declared there could be no meddling with the settlement of Brest-Litovsk and the peace treaties with the Ukraine, Russia and Roumania. "In the East we have peace, and it remains for us peace, whether it pleases our western neighbours or not." All the German colonies must be restored and every inch of territory belonging to Germany and her allies — which, of course, included all former Turkish territory in Arabia, Mesopotamia and Palestine. Germany would naturally refuse to surrender Alsace-Lorraine. He held out a hope that they might release Belgium: —

"We can, when things have got to that stage, restore Belgium. If we and our allies are once again in possession of what belonged to us, if we are first sure that in Belgium no other State will be more favourably placed than we, then Belgium, I think I may say, can be given back without encumbrance and without reserve. The requisite understanding between Belgium and ourselves will be all the easier because our economic interests are frequently parallel, and Belgium is even directly dependent on us as a Hinterland. We have also no reason to doubt that the Flemish question will be solved in accordance with the dictates of justice and wise statesmanship. It is hypocrisy to represent Belgium as the innocent victim of our policy, and to clothe her, as it were, in the white garment of innocence. . . ."

Von Payer claimed that Germany was entitled to indemnities from her enemies, but would be willing to forgo them for the sake of peace! There was, of course, no suggestion on his part of indemnifying Belgium in any way. Germany would also be willing to join a League of Nations, and to join in disarmament, provided this included the freedom of the seas and abolition of Britain's naval pre-dominance.

"We desire to have a disarmament agreement on the condition of complete reciprocity, applied not merely to the land armies but even to naval forces. In pursuance of the same idea, and going even beyond it, we will raise in the negotiations a demand for the freedom of the seas and sea routes, for the open door in all over-sea possessions, and for the protection of private property at sea; and, if negotiations take place in regard to the protection of small nations and of national minorities in individual States, we shall willingly advocate the international arrangements which will act like a deliverance in countries under Great Britain's domination."

The intransigeance of manner of this speech might have been discounted, had the substance of the terms offered been satisfactory. But it was quite evident that Germany was not as yet prepared to consider the terms which we regarded as just and now within our reach — such matters as not only the unconditional evacuation of Belgium, but compensation to her for the wrong committed against her; the restitution of France's lost provinces of Alsace-Lorraine; rehabilitation of Serbia; freedom for the Czechs, and for the Italian Trentino, and the emancipation of the Arabs. The voice we heard was still that of an arrogant military Imperialism, irritated by the temporary check to its ambitions, but un-mollified in heart and immutable in purpose.

It is symptomatic of the unchanged quality of the German Government up to this point that although the former Chancellor, von Bethmann-Hollweg, had induced the Kaiser at Easter, 1917, to promise a reform of the extremely unequal and undemocratic Prussian franchise, that pledge had still remained unhonoured and unimplemented. Not until after the Supreme Army Command had reached the stage of despair and insistence upon an armistice was Wilhelm ultimately compelled by the stubborn insistence of von Hintze to sign a decree authorising a new constitution. In mid-September, 1918, we were still dealing with a Germany which in the last resort was in effect autocratic with its titular head, the Kaiser, completely under the thumb of the military leaders. We were reluctant to enter into a conference which did not commit the Central Powers beforehand to concessions which we regarded as essential, and at which the discussions would inevitably give the Germans a whole winter to reform their broken armies, to throw up a new line of defence, to replenish their exhausted stores of food and material and to recover their lost morale.

Speaking in Manchester on the same day as Herr von Payer made his statement at Stuttgart, and therefore without knowledge of it, I said: —

"The first indispensable condition, in my judgment, is that civilisation shall establish beyond doubt its power to enforce its decrees. . . . Prussian military power must not only be beaten, but Germany herself must know that. The German people must know that if their rulers outrage the laws of humanity, Prussian military strength cannot protect them from punishment. There is no right you can establish, national or international, unless you establish the fact that the man who breaks the law will meet inevitable punishment. Unless this is accomplished, the loss, the suffering, and the burdens of this war will have been in vain."

Clearly there was a great gulf between the viewpoint expressed here by me, and that to which von Payer was on the same day giving utterance. If the Vice-Chancellor was voicing the official opinion of the German Government, then we were not as yet near enough to a common mind upon peace issues to hope for favourable results from a conference. The Austrian Note was, in fact, issued in defiance of Berlin, but we were not aware of that. We had already received so many overtures from Austria which turned out on the test to be illusive that we were not disposed to waste time on any more vague suggestions for secret conferences.

Accordingly, Mr. Balfour, speaking at the Savoy Hotel on September 16th, declared: —

"I cannot bring myself to believe that this is an honest desire on the part of our enemies to arrive at an understanding with us on terms which it would be possible for us to accept. . . . This is not an attempt to make peace by understanding, but an attempt to weaken forces which are proving too strong for them in the field, by working upon those sentiments, honourable in their origin, mistaken in development, which they believe to exist in all countries, and which they think capable of being turned to their purpose to work out their end. . . ."

Although Mr. Balfour described his speech as merely that of "an individual Minister", it expressed the general view of his colleagues. And that view was shared by the country at large. Mr. Asquith, the leader of the Opposition, spoke at Manchester eleven days later, on September 27th, and adopted the same attitude. He said: —

"I am bound to say that, whatever its motive, Count Burian's present suggestion does not commend itself to me as a practical proposition. . . . I do not want to find myself bogged and befogged in a jungle. . . . Our objects have (as we think) been plainly stated both here and in America. . . ."

The United States Government sent a prompt reply to the Austrian Note, pointing out that its peace aims had already been clearly set out in President Wilson's Fourteen Points, and that the United States "can and will entertain no proposal for a Conference upon a matter concerning which it has made its position and purpose so plain." Seeing that the Fourteen Points included such items as the evacuation of all Russian territory, the independence of Poland, the evacuation and restoration of Belgium, the return to France of Alsace and Lorraine, incorporation of the Trentino with Italy, freedom for the Balkans and autonomy for the subject populations of Austria and Turkey — all of them matters to which von Payer had at Stuttgart returned an emphatic and implicit "No!" — it was evident that for the moment no peace was in prospect to which America would agree.

President Wilson followed up this reply in a speech at New York on September 27th, in which he laid down five essential conditions of peace: —

"First, the impartial justice meted out must involve no discrimination between those to whom we wish to be just and those to whom we do not wish to be just. It must be a justice that plays no favourites and knows no standards but the equal rights of the several peoples concerned.

"Second, no special or separate interest of any single nation or any group of nations can be made the basis of any part of the settlement which is not consistent with the common interest of all.

"Third, there can be no leagues or alliances or special covenants and understandings within the general and common family of the League of Nations.[1]

"Fourthly, and more specifically, there can be no special, selfish economic combinations within the League, and no employment of any form of economic boycott or exclusion, except as the power of economic penalty, by exclusion from the markets of the world, may be vested in the League of Nations itself as a means of discipline and control.

"Fifthly, all international agreements and treaties of every kind must be made known in their entirety to the rest of the world."

[1] Arrangements like the Locarno Treaty, the Stresa Pact, the Franco-Russian Pact, the Treaty between Italy and Austria, the Petite Entente and other particularist undertakings of that kind constitute a departure from this principle.

These five principles are of interest as setting out the attitude, entirely different from that of traditional "Power Diplomacy", which both America and Britain had come to adopt towards the problems of war and peace. They were principles which we later sought, with some measure of success, to incorporate in the Peace Treaty. The measure in which the world has departed from them in subsequent years is the measure of the chaos and trouble into which it has been plunged.

President Wilson made in this speech another pronouncement which indicated the real difficulty we had in any approach to peace negotiations. He said: —

"We are all agreed that there can be no peace obtained by any kind of bargain or compromise with the Governments of the Central Empires, because we have dealt with them already and have seen them deal with other Governments that were parties to this struggle, at Brest-Litovsk and at Bukharest. They have convinced us that they are without honour and do not intend justice. They observe no covenants, accept no principle but force and their own interest. We cannot 'come to terms' with them. They have made it impossible. The German people must by this time be fully aware that we cannot accept the word of those who forced this war upon us. We do not think the same thoughts or speak the same language of agreement."

This was in fact our greatest problem. We had no desire to go on fighting the Germans or Austrians a needless hour. Nor, when this war ended, would we have any lust to plot for another. But we knew that if this war ended in a sort of armed truce, leaving the present militarist régime of the Central Empires still in authority and undefeated, they would have only one purpose — to prepare for a renewal of the conflict at a more favourable moment, with more formidable arms and better-laid plans. Thus our only hope was to keep on till they had been defeated in the field and discredited at home. Had they been able to boast that they had successfully defied the Armies and Navies of two continents and, still unbeaten, made peace on foreign soil they had conquered, and from which they could not be driven, their power for mischief would have been unbroken.

The British Trade Union Congress passed on September 6th a resolution calling for —

". . . the destruction of every arbitrary power anywhere that can separately, secretly, and of its single choice disturb the peace of the world, or if it cannot be presently destroyed, at the least its reduction to virtual impotence. . . . The Congress urges the Government to establish peace negotiations immediately the enemy either voluntarily or by compulsion evacuates France and Belgium. . . ."

That substantially poses the problem. We could only make peace when the defeat of the Central Powers was a fact patently established, and their forces withdrew or were driven from France and Belgium. Without fulfilment of those conditions, a peace would be only a truce, under cover of which the redoubtable military leaders of Germany would gather up her strength for a renewed conflict and we should be compelled to prepare for the next struggle.

As it happened, the Note of Count Burian was not a blow in service of Germany's "Peace Offensive" strategy. It was a cry of despair. Its appearance on September 15th in the Berlin Press struck public opinion in Germany with the shock of a thunderbolt, and the Reichstag party leaders rushed together and demanded an interview with the Chancellor. He succeeded in calming them, and von Hintze worked to utilise the Austrian Note as a basis for arranging a Peace Conference at The Hague. On September 28th the Dutch Government announced that the Queen of the Netherlands would place her residence at the disposal of the Powers for Conferences on the lines of the Note.[1]

But events were moving too fast for von Hintze. On September 15th, the day after Burian despatched his Note, General Franchet d'Esperey launched a great attack on the Salonika Front which routed the Bulgars and sent the Allied forces sweeping forward to victory. On September 28th the envoys of the Bulgarian Government reached Salonika to sue for an armistice and abandon hostilities. On September 28th the German Foreign Office produced a Memorandum setting out the necessity for an immediate reconstruction of the Government on a broad democratic basis as a preliminary to the peace negotiations which were essential. That morning, von Hintze started for Spa to find out the full truth about the military situation, and the next train found Count Hertling, the Chancellor, heading in the same direction to discover if it was really true that Ludendorff was in agreement with the proposal for a Government reconstruction — to which Hertling was unalterably opposed. And on September 28th, Ludendorff and Hindenburg took stock of the outlook and reached the despairing conclusion that the War was lost, and that there was nothing for it but to appeal at once to the enemy for an armistice. In his Memoirs, "Out of My Life", Hindenburg describes this decision in the following terms: —

"It was on 28th September that this inward battle raged most fiercely. Though German courage on the Western Front still denied our enemies a final break through, though France and England were visibly tiring and America's oppressive superiority bled in vain a thousand times, our resources were patently diminishing. The worse the news from the Far East, the sooner they would fail altogether. Who would close the gap if Bulgaria fell out once and

[1] "Die Ursachen des Deutschen Zusammenbruchs im Jahre 1918", Vol. II, p. 246.

for all? We could still do much, but we could not build up a new front. It was true that a new army was in process of formation in Serbia, but how weak these troops were! Our Alpine Corps had scarcely any effective units, and one of the Austro-Hungarian divisions which were on their way was declared to be totally useless. It consisted of Czechs, who would presumably refuse to fight. Although the Syrian theatre lay far from a decisive point of the War, the defeat there would undoubtedly cause the collapse of our loyal Turkish comrades, who now saw themselves threatened in Europe again. What would Roumania, or the mighty fragments of Russia do? All these thoughts swept over me and forced me to decide to seek an end, though only an honourable end. No one would say it was too soon.

"In pursuance of such thoughts, and with his mind already made up, my First Quartermaster-General came to see me in the late afternoon of 28th September. I could see in his face what had brought him to me. As had so often happened since 22nd August, 1914, our thoughts were at one before they found expression in words. Our hardest resolve was based on convictions we shared in common." [1]

The 28th of September, 1918, thus becomes a very important date in the history of the War, and of the coming of peace. On the German side, the blame for the final collapse of her war effort has been variously attributed by apologists for her military leaders to the collapse of the home front, the flight of the Kaiser, the mutiny at Kiel, the weakness of Prince Max of Baden, the base machinations of the Socialists, and so on. Before any of these causes operated, Hindenburg and Ludendorff reached the conclusion that the War was hopelessly lost, and that the future could hold out nothing for Germany but a rapid mounting of calamities and defeats. As Ludendorff himself admits, on the Western Front their forces were fading away; battalions reduced from four companies to three; divisions from three brigades to two, of

[1] Von Hindenburg: "Out of My Life", pp. 428 and 429.

weary, exhausted, underfed men, who were being defeated and driven back at an ever-accelerating pace. As I describe in another chapter, their need for food supplies from the Ukraine made it impossible for them to bring west the troops they had stationed there. Bulgaria had gone. Turkey was going. That meant that Entente troops would soon be on the Danube, and Entente fleets in the Black Sea. Roumania would reënter the War, and Germany would then be unable to get any petrol — of which she had barely enough to last her aeroplanes for two months.

"The War was now lost. Nothing could alter that. If we had the strength to reverse the situation in the West, then of course nothing would yet have been lost. But we had not the means for that. After the way in which our troops on the Western Front had been used up, we had to count on being beaten back again and again. Our situation could only get worse, never better. There was no hope of further reinforcements for the time being from home. Independently of each other, the Field-Marshal and I came to the conclusion that we must bring things to an end." [1]

Thus Ludendorff. And the conclusion is inescapable that Germany and her allies were in fact defeated in the field, whatever civil collapse was superimposed in November to make her completely helpless before the Entente. Even had that civil collapse not intervened, the following months could only have witnessed the fuller materialisation of the ruin which Ludendorff foresaw.

The Bulgarian Armistice was not, of course, the first breakaway in the World War; Russia and Roumania had ceased fighting months previously. But it was the first collapse on the side of the Central Powers or their allies, and it was, as we have seen, of immense significance in that it led directly to general peace approaches from them. The Allies immediately made arrangements to take full ad-

[1] "Die Ursachen des Deutschen Zusammenbruchs im Jahre 1918", Vol. II, p. 256.

vantage of Bulgaria's elimination to march to the Danube and attack Austria on that front. On September 27th, as soon as Clemenceau knew that there was a prospect of a Bulgarian surrender, he asked both General Franchet d'Esperey, the G.O.C. at Salonika, and General Guillaumat, his predecessor, to submit memoranda setting out their recommendation for the further course of operations. Guillaumat, who was now in Paris, promptly prepared a document which Clemenceau forwarded to me for comments. But while this document was on its way to Signor Orlando in Italy and to me in London, the Bulgarian emissaries were negotiating an armistice with Franchet d'Esperey at Salonika. On September 26th an envoy from the Bulgarian Government arrived at General Milne's Headquarters to ask for a suspension of hostilities. Milne referred him to General Franchet d'Esperey, the Commander-in-Chief of the Salonika forces, and d'Esperey thereafter took in hand the further negotiations, about which he did not consult Milne at all. The envoys reached him on September 28th, and signed the Armistice on the following day. It came into force on the 30th. Its terms, which constituted an abject surrender, were as follows: —

"Armistice Convention with Bulgaria,
Signed 29th September, 1918.

"1. Immediate evacuation of the territories still occupied in Greece and Serbia in conformity with an arrangement to be concluded. No cattle, grain or stores of any kind are to be removed from these territories. No destruction shall be caused by the Bulgarian troops on their departure. The Bulgarian Administration shall continue to carry on its functions in the parts of Bulgaria at present occupied by the Allies.

"2. Immediate demobilisation of all the Bulgarian Armies, with the exception that a group of all arms, comprising three divisions of 16 battalions each and four regiments of cavalry, shall be maintained on a war footing, of which two divisions shall be allocated to the defence of the eastern frontier of Bulgaria and of the Dobrudja, and the 148th Division to the protection of the railways.

"3. The arms, ammunition and military transport belonging to the demobilised units shall be deposited at points to be indicated by the Supreme Command of the *Armées d'Orient*. They will then be stored by the Bulgarian authorities, and under the control of the Allies.

"The horses will likewise be handed over to the Allies.

"4. The material belonging to the Fourth Greek Army Corps, which was taken from the Greek Army at the time of the occupation of Eastern Macedonia, shall be handed over to Greece, in so far as it has not been sent to Germany.

"5. Those portions of the Bulgarian troops at the present time west of the meridian of Uskub, and belonging to the Eleventh German Army, shall lay down their arms and shall be considered until further notice to be prisoners of war. The officers will retain their arms.

"6. Bulgarian prisoners of war in the East shall be employed by the Allied Armies until the conclusion of peace, without reciprocity as regards Allied prisoners of war in Bulgarian hands. These latter shall be handed over without delay to the Allied authorities, and deported civilians shall be entirely free to return to their homes.

"7. Germany and Austria-Hungary shall have a period of four weeks to withdraw their troops and military organisations. The diplomatic and consular representatives of the Central Powers, as well as their nationals, must leave Bulgarian territory within the same period. The orders for the cessation of hostilities will be given by the signatories of the present convention.

General FRANCHET D'ESPEREY.
ANDRE LIAPCHEF.
E. T. LOUKOF.

"General Headquarters,
    29th September, 1918, 10.50 P.M."

On October 5th I arrived at Versailles for a series of conferences with Clemenceau and Orlando and our military advisers about the situation arising from the termination of hostilities in Bulgaria. We recognised that this success must be exploited in three directions: first of all we must cut the communications between Turkey and the Central Powers, and force Turkey out of the War; then we must push up to Roumania and help her to drive out the garrison of Austrian troops and reënter the War on the Allied side; and finally, by advancing up to the Danube we could menace Austria herself. Of these developments, the earliest in point of time was likely to be the overthrow of Turkey, and we proceeded to discuss the terms on which Turkey might be granted an armistice. Marshal Foch's advice was summed up in a series of short sentences scribbled by him upon a sheet of notepaper, which is before me as I write. It was as follows: —

"Mon Conseil.

"1. Couper les chemins de fer du territoire allemand à Constantinople.

"A Nisch, on en coupe une partie.

"Sur la Maritza, en amont d'Adrianople on les coupe tous.

"2. Prendre possession des points stratégiques de la Bulgarie qui assurent le désarmement de l'Armée bulgare.

"3. Jeter une A.C. au Danube pour y couper les communications fluviales de l'ennemi et au besoin tendre la main à la Roumanie.

"4. Ultérieurement, ces conditions réalisées, entrevoir, étudier, préparer action contre Turquie.

F. FOCH.

"4/10/18."

TRANSLATION: —

"My Advice.

"1. Cut the railway lines running from German territory to Constantinople.

"At Nish, a section is to be cut.

"On the Maritza, upstream from Adrianople, all are to be cut.

"2. Take possession of strategic points in Bulgaria that will ensure the disarmament of the Bulgarian Army.

"3. Fling an army corps to the Danube to cut the enemy's river communications there and if necessary to lend a hand to Roumania.

"4. Thereafter, when these conditions are carried out, examine, study, prepare an action against Turkey."

At this time, Allenby was pursuing his victorious campaign in Syria. Damascus had fallen on October 1st, and on October 6th I heard, while at Versailles, that a Turkish emissary had reached Mytilene on his way to Athens. I had with me a draft of armistice terms for Turkey which had been already approved by the British War Cabinet, and I laid this before the Conference. It was referred to the military experts, and with their emendations was ultimately as follows: —

"1. Immediate demobilisation of the Turkish Army, except for such troops as are required for the surveillance of the frontiers, and for the maintenance of internal order (effectives to be determined by the Allies).

"2. Opening of the Dardanelles and Bosphorus, and access to the Black Sea. Allied occupation of Dardanelles and Bosphorus forts.

"3. Free use by Allied ships of all ports and anchorages now in Turkish occupation and denial of their use by the enemy.

"4. Surrender of all war-vessels in Turkish waters, or in waters occupied by the Turks. These ships to be interned at such port or ports as may be directed.

"5. Wireless telegraph and cable stations to be administered by the Allies.

"6. Positions of all minefields, torpedo tubes, and other obstructions in Turkish waters to be indicated, and assistance given to sweep or remove them as may be required.

"7. All available information as to mines in the Black Sea to be communicated.

"8. Use of Constantinople as a naval base for the Allies and use of all ship repair facilities at all Turkish ports and arsenals.

"9. Facilities to be given for the purchase of coal, oil fuel and naval material from Turkish sources.

"10. Occupation by Allied troops of important strategical points.

"11. Allied Control Officers to be placed on all railways including such portions of the Trans-Caucasian railways now under Turkish control, which must be placed at the free and complete disposal of the Allied authorities. This clause to include Allied occupation of Baku and Batoum.

"12. Allied occupation of the Taurus tunnel system.

"13. Immediate withdrawal of Turkish troops from North-West Persia and Trans-Caucasia to behind the pre-War frontier.

"14. The surrender of all garrisons in the Hejaz, Assir, Yemen, Syria, Cilicia, and Mesopotamia to the nearest Allied Commander or Arab representative.

"15. The surrender of all Turkish Officers in Tripolitania and Cyrenaica to the nearest Italian garrison.

"16. The surrender of all ports occupied in Tripolitania and Cyrenaica, including Misurata, to the nearest Allied garrison.

"17. Surrender of all Germans and Austrians, naval, military and civilian, to the nearest British or Allied Commander.

"18. Compliance with such orders as may be conveyed for the disposal and disposition of the Turkish Army and its equipment, arms and ammunition, including transport.

"19. Appointment of Allied Officers to control army supplies.

"20. All Allied prisoners of war, and Armenian interned persons and prisoners, to be collected in Constantinople and handed over unconditionally to the Allies.

"21. Obligations on the part of Turkey to cease all relations with the Central Powers."

We had received information that the Sultan was anxious to ensure the guarantee of two points in any terms accorded him: first, that he should retain his throne; and second, that Turkey should remain an independent nation. It will be seen that the above armistice provisions did not affect either of these two issues.

Turkish Armies were offering a weakening resistance to our progress in Syria and Mesopotamia, and might continue to do so for some time. It was clear to us that our success in Bulgaria would now enable us to exert considerable additional pressure on Turkey from the north, with a view to hastening her surrender. General Franchet d'Esperey had not only replied to Clemenceau's request for a Memorandum sketching out the further action to be taken, but we learned that without waiting for confirmation he had begun to put his programme into action. The British Army had hitherto occupied the right flank of the Allied line and by no means the most salubrious sector of the front. General Franchet d'Esperey now proposed to break up the British forces at Salonika under General Milne, and diverting some of them up in Bulgaria while placing a part under a French General, to march along with French troops on Constantinople. The French were very anxious to get that city into their own hands. They seem to have had a secret fear that if once the British got hold of it we might develop independent plans for its ultimate disposal. Needless to say, such an idea was completely without foundation, and I raised the strongest protest against the cavalier treatment being meted out by d'Esperey to our forces and their General. Clemenceau gave way at once, and sent instructions to d'Esperey to re-group the British forces in their original position on the east of the Allied line. In a further telegram he sent the decisions of the Conference as to the further course of operations on the Balkan Front. These ran: —

"The British, French and Italian Governments agree that the immediate action of the Allies for exploiting the situation in the Balkans shall be developed on the following bases: —

"1. The section of the Allied Army of the East marching on Constantinople shall be under the immediate command of a British General, who shall himself be under the orders of the Allied Commander-in-Chief;

"2. The section of the Army of the East marching on Constantinople shall consist mainly of British troops, but shall also include French, Italian, Greek and Serbian troops;

"3. Reciprocally, some British troops shall take part in the operation in the North."

Two days later, on October 9th, at the end of the last meeting of the Conference, it was agreed, on my proposition: —

"To refer to the Military Representatives at Versailles, with whom should be associated representatives of the American, British, French and Italian Navies, the question of the liaison between the naval and military forces of the Allies in the forthcoming operations against Constantinople, together with the question of the command of the Allied naval forces engaged in these operations."

But if the fall of Bulgaria thus enabled us to concert fuller measures for achieving victory in the south-east of Europe, its effects were even more immediately apparent in the main theatres of war. Ludendorff and Hindenburg had already been forced to the conclusion that there was nothing for them to do but to abandon the fight. And even before the Conference at Versailles of October 5th–9th had assembled, this decision of theirs had borne fruit.

The course of events in Germany between September 29th and October 4th may be briefly summarised. It involved an internal political crisis which changed the constitution of the Empire. And it provided a further illustration of the completeness with which Germany's affairs were at this time dominated by the Military High Command. Theirs was the only voice that counted — even to ordering a revolution.

On September 29th there was a conference at Spa, when Ludendorff set out his reasons for requiring an immediate armistice — a pre-condition of which, he recognised, must be the reconstruction of the Government on a democratic basis.[1] There were really a series of conferences: first between the Army Heads and von Hintze, the Foreign Secretary; then another with the Kaiser; and in the afternoon the Chancellor, Count Hertling, arrived to hear the story again. Ludendorff was extremely emphatic that there was no time to lose; that "every hour of delay is dangerous!" He gave von Hintze the impression that imminent catastrophe threatened the Army. When the Kaiser arrived, he heard the same story, with the same complete surprise and dismay. At midday the elderly Chancellor turned up and heard the news. He came out of the room and said to his son: "It's absolutely terrible! The Supreme Army Command demands that *as soon as it can possibly be done,* a request for peace be sent to the Entente!"

In the afternoon, they talked over the political situation. Count Hertling, an old reactionary, refused to remain Chancellor with a democratic, parliamentary government, and tendered his resignation, which the Kaiser accepted. Among the names suggested for his successor was Prince Max of Baden. Von Hintze also offered his resignation; for he too represented the old traditions of the Empire; but the Kaiser refused to accept it. Hertling was unwilling to believe too seriously in the need for revolutionary reforms, and the Kaiser took courage from his attitude to suggest that they

[1] "Die Ursachen des Deutschen Zusammenbruchs im Jahre 1918", Vol. II, pp. 260 *et seq.*

might leave over the transition to democracy for another fortnight or so. A draft decree lay on the table, authorising the political transition. It was dated September 30th. The Kaiser let it lie, and went to the door. Von Hintze followed him, reminding him that the Supreme War Command insisted on an immediate appeal for an armistice, and on the necessity for any application to the enemy for armistice or peace negotiations being sent by a democratically constituted Government. Tired, bewildered, the Kaiser turned back and affixed his signature. It was not a very big reform. Its purport was that the Kaiser was willing to call into his Government the representatives of the majority parties in the Reichstag: but he still retained in his own hands the appointment of the Chancellor. Addressed to Count von Hertling, it accepted his resignation, and went on to say: —

"I desire that the German people shall coöperate more effectively than heretofore in the determination of our country's fate. It is therefore my wish that men who are supported by the confidence of the people shall take part in wide measure in the rights and duties of the Government. I beg you to conclude your work by carrying on the business of Government and initiating the measures which I intend to introduce until I have found your successor. I look forward to your proposals in this matter.

With the signature in his pocket, von Hintze dashed back that same night by a special train to Berlin, to get the party leaders to come together to form a ministry, and to find someone to take over the post of Chancellor. Before leaving the German H.Q., he had sent off telegrams to Vienna and Constantinople, urging that Austria and Turkey should join with Germany in an appeal to President Wilson for peace on the basis of the Fourteen Points, and an invitation to him to summon a Peace Conference at Washington, subject to an immediate armistice. He had now to form a Government and find a Chancellor that would undertake to carry out this approach to America without a moment's delay. He was pursued, on October 1st, by a telegram from Hindenburg which said: —

"If by seven or eight o'clock this evening it is certain that Prince Max of Baden will form the Government, I agree to the postponement till to-morrow forenoon.

If, on the contrary, the formation of the Government should be in any way doubtful, I consider it desirable that the declaration should be issued to foreign Governments to-night." [1]

Hindenburg had, of course, no conception of the time it takes to form a Government on democratic lines, especially when it is a Coalition Government. Neither he nor Germany had the experience in such matters which accumulates in a country subject to parliamentary government. Prince Max had as yet no intimate knowledge of the military situation or the international outlook, but had a very definite idea that it would be impolitic to appeal for an armistice with the impetuous haste counselled by the Supreme Command. According to his own account, he in the end accepted the post of Chancellor mainly in order to be in a position to delay such an act.

The Reichstag Committee notes in its findings that —

"The Chancellor, Prince Max von Baden, exhausted every resource open to him, to avoid what he regarded as the false step of appealing for an immediate armistice." [2]

At a Crown Council held on the evening of October 2nd, he began to protest against an immediate appeal for an armistice, but the Kaiser promptly silenced him with the

[1] "Memoirs of Prince Max of Baden", Vol. II, p. 4.
[2] "Die Ursachen des Deutschen Zusammenbruchs im Jahre 1918", Vol. II, p. 24.

PRINCE MAX OF BADEN

reminder that the Supreme Command held it necessary. He appealed in writing to Hindenburg, and got back a reply next day, saying: —

"The Supreme Command insists on its demand of Sunday, 29th September, that a peace offer to our enemies be issued at once." [1]

Prince Max made yet another appeal to Hindenburg on the 3rd of October, and when it was rejected at a Conference, he suggested that the peace offer should be sent without an appeal for an armistice. That suggestion also was turned down. So on October 4th he duly dispatched the Note, the text of which had been agreed upon by the Supreme Command. It was addressed to President Wilson, and was as follows: —

"The German Government requests the President of the United States of America to take in hand the restoration of peace, acquaint all belligerent States with this request, and invite them to send plenipotentiaries for the purpose of opening negotiations. The German Government accepts the programme set forth by the President of the United States in his message to Congress of January 8th, 1918, and in his later pronouncements, especially his speech of September 27th, as a basis for peace negotiations.

"With a view to avoiding further bloodshed, the German Government requests the immediate conclusion of an armistice on land and sea and in the air.

MAX, PRINCE OF BADEN,
Imperial Chancellor."

Simultaneously with the despatch of this note, a note couched in similar terms was also dispatched by Austria. It ran as follows: —

"The Austro-Hungarian Monarchy, which has always waged the war solely as a defensive war, and has repeatedly announced its readiness to put an end to the bloodshed and to attain a just

[1] "Memoirs of Prince Max of Baden", Vol. II, p. 19.

and honourable peace, approaches herewith the President of the United States of America with a proposal to conclude with him and his allies an immediate armistice on land and sea and in the air, and immediately thereupon to enter into negotiations for the conclusion of peace, for which the Fourteen Points of President Wilson's message to Congress of the 8th January, 1918, and the Four Points in his speech of the 12th February, 1918, should serve as a basis, while attention will likewise be paid to the declarations by President Wilson on the 27th September, 1918."

On the day when these two peace notes, from Germany and Austria, were published, I was on my way to Paris to take part in the Conference with the French and Italian Governments about the situation in Bulgaria and in Turkey to which I have already referred. For the first days of this Conference we were without any official notification about the Peace Notes. President Wilson was sitting on them, despite the request in the German Note that he should "acquaint all belligerent States with this request." He decided to frame and dispatch his own reply without any consultation with his associates in the common enterprise.

Until we were officially seized of the Notes, we could not, of course, officially decide on our attitude. But, as I informed the Imperial War Cabinet on my return: —

"The representatives of the three Governments, however, met every day and discussed the situation. They also conferred with Marshal Foch and his Chief of Staff, and with the Military Representatives at Versailles, and as a preliminary step, directed their attention to the terms of an armistice."

The principles upon which the terms of an armistice with Germany and Austria were to be drawn up were indicated to the Military Representatives as follows: —

1. Total evacuation by the enemy of France, Belgium, Luxemburg and Italy.

2. The Germans to retire behind the Rhine into Germany.

3. Alsace-Lorraine to be evacuated by German troops without occupation by the Allies.

4. The same conditions to apply to the Trentino and Istria.

5. Serbia and Montenegro to be evacuated by the enemy.

6. Evacuation of the Caucasus.

7. Immediate steps to be taken (*"mise entrain"*) for the evacuation of all territory belonging to Russia and Roumania before the War.

8. Immediate cessation of submarine warfare.

(It was also agreed that the Allied blockade should not be raised.) This decision seems harsh but we were anxious that the period of the Armistice should not be utilised to reëquip Germany for a renewal of the War.

At our discussion on October 8th, we had before us a note from Marshal Foch, on the conditions which he regarded as requisite for an armistice with Germany. These were: —

"There can be, for the armies operating in France and Belgium, no question of ceasing hostilities without having: —

"1. *Liberated the countries invaded* contrary to all right — namely, Belgium, France, Alsace-Lorraine, Luxemburg — and brought back their population. The enemy will have to evacuate these territories within a fortnight, and their population will have to be immediately repatriated.

First condition of the Armistice.

"2. *Assured a suitable military base of departure,* permitting us to pursue the War up to the destruction of the enemy force in case the peace negotiations should lead to no result.

"For this we must have two or three bridgeheads on the Rhine as high up as Rastadt, Strassburg, and Neu Breisach (bridgehead of a semicircle traced on the right bank with a radius of 30 kilometres with the end of the bridge on the right bank as centre) within a delay of a fortnight.

Second condition of the Armistice.

"3. *Taken possession of security for the reparations* to be exacted for the destruction perpetuated in Allied countries, the demand for which will be presented in the course of the negotiations of the Peace Treaty.

"For this the countries on the left bank of the Rhine will be evacuated by enemy troops within a delay of thirty days; they will be occupied and administered by the Allied troops in concert with the local authorities up to the time of the signature of peace.

Third condition of the Armistice.

"Beyond this, it will be necessary to impose the following complementary conditions: —

"4. All material of war and supplies of every kind which cannot be evacuated by the German troops within the period fixed must be left in place; it will be prohibited to destroy them.

"5. The units which will not have evacuated the prescribed territories within the period fixed will be disarmed and made prisoners of war.

"6. The railway material, both permanent way and materials of all kinds, will be left in place, and must not be the object of any destruction. All the Belgian and French material seized (or its numerical equivalent) will be immediately restored.

"7. The military installations of every kind for the use of troops, camps, barracks, parks, arsenals, etc., will be abandoned intact, with prohibition to remove or destroy them.

"8. The same will apply to industrial establishments and factories of every kind.

"9. Hostilities will cease twenty-four hours after the day on which the conditions of the armistice shall have been approved by the contracting parties.

FOCH."

When these conditions were read out, Mr. Bonar Law remarked that this amounted virtually to unconditional capitulation. Baron Sonnino thought that both Foch and the Military Representatives were asking too much. I inclined to the same view. We felt, however, that it was not much good at this stage discussing the matter at length, for we were still in the dark as to what President Wilson proposed to say in reply to the German and Austrian Notes. The American Press took it for granted that he would reject their offer, which was regarded there as a manœuvre to trick the Allies into a negotiated peace without victory. And in this there was this measure of truth, that Ludendorff and Hindenburg saw in an immediate armistice the only hope of rescuing their army intact, so as to be able to maintain resistance afterwards, if necessary, to peace terms which they could not bring themselves to accept. But neither the Americans nor ourselves knew then how near to collapse Germany was, and how hopeless the prospect facing her Supreme Command.

On Tuesday, October 8th, Lansing handed to the Swiss Chargé d'Affaires at Washington, who acted as intermediary for communications between the United States and Germany, President Wilson's reply to the German appeal for an armistice. It was as follows: —

> "The Department of State,
> 8th October, 1918.

"Sir,

"I have the honour to acknowledge, on behalf of the President, your note of the 6th October, enclosing a communication from the German Government to the President; and I am instructed by the President to request you to make the following communication to the Imperial German Chancellor: —

"Before making a reply to the request of the Imperial German Government, and in order that that reply shall be as candid and straightforward as the momentous interests involved require, the President of the United States deems it necessary to assure himself of the exact meaning of the note of the Imperial Chancellor.

Does the Imperial Chancellor mean that the Imperial German Government accepts the terms laid down by the President in his address to the Congress of the United States on the 8th January last, and in subsequent addresses, and that its object in entering into discussions would be only to agree upon the practical details of their application? The President feels bound to say, with regard to the suggestion of an armistice, that he would not feel at liberty to propose a cessation of arms to the Governments with which the Government of the United States is associated against the Central Powers so long as the armies of those Powers are upon their soil. The good faith of any discussion would manifestly depend upon the consent of the Central Powers immediately to withdraw their forces everywhere from invaded territory.

"The President also feels that he is justified in asking whether the Imperial Chancellor is speaking merely for the constituted authorities of the Empire who have so far conducted the War. He deems the answer to these questions vital from every point of view.

"Accept, Sir, the renewed assurances of my high consideration.

ROBERT LANSING."

At the last meeting of our Conference at Versailles, on October 9th, we had before us the text of this reply.

M. Clemenceau said he thought it was an excellent document. Without consulting the Allies, President Wilson had demanded the evacuation of France, Belgium, Italy and Luxemburg. When a reply was received, it might suggest to us the discussion of armistice conditions. We naturally would then turn to our military advisers and ask what conditions they considered necessary. If we were to speak now without waiting to be asked, it would be a mistake, and would play into the hands of the Germans; hence he considered that our present condition was quite satisfactory, and that no action need be taken.

I could not quite agree with this view. I pointed out that the speech in which Prince Max of Baden had defended and explained the German Peace Note to the Reichstag on

October 5th was the speech of the Chief Minister of a defeated Empire. Had either Clemenceau or I made such a speech, the world would say that we were defeated. In Prince Max's place I would accept President Wilson's proposals without alteration. The Prince would no doubt readily accept the Fourteen Points; but there were matters in them of which I would like to know a little more — for example, the Freedom of the Seas in war-time. This was quite unacceptable to the British nation. Prince Max would also no doubt readily accept the evacuation of occupied territories as a condition of the Armistice. In fact, the Germans were even now evacuating their territory, and it was only Marshal Foch who was delaying them and knocking them about in the process. A difficulty arose regarding the first point in the President's letter, because of the uncertainty of interpretation of the Fourteen Points; there was vagueness, for instance, about Alsace-Lorraine. His second point, however, dealing with the Armistice, was more serious, for if the Germans accepted this view, they could say they had accepted President Wilson's proposal, and if we had said nothing they could maintain that nobody had protested against it, and that they were entitled to regard it as the sum of the Allied conditions for an armistice.

I went on to point out that the American Government had formally sent us their reply, and we must send back some sort of answer. Moreover, the American reply had appeared in the Press before it reached the Governments. If we simply let the matter pass after this publication, and said nothing, I thought we should be, to a great extent, committed to it. Accordingly, I submitted to the Conference a rough draft I had made of the sort of reply which I felt we ought to send to Wilson. This was considered by the Conference, and on the basis of it a formal reply was drawn up and approved. The following is a translation of its text: —

"The Allied Governments have taken note with the greatest interest of the reply addressed by President Wilson to the Chancellor of the German Empire.

"They appreciate the lofty sentiments which have inspired this reply. Confining themselves to the most urgent question, that of the Armistice, they share the opinion of the President of the United States, that the preliminary condition for any discussion of this question is the evacuation by the enemy of all invaded territories. But for the conclusion of the Armistice itself, they consider that this condition, essential though it is, not sufficient.

"It would not prevent the enemy from taking advantage of a suspension of hostilities to place himself, at the expiration of an armistice not followed by peace, in a better military situation than at the moment of the interruption of hostilities. They might be enabled to withdraw from a critical situation, to save their stores, to reform their units, to shorten their front, to retire without loss of men upon new positions which they would have time to select and fortify.

"The conditions of an armistice can only be fixed after consultation with the military experts and in accordance with the military situation at the actual moment when negotiations are entered on.

"These considerations have been strongly urged by the military experts of the Allied Powers, and particularly by Marshal Foch. They equally concern all the armies of the Governments associated in the fight against the Central Empires.

"The Allied Governments commend them to President Wilson for his fullest attention."

Along with this message we decided to send to the President a further telegram on the need for closer co-operation in the conduct of peace negotiations. This was as follows: —

"The Allied Governments venture to point out to President that time has come when decisions of supreme importance in regard to War may have to be taken at very short notice. They therefore think it would be of very great assistance if an American representative possessing the full confidence of the United States Government could be sent to Europe to confer, when occasion arose, with the other associated Governments so as to keep them accurately and fully informed of the point of view of United States Government."

It was clear that the end was now in sight. It was no less clear that we must move with the utmost care at this critical juncture, making sure of our footing at every stride, lest by a false step we should imperil the full harvest of our long effort. We wanted to make a clean finish to the War, in such a manner that its lesson would be driven home and there would be no danger of it breaking out afresh. And, as President Wilson had hinted in his Reply to the German note, we were really still dealing with the old military Imperialist clique there. The democratisation of the German Government was at this stage no more than a dummy façade, imposed as an emergency war measure by the Emperor to meet Allied criticism. Its composition had in the main been determined by the reactionary retiring Chancellor, Hertling, and the new Chancellor, Prince Max, was selected by a Council of War and not nominated by a democratic body. The terms and the despatch of the appeal for an armistice had been dictated by the same Council of War. The hands might be sketchily gloved in a democratic pelt, but the voice was the voice of Ludendorff.

This situation has to be borne in mind in considering how it came about that hostilities were allowed to continue unchecked for more than a month after the Germans made their appeal for peace. All the world was panting for peace. Yet for weeks the fighting went on. The fact was that we did not feel ready to commit ourselves to negotiations with Ludendorff until we were in a position to ensure that our main peace terms were sure of acceptance. As for Wilson's Fourteen Points, they might be, and in the main were, in harmony with our desired terms, but they were in places phrased in the language of vague idealism which, in the absence of practical application, made them capable of more than one interpretation. It was not sufficient for Germany to express readiness to negotiate on the basis of the Fourteen Points, unless we were in a position to insist on her accepting our exegesis of the sacred text.

The policy Committee of the British War Mission in America produced on October 9th a Memorandum about the German Note — the first of many memoranda that were to be poured in from various advisory quarters on that theme — in which it underlined the fact that —

". . . the pronouncements of President Wilson were a statement of attitude made before the Brest-Litovsk Treaty, the enforcement of the peace of Bukharest on Roumania, and the German statement of their intentions at the outset of the spring offensive. They cannot, therefore, be understood as a full recitation of the conditions of peace.

"The phrasing of the German acceptance of them as a 'basis for peace negotiations' covers every variety of interpretation from sincere acceptance to that mere desire for negotiations which is the inevitable consequence of the existing military situation. It is, therefore, impossible to grant any armistice to Germany which does not give the Entente full and acceptable guarantees that the terms arranged will be complied with. There must be a clear understanding that Germany accepts certain principles as indisputable, and reserves for negotiation only such details as, in the opinion of the Associated Powers, are negotiable."

How truly we interpreted the temper of the German High Command at the moment when they launched their armistice proposal has since been admitted by Prince Max himself. In his Memoirs he states that: —

"The Supreme Command had probably no clear idea at first as to the fateful conditions to which the Fourteen Points must in any case commit Germany. They probably saw in Wilson's programme a mere collection of phrases, which a skilful diplomacy would be able to interpret at the conference table in a sense favourable to Germany. I had put them the question whether the Supreme Command were aware that the course they were entering upon might lead to the loss of colonies and even of German soil — in particular of Alsace-Lorraine and of the purely Polish districts of our eastern provinces. I received from them the evasive reply: 'The Supreme Command is ready to consider the cession of some small French-speaking parts of Alsace-Lorraine, if that is unavoidable. The cession of German territory on the eastern frontier is for them out of the question.' At the last moment the Supreme Command tried to give expression to this mental reservation of theirs, in the wording which they proposed for our Note: 'The German Government agrees that Wilson's Fourteen Points shall "serve as the basis of conversations." ' But the Ministers were — from their point of view rightly — of the opinion that no formulation should be used which would make Wilson suspicious and might provoke inconvenient questions. They supposed that they had avoided this in the final wording of the Note: as it afterwards appeared, they underrated the alertness of our opponents."[1]

Dealing with opponents who asked for an armistice in so insincere a frame of mind, it is obvious that we should never have secured those terms which we regarded as quite indispensable for a genuine peace — terms such as the full release and restoration of Belgium, the return of Alsace-Lorraine to France, the rectification of Italian, Polish and Roumanian frontiers and so on — if they retained the power of effective refusal. Had they when asking for an armistice come forward with an honest, unequivocal offer in set terms to satisfy us on these points, the case would have been different. But we were, as is now known, quite right in suspect-

---

[1] "Memoirs of Prince Max of Baden", Vol. II, p. 24.

ing that they had on October 4th no intention of agreeing to our demands. There was nothing for it but to fight on until they were compelled to accept armistice terms which put us in a position to insist on the objects which we had throughout the War openly announced to be those for which we were fighting.

The vague and unprecise character of the various speeches by President Wilson cited in the German Peace Note, if viewed as a final definition of the nature of the peace the Allies were prepared to make, was brought out in a Memorandum from the Political Intelligence Department of the Foreign Office, produced on October 12th.

Meantime, the German Government issued on October 12th a reply to President Wilson's Note of October 8th. They declared that they "accepted the propositions laid down by President Wilson in his address of January 8th, and in his subsequent addresses as the foundation for a permanent peace of justice." They took it that the Entente Powers associated with America in the War also accepted these propositions. They were ready to evacuate the occupied territory as a condition of an armistice, and suggested a mixed commission to supervise the arrangements for the evacuation. And they concluded with the assertion that the German Government represented the views of the majority of the Reichstag, and thus spoke for the German people.

It was unfortunate that these smooth approaches to peace by the German Government coincided with incidents which exasperated Allied opinion and were responsible for stiffening Allied demands. As the German Army retreated in France and Belgium they deported civilian populations and wrought havoc and destruction on their property far beyond anything which military exigencies could warrant. Every fruit tree in the orchards, for instance, was ringed; even the innocent rose trees round cottage doors were often destroyed. At sea, not only did the practice of sinking ships without warning continue, but there was just at this time a crop of sinkings of passenger vessels with heavy loss of life. On October 10th the passenger steamer *Hiramo Maru* was sunk off the Irish coast, and of 320 persons on board, only 28 were saved; and on the same day the Irish Mail Boat *Leinster* was torpedoed without warning, and when beginning to sink was torpedoed a second time, thus being sunk in a few minutes with a loss of lives reported at the time as 520. There was a howl of indignation, which drowned the welcome that might otherwise have been given to the German Peace Note.

President Wilson replied at some length on October 14th to Germany. He made it clear that for armistice conditions they would have to deal with the military authorities on the Allied side, and that these conditions would have to "provide absolutely satisfactory safeguards and guarantees of the maintenance of the present military supremacy of the Armies of the United States and of the Allies in the field." He went on to draw attention to the German atrocities and to demand that they should cease.

"The President feels that it is also his duty to add that neither the Government of the United States nor, he is quite sure, the Governments with which the Government of the United States is associated as a belligerent will consent to consider an armistice so long as the armed forces of Germany continue the illegal and inhuman practices which they still persist in. At the very time that the German Government approaches the Government of the United States with proposals of peace, its submarines are engaged in sinking passenger ships at sea — and not the ships alone but the very boats in which their passengers and crews seek to make their way to safety; and in their present enforced withdrawal from Flanders and France the German Armies are pursuing a course of wanton destruction which has always been regarded as in direct violation of the rules and practices of civilised warfare. Cities and villages, if not destroyed, are being stripped not only of all they contain but often of their very inhabitants. The nations associated against Germany cannot be expected to agree to a cessation of arms while acts of inhumanity, spoliation and desolation are being continued which they justly look upon with horror and with burning hearts."

He rounded off his Note by pointing out that this was the kind of thing we had learned to expect from the authorities which had hitherto controlled Germany; and if there was a real change in the character of the German Government, he hinted that they should bring forth fruits meet for repentance if they wanted a merciful peace.

I received at this time a telegram from Sir Eric Geddes, then in the United States, reporting a talk he had had with the President, whose attitude, since receiving the last German Note, appeared to be hardening towards caution. The telegram, which I read to the Cabinet on October 15th, stated that: —

"(*a*) President Wilson was fully alive to the need for continuing the prosecution of the War. He proposed shortly to announce the undiminished despatch of troops and war effort of the United States.

"(*b*) He realised that the time had arrived when consultation with the Allied Powers was essential.

"(*c*) He had stated that our armistice terms, framed by naval and military officers, must be viewed in the spirit that undue humiliation would be inexcusable, except in so far as the enemy must be prevented from taking advantage of the Armistice to reform their forces and better their position.

"(*d*) He inclined to take Germany to task for recent atrocities, *e.g.*, the sinking of the *Leinster*.

"(*e*) In talking of his Fourteen Points, the President's views on the Freedom of the Seas appeared to be unformed.

"(*f*) The President had referred to the absolute necessity for the break-up of Austria, owing to commitments to oppressed nationalities."

Sir Eric Geddes further recorded that the whole tone of the discussion had been most cordial, but that the President was outstandingly fearful, lest the naval and military authorities might urge an armistice so humiliating that the German nation could not accept it. His mind appeared to be set upon the kind of armistice which would leave no rancour, and demonstrate the high plane upon which the Allies stood.

In a Memorandum which he wrote on October 15th for the War Cabinet about the conditions of an armistice, Lord Curzon stressed the fact that from this stage onwards, any decision as to terms to be laid down for an armistice must be jointly discussed and settled among the Allies, not negotiated by the President alone. His Memorandum went on to suggest that the Armistice ought to contain in it a summary of the main items we should insist on in our peace terms — among which he referred not only to the matters contained in the Fourteen Points, but others which he thought should be included — surrender of Heligoland, the German Fleet and part of its mercantile marine; compensations, reparations, indemnities to the Allies for the cost of the War; and the trial and punishment of the principal criminals, possibly including the Kaiser, unless he abdicated. Lord Curzon's document was symptomatic of the hardening of the public attitude and its insistence upon an uncompromising victory.

In Germany, on the other hand, it was being slowly forced upon those in authority that they were facing certain defeat and were on the brink of collapse. Before sending his second Note to Wilson, Prince Max had held a consultation with Ludendorff, from which he was forced to conclude that if the Allies continued to attack without giving the Germans any respite, the German Army could not hold out, and might at any time be penetrated and broken up. In his Memoirs, Max states that he finally asked Ludendorff point-blank: —

" '*If the present peace action should fail,* could the War be carried on by us alone till the spring, in spite of the desertion of one of the two allies that remain to us?'

"I received the answer: 'We need a breathing-space; after that we can re-form.'

" 'In other words,' I asked, 'can we hold out if we do *not* obtain a breathing-space?' and received the answer: 'Yes, if we obtain a breathing-space, we can hold out.'

"Our situation was therefore dark and difficult indeed." [1]

Prince Max declares that the real truth was that General Ludendorff believed he could hold the frontiers if the Army could be led back in good order, but not if it had been beaten back. And he seriously thought the Allies would grant him an armistice that would enable him to carry out this manœuvre. To get that armistice he would now have been willing to promise peace terms that would involve the loss of Alsace-Lorraine and payment of a heavy indemnity. It is clear therefore that from a military standpoint the German Army was not now in a position to guarantee continued resistance. On the political side, the home front was rapidly disintegrating. Up till the end of September the nation had been carefully blinded by the Supreme Command as to the seriousness of the situation. Not even the civilian Ministers had been given any inkling of its real gravity, and they were dumbfounded by Ludendorff's demand for an armistice. Up till the middle of July the German Army had been marching from victory to victory. Allied entrenchments were stormed, Allied fronts broken, Allied guns captured and

---

[1] "Memoirs of Prince Max of Baden", Vol. II, p. 68.

hundreds of thousands of Allied troops made prisoners. The mass of the nation, that had suffered so long and so resolutely, with a grim confidence in their military leaders, which seemed to have been so brilliantly justified by the recent offensives, could not understand the sudden change in the prospect, and they were utterly shattered by the publication of the Note to America. They swung round to the deepest distrust of those who had hitherto been their idols — especially of Ludendorff, whom they dissociated from Hindenburg and recognised as the man who had dominated German policy during the latter part of the War, whereas Hindenburg rather embodied the nation's patriotic spirit. In this connection it is interesting to recall a comment made by Marshal Foch, when I asked him his opinion in June 1918 about the two outstanding German military leaders. What, I said, did he think of Ludendorff? His reply was: *"Un bon soldat!"* And how, I continued, would he describe Hindenburg? He answered: *"Un grand patriote!"* The mass of the nation could no longer be relied on to support Ludendorff in fresh military ventures. Prince Max toyed with the idea of a *levée en masse* as an alternative to continuing the peace negotiations, but could find no one to support the suggestion.

The very broad hint contained at the end of Wilson's second Note, that there was not much hope of the War ending so long as the Kaiser and his military advisers were in charge of Germany's policy, acted like a bombshell on public opinion there, and set all Berlin talking about the possible abdication of the Kaiser. At a meeting of the German War Cabinet, held on October 17th to consider President Wilson's latest Note, Ludendorff swung round to an attitude of intransigence; but Prince Max notes his own impression that Ludendorff, having in the first place compelled him to send off the first Peace Note, now wanted to score credit for opposing actual surrender. "I cannot deny

that the impression gained on me that General Ludendorff
was less concerned to alter our decision than to register a
protest against it." [1]

Although at the meeting of October 17th Ludendorff
sounded a note of optimism, he was unable to adduce any
sound reason for it. A note written on the following day to
Prince Max by Crown Prince Rupprecht gives a picture of
the Army from which little optimism could be deduced.
He says: —

"Our troops are exhausted and their numbers have dwindled
terribly. The number of infantry in an Active Service Division
is seldom as much as 3,000. In general the infantry of a division
can be treated as equivalent to one or two battalions, and in
certain cases as only equivalent to two or three companies. Quantities of machine-guns have been lost, and there is a lack of
trained machine-gun teams. The artillery has also lost a great
number of guns and suffers from a lack of trained gun-layers.
In certain armies 50 per cent. of the guns are without horses!
There is also a lack of ammunition. . . .

"The morale of the troops has suffered seriously and their
power of resistance diminishes daily. They surrender in hordes,
whenever the enemy attacks, and thousands of plunderers infest
the districts round the bases. . . .

"I do not believe that there is any possibility of holding out
over December. . . . Our situation is already exceedingly dangerous. . . . Ludendorff does not realise the whole seriousness
of the situation. Whatever happens, we must obtain peace, before
the enemy breaks through into Germany; if he does, woe on us! [2]

Prince Max's first draft for a reply to President Wilson
was rejected by the Cabinet as too abject, and for a short
time it looked as though the military chiefs would demand his resignation — so little had the effective Govern-

[1] "Memoirs of Prince Max of Baden", Vol. II, p. 68.
[2] *Ibid.*, p. 157.

ment of Germany yet changed as a result of the pseudo-democratisation authorised by the Kaiser. Finally a Note in a less complaisant vein was drafted and agreed, and on October 20th it was send off by Solf.

As regards the terms of the Armistice for which Germany was asking, their Note accepted the condition that it should be arranged by military advisers, but demanded that "the present relative strength on the fronts must be made the basis of arrangements that will safeguard and guarantee it." President Wilson was asked to have the matter settled on this basis, and to approve no demand "that would be irreconcilable with the honour of the German people and with paving the way to a peace of justice." The Note went on to deny the charges of illegal and inhuman practices on land or sea, but promised to order U-boat commanders not to sink passenger ships in future. In conclusion, it asserted that the new Government involved a fundamental change in the constitution of Germany, and that a Bill had been introduced to make the decision on war and peace subject to approval by the Reichstag.

To this note Wilson replied on October 23rd. He accepted the German promise to observe the humane rules of civilised warfare, and also their assertion that their Government included Ministers representing the Reichstag majority and the opinion of the nation. But as for the Armistice's terms, he declared that: —

"The only Armistice he would feel justified in submitting for consideration would be one which should leave the United States and the Powers associated with her in a position to enforce any arrangements that may be entered into, and to make a renewal of hostilities on the part of Germany impossible."

So he was sending the correspondence to the Associated Governments, for their military advisers to work out armistice terms such as "will fully protect the interests of the peoples involved and ensure to the Associated Governments the unrestricted power to safeguard and enforce the details of the peace. . . ." He went on to point out that he did not put much confidence in the professed change of Government; that the world could not trust the word of those who had hitherto dictated German policy, and that if the United States had to deal: —

"with the military masters and the monarchial autocrats of Germany now, or if it is likely to have to deal with them later in regard to the international obligations of the German Empire, it must demand, not peace negotiations but surrender."

As a matter of fact, quite irrespective of his final dig at the German autocracy, Wilson had intimated in this note that the Armistice terms would involve a complete surrender by the Central Powers. But when news of the terms of his reply got abroad among the German people, there were clamours from many quarters for the Kaiser's abdication as a means to secure better terms for the country. Even prominent military figures like Colonel von Haeften were eager that Wilhelm should abdicate before he was forced to do so by popular clamour. Ludendorff, on the other hand, issued a defiant order to the Army calling on them to refuse Wilson's terms. On this Prince Max asked the Kaiser to dismiss Ludendorff. He did so on the 26th, and on the following day a further note was dispatched by Germany to the President, asserting that the constitution was being duly changed as he had required, and that the military powers were now subject to it. Accordingly, the German Government —

". . . now awaits proposals for an armistice, which shall be a first step towards a just peace, as the President has described it in his proclamations."

After this, the next step as regarded Germany rested with the Allied Governments and their military advisers, to whom Wilson had passed the previous correspondence on October 23rd. Some few days had to elapse while each of the Allied Governments considered its attitude and while arrangements were being made for them to meet together in conference to discuss the situation.

2. THE TERMS OF THE ARMISTICE

Attitude of British Government — Sir Douglas Haig's statement — Condition of Allied Armies — Haig's suggestion for armistice terms — Cabinet depressed — Victory not expected before 1919 — Cabinet approves Wilson's note — Further memoranda — Smuts under spell of G.H.Q. — Post-War perils in Europe — Moderate peace not attainable — Turkey's collapse — A breeze with Clemenceau — My insistence on British command in Aegean — French suspicion — Calthorpe takes charge of armistice negotiations — Clemenceau's protest — Austria gives in — Appeal by the Pope — Drastic terms — Italian fear of Germany — Provisional scheme for crushing German resistance — Allied response to President Wilson — Terms of the Note — Wilson's final Note to Germany — Germany in chaos — Delegates meet Foch — Abdication of the Kaiser — The Armistice signed — Its main conditions — Clemenceau's account of the negotiations — Germany's acceptance — Protest of German signatories — News of the signature — Final modifications — Parliament gives thanks — Problems of Peace.

The British Government had been following the developments of the situation with the closest attention. They were anxious not to prolong the slaughter one hour beyond the moment when victory was so assured that the Germans could not by a short period of rest put a complete triumph in jeopardy. If a few more weeks would place the Allies in that position, then a premature armistice would be a blunder. On the other hand, if the German Army were still capable of holding on behind the Rhine until the winter came and the condition of the roads made a further advance impracticable, then we should have to face the prospect of a renewal of the campaign in 1919. With the Germans driven out of France and Belgium, I was more than doubtful whether public opinion either in Britain or in France would face the sacrifices of another campaign merely to force Germany to disgorge her Eastern conquests. Our decision as to the terms of the Armistice therefore depended on the military prospects. I invited the Commander-in-Chief to come over to London to enlighten the Government on this subject. On October 19th, Marshal Haig attended a meeting of the War Cabinet and gave us his views on the military position and the prospects of a satisfactory armistice. He confirmed Sir Henry Wilson's appreciation in every particular. The statement he made to the Cabinet on this occasion had a special interest as showing how little weight our military leaders attached to the abandonment of Germany by her allies. Their minds were focussed on the trenches in front of them, they had no eyes for the facts and considerations outside which were directly responsible for the immediate collapse of the German resistance. Sir Douglas Haig gave us a pessimistic appreciation of the military situation which is extraordinary in view of the actual condition of the Germany Army. Here is a résumé of his statement: —

"In the event of the enemy asking for an armistice the nature of the reply should depend greatly on the answers which we can make to the two following questions: —

1. Is Germany so beaten that she will accept any terms dictated by the Allies?

2. Can the Allies continue to press the enemy sufficiently vigorously during the coming winter months to cause him to withdraw so quickly that he cannot destroy the railways, roads, etc., up to the German frontier?

"A very large part of the German Army has been badly beaten, but the whole Field Army has not yet been broken up. Owing to the large numbers of divisions of which it consists, *general disorganisation* (which follows a decisive defeat) is not yet apparent.

"In my opinion the German Army is capable of retiring to

its own frontiers and holding that line against equal or even superior forces.

"The length of that line is about 235 miles as against the front of 400 miles which he was holding only a week ago.

"The situation of the Allied Armies is as follows: —

"The French Army seems greatly worn out. Many of the rank and file seem to feel that the War has been won. Lille, Roubaix, Tourcoing and other big centres of industry have been taken. Reports say that many of their men are disinclined to risk their lives. Certainly neither on the right nor on the left of the British have the French attacked vigorously during the last six weeks. Even in July it was the British and American divisions which carried the French forward on the Marne. Next year a large proportion of the French Armies will probably be Black!

"*American Army* is disorganised, ill-equipped and ill-trained with very few N.C.O.'s and officers of experience. It has suffered severely through ignorance of modern war and it must take *at least a year* before it becomes a serious fighting force.

"*The British Army* has fought hard. It is a veteran force, very confident in itself but its infantry is already 50,000 under strength. If infantry effectives could be maintained and rest given during winter it would remain what it is now, the most formidable fighting force in the world. On the other hand with diminishing effectives we must expect morale to decline.

"If the French and American Armies were capable of a serious offensive *now*, the Allies could completely overthrow the remaining efficient enemy divisions before they could reach the line of the Meuse.

"They are not. We must reckon with that fact as well as with the fact that the British Army alone is not sufficiently fresh or strong to force a decision by itself.

"This means that the Allies are not in a position to prevent the enemy from doing an immense amount of material damage to railways, roads, etc., during the winter months *and during his retirement.*

"The advance of the Allies, when active operations again begin, will, therefore, be greatly hampered and progress must be slow.

"In the coming winter, too, the enemy will have several months for recuperation, and absorption of the 1920 class, untouched as yet.

"So we must conclude that the enemy will be able to hold the line which he selects for defence for some time after the campaign of 1919 commences." [1]

Having regard to the fact that we were within a fortnight or three weeks, at the outside, of the complete break-up of the German Army, and that all Germany's allies had already given up the struggle, Haig's view of the military prospects was, to say the least, unduly restrained. He advised us that in his view it would be best to offer armistice terms which involved no more than the retirement of the enemy to his own frontiers, evacuating Belgium, France and Alsace-Lorraine, and returning the commandeered Belgian rolling stock and the deported Belgian citizens. If Germany rejected satisfactory peace terms we could then resume the War in 1919 on enemy soil.

Mr. Bonar Law pointed out that such terms really amounted to complete defeat, and that in the military situation which Haig described there was nothing which should compel the Germans to accept such terms.

The Field-Marshal's reply to this was that —

. . . the enemy might think that the Allies were stronger than they were in reality.

Discussion followed as to the naval terms we might hope to impose, and also as to the state of the German

---

[1] His estimate of the contribution made by the French Army is very ungenerous, seeing that the total casualties suffered by the French between July and November, 1918, were 531,000, as compared with 411,000 suffered by the British — and that, after France had already suffered some 2,157,000 casualties in the previous fighting.

morale, which I pointed out was the crucial issue at this stage. Feeling was general that it was unlikely hostilities would be resumed once the "cease fire" had sounded; and on that account we ought to hold pledges for the fulfilment of our peace terms. Milner suggested occupying the Western Rhineland, and Wilson the Saar; but I remarked that on the evidence furnished by Field-Marshal Haig, the Germans were not sufficiently defeated to concede such terms. In that case the continuance of the blockade would be our most effectual guarantee.

We passed under review the military terms which Foch had suggested for an armistice, and the naval terms which our Admiralty demanded. These anticipated the main features of the Armistice ultimately imposed, and I pointed out that they amounted to abject surrender. I asked Haig what would be the effect on our Army if we insisted on such terms and the enemy refused them. He hinted that the effect of their morale would be bad. As to a continuance of the blockade, Mr. Bonar Law doubted whether America would agree to it if the Germans surrendered their submarines.

On the whole, the military advice we obtained did not encourage us to expect an immediate termination of the War. All our plans and preparations at that date were therefore made on the assumption of all our military advisers that the War would certainly not conclude before 1919. We were not fully informed as to the internal conditions in Germany and we underestimated the effect of the Balkan and Turkish victories on the military situation. Our military counsellors attached little importance to the events in the East which the German Staff considered decisive. If Haig and Wilson correctly read the military situation on October 19th, it would not, at that date, have been possible to conclude an armistice which would afford any satisfactory guarantee to the Allies that their essential peace terms would be attained, or that we might not find the enemy at the end of it in a stronger position for defying us and holding out against us than he had been when hostilities were broken off.

Matters had advanced a stage further when the Cabinet assembled to review the situation on the morning of October 24th. In the meantime, the German Note of October 20th had been sent to President Wilson, and he had answered it on the 23rd as already noted. We had before us the text of Wilson's latest note to Germany, though his official communication to us was not yet to hand. I stated that I welcomed the terms of his reply and liked the tenor of the President's proposals. If Germany meant peace, she would accept, and the acceptance would be equivalent to military surrender. I was glad that the diplomatic wrangle was over, and that the President had made it clear that the terms of an armistice must be such as would prevent the resumption of hostilities by the Germans.

The general opinion of the Cabinet was in accord with this view. Mr. Bonar Law expressed his pleasure that President Wilson had been firm enough when it came to the point to insist on what practically amounted to unconditional surrender. Some members of the Ministry were impatient with Wilson's attempts to interfere with the internal affairs of Germany. Their view was that democratic government was no guarantee against war, though it checked the tendency to plot and prepare for war. Further discussion was adjourned until the President's official communication to the Allied Governments should be available. A good deal of preliminary work had already been done in examining the problem of an armistice. Foch's terms were confined to the position on land. On October 20th, Mr. Balfour submitted a Memorandum suggesting further points for the Armistice, such as the surrender of the German Navy, and the occupation of parts of Germany other than those it was proposed to detach — such as Alsace-Lorraine — with a view to holding them as pledges for payment of reparations and the settlement of the eastern frontier. On October 22nd, Lord Fisher submitted a characteristic Memorandum of five naval points he wished to see dealt with: —

"1.   The German High Sea Fleet to be delivered up intact.
"2.   Ditto — Every German Submarine.
"3.   Ditto — Heligoland.
"4.   Ditto — The two flanking islands of Sylt and Borkum.
"5.   No spot of German Jesuitry in the wide world to be permitted: It would infallibly be a Submarine base."

The Ministry of Shipping, the Air Ministry, and the War Office all submitted memoranda indicating the points which they wanted to see covered by the armistice terms.

On the other hand, we had two Notes laid before us by General Smuts on October 23rd and 24th, in which he accepted without doubt or demur Haig's estimate of the military position. We have seen in previous chapters how very greatly this otherwise acute observer had fallen under the spell of G.H.Q. opinion. In view of the account of the military situation given to the Government by Haig on October 19th which I have described above, Smuts thought we were foolish to suppose that Germany would sign an armistice that involved a surrender. His memorandum of October 23rd declared that: —

"The result of these discussions on an armistice is that the various drafts before us differ in no material respect from an unconditional surrender, which is not justified by the present relative military positions of the belligerents. . . .

"An armistice conference between the military leaders on these lines is, therefore, bound to prove abortive. . . ."

Accordingly, he urged that instead of concluding an armistice we should make peace — put forward moderate peace terms on the lines of the Fourteen Points and get Germany to accept them while hostilities still continued — unless we intended to carry on the War into 1919. In his second Memorandum of the following day, he continues in this strain, reminding us of —

". . . the very sober statement which Sir Douglas Haig made to the Cabinet on the 19th October, and which inspires no extravagant hopes for the immediate future from purely military effort on the Western Front."

In this second Memorandum he warned us against trying to defeat Germany, as that might mean dragging on the War for another year. There was considerable shrewdness and foresight in his warning against the disintegration of Central Europe which had now become imminent: —

"There is serious danger that the bad, but more or less orderly, political pre-War system of Europe may give place to a wild disorder of jarring and warring state fragments, such as we now see on a vast scale in Russia. . . . What is going to happen when, as now seems probable, Austria breaks up and becomes a 'Balkans' on a vaster scale? With the creation of an 'independent' Poland, there will be a chain of these discordant fragments right across Europe from Finland in the north to Turkey in the south. No League of Nations could hope to prevent a wild wardance of these so-called free nations in future. . . ."

In the economic realm, though not as yet in the martial, we have witnessed in post-War Europe that wild war-dance of the new powers which Smuts foretold, but the smaller States who were liberated by the Treaty are not mainly or largely responsible. The most serious trouble has been created by the rivalries, jealousies and disagreements of the greater powers of Europe and Asia.

Smuts wanted us to make the best peace we could, without demanding surrender from Germany.

"The popular cry for justice is very insistent, but two governing considerations should be kept steadily in view. Firstly, the evil of continuing the War is rapidly beginning to outweigh the good to be achieved by a more complete measure of victory or justice. Secondly, the British Empire should not pursue justice at the expense of its own legitimate future. . . ."

That last observation sounds a little cynical. But Smuts doubtless had in mind the advice of Ecclesiastes: —

"Be not righteous overmuch . . . why shouldest thou destroy thyself?"

He was misled by Haig and Wilson into failing to realise how incapable Germany was of prolonging the struggle. Beyond question, it was a disaster that we had to lay Germany prostrate before we could reach a peace settlement. Had Ludendorff retreated earlier to strong lines within the German frontier and there held out against us, a peace settlement might have been reached that contained fewer roots of bitterness than one dictated to a foe who even in defeat clung with his claws to the foreign lands he had invaded and devastated and in the process of liberating his hold increased the desolation. Unhappily, for the peace of the world, the hostile armies were still on the soil of France and Belgium when the end came, and the surrender had to be complete enough to guarantee the aims for which we fought.

While the Allies were considering with their military advisers what form the armistice terms should take, Germany's remaining associates were tumbling down. Turkey had addressed a Peace Note to President Wilson as far back as October 14th, patterned on those of Germany and Austria. But we dropped him a hint that as Turkey was on the point of collapse, he need do no more than refer her to which-ever Allied commander, naval or military, of the forces at-tacking her, she cared to approach, to receive our terms for an armistice.

The Turkish Armistice led to the only real unpleasant-ness I ever had with Clemenceau. At this time, while the Commander-in-Chief of the Allied Naval forces in the Mediterranean was French, the naval forces located in the Aegean were under a British Admiral, Sir S. A. Gough-Calthorpe. When a prospect arose in October of an early victory over Turkey, the question was discussed at our Con-ference of October 9th as to who should command the Allied naval forces operating at Constantinople. We naturally in-sisted that he should be British, in view of the fact that the Allied Fleet in the Aegean was at least 75 per cent. British, and that this country had been responsible for practically all the military operations against Turkey — alike at Gal-lipoli, in Egypt and Palestine, and in Mesopotamia. Clemen-ceau was anxious to put a French Admiral in charge, and the French representative at Versailles held out for this. Accordingly I wrote a strong letter to Clemenceau on Octo-ber 15th, urging him to agree without further delay to our proposition. In this letter I pointed out that: —

"We have taken by far the larger part of the burden of the war against Turkey in the Dardanelles and in Gallipoli, in Egypt, in Mesopotamia and in Palestine. The British Government has agreed that the Commander-in-Chief of the Allied Armies in France should be a French General; it has agreed that the Commander-in-Chief of the Allied Armies in the Balkans should be a French General. I do not see how I could possibly justify to the people of the British Empire that at the moment when the final attack upon Turkey was to be delivered, the command of Naval Forces which are overwhelmingly British, in a theatre of war associated with some of the most desperate and heroic fighting by troops from nearly every part of the British Empire, should be handed over to a French Admiral as well."

Clemenceau replied on the 21st asserting that if we had borne the lion's share of the fighting against the Turks we had to that extent been compelled to limit the help we might otherwise have given them in France! And he declared that as France was Turkey's principal creditor, and most of the banks and business concerns in Constantinople were French owned, they had the greatest interest there. He had agreed that General Milne should command the operations in the Balkans against Turkey; he could not agree that the naval operations should also be in British hands.

I sent him an emphatic reply on October 25th, in which I answered his arguments, point by point, and ended by saying: —

"The British Government have agreed to a French Commander-in-Chief on the Western Front; they have agreed to a French Commander-in-Chief in the Balkans; they have agreed to a French Commander-in-Chief in the Mediterranean. Unless it is to be contended that unity of command means that one nation alone among the Allies is to have not only the supreme but the subordinate command wherever Allied forces are employed on a common enterprise together, I do not understand why it is that you wish to deprive the British of a naval command which they have exercised ever since 1915 in order that a French Admiral may be placed in control of an expedition, three-quarters of which is British in material and personnel. I assure you that insistence on such a view must inevitably imperil the operation of the all-important principle of unity of command in every department of the War, for public opinion will never tolerate the relinquishment by the British of the naval command in a theatre in which the British arms have throughout the War made the heaviest sacrifices, and to which the people, not of Great Britain alone but of Australia, New Zealand and India, have sent so many of their sons to die. I earnestly trust, therefore, that you will see your way to consent to the arrangement whereby the command in the Aegean and of the attack on Constantinople by sea is to remain in the hands of a British Admiral acting under the general direction of the Allied Commander-in-Chief in the Mediterranean."

Unquestionably the French were, at this time, very jealous of the position we had won in Egypt, Palestine and Mesopotamia, and were most anxious to keep in their own hands all the negotiations in the Balkans and with Turkey. The Turks, on the other hand, preferred to do their business with us. The upshot was that Turkey short-circuited my dispute with Clemenceau by directly approaching Admiral Calthorpe at Mudros with a request for an armistice. On October 20th, General Townshend, who had remained in Turkish hands since the fall of Kut on April 29th, 1916, arrived at Mudros as an emissary from Izzet Pasha to ask for peace terms. Calthorpe cabled us the news, informing us also that the Turks particularly wanted to deal with us, not with the French, and that —

". . . the effect of a Fleet under French command going up to Constantinople would be deplorable, nor could anything be more unpopular with the Greeks in Turkey. General Townshend thinks that the Turks would be willing to send plenipotentiaries now to treat for peace with British representatives and that they would allow the British to take over the Forts of the Dardanelles if they were assured of support against the Germans in Turkey and the Black Sea."

Calthorpe was told to inform the Turkish Government that he was empowered to sign an armistice, and on October 26th, three envoys from Turkey reached Mytilene and were brought to Mudros. The main features of the armistice terms to be granted to Turkey had already been settled, as we have seen, at the Inter-Allied Conference of October 7th–9th.

The French, on learning of this, promptly sent their Admiral Amet to associate himself with Calthorpe in the negotiations; but Calthorpe firmly refused to share the business with him. The discussions were long and difficult. The Turks particularly objected to Clause I of the proposed terms, which involved Allied occupation of the Dardanelles and Bosphorus forts. They said they would rather dismantle them and in any case would never agree to Greeks occupying them, and they had an almost equal objection to Italians. On our instructions, Calthorpe gave an undertaking that only British and French troops would take part in this occupation, and in the small hours of the morning of October 29th, Calthorpe wired us that subject to Constantinople agreeing to Clause I in the light of this guarantee, the Armistice was now agreed. It was, in fact, signed on October 30th, and Turkey withdrew from the War.

On that day I was attending an Inter-Allied Conference in Paris, and I reported to it that the Armistice would be signed before evening. Clemenceau and his Foreign Secretary, Pichon, at once raised the question of Calthorpe's action in refusing to associate Admiral Amet with himself in the conduct of the negotiations, and a somewhat heated argument ensued, the French taking their stand on the legal point that the supreme command in the Mediterranean was held by them, while I maintained that the local command in the Aegean, and the whole of the operations against Turkey, were in British hands. There was a certain amount of recrimination, and I see that the official minutes record me as remarking at one point of the discussion that: —

". . . except for Great Britain no one had contributed anything more than a handful of black troops to the expedition in Palestine. I was really surprised at the lack of generosity on the part of the French Government. The British had now some 500,000 men on Turkish soil. The British had captured three or four Turkish Armies and had incurred hundreds of thousands of casualties in the war with Turkey. The other Governments had only put in a few nigger policemen to see that we did not steal the Holy Sepulchre! When, however, it came to signing an armistice, all this fuss was made."

Mr. Balfour supported me, and declared that if the French made a point of it, we would refer the question to Versailles for a general ruling whether an armistice must be signed by representatives of all the Allies. The Armistice with Bulgaria had been negotiated by Franchet d'Esperey single-handed, Milne not having been associated with him, although the Bulgarian peace overtures had been made to the British Government. In the end, Clemenceau consulted with Pichon and then said that as in this case the armistice had probably been signed already they would agree to accept the *fait accompli*, and the incident closed.

While the negotiations with Turkey were being concluded yet another of our enemies, Austria-Hungary, was suing out her armistice. The Italian advance of Vittorio Veneto had begun on October 24th, and on the 29th an Austrian officer crossed the Italian lines with a white flag, asking for armistice terms. He only represented the local Austrian general, not their Commander-in-Chief, so he was sent back; but next day a fully accredited mission arrived under a flag of truce.

The Austrian Peace Note of October 4th to President Wilson had been answered by him on October 18th with the statement that his Fourteen Points no longer applied to Austria in their original form, as he had since recognised the independence of the Czecho-Slovaks and the Yugo-Slavs. On October 27th, they replied that they were willing to accept this; but there was no need for him thereafter to refer them to the military for armistice terms, as their necessities drove them to do this spontaneously. On November 1st, the Pope sent to us a special appeal on behalf of the crumbling Empire. This ran: —

"The Holy Father, in his most earnest desire to see an end put as soon as possible to the War which for too long has devastated Europe, begs His Britannic Majesty's Government to give benevolent and immediate consideration to the request for a separate peace put forward by Austria-Hungary. After a request of this nature, the cessation of the sanguinary conflict appears to be imperiously called for by every principle of humanity.

"Further, the August Pontiff, with a strong feeling for the sufferings of poor prisoners of war, especially on the approach of severe weather, trusts that, thanks especially to the noble and efficacious intervention of His Majesty's Government, these unfortunate people can by both parties be restored to their families."

When we received this Note, the negotiations for an armistice were already well under way, and our Inter-Allied Conference at Paris had given place to a meeting of the Supreme War Council at Versailles, where the actual terms were being agreed. They were drastic. M. Clemenceau himself remarked of the naval terms that "they had left the breeches of the Emperor and nothing else!" But Austria was in no mood to boggle at the conditions. On November 3rd, the Armistice was signed, and hostilities ceased on the following day.

There was a meeting of Allied Premiers, Clemenceau, Orlando and myself at Colonel House's rooms in Paris when the fate of the Austrian Armistice was in the balance. We were discussing the conditions to be imposed on Germany. We decided to adjourn the discussions to the following morning in the confident expectation that by the following day there would be some definite news as to the Austrian negotiations. I had packed up my papers and was passing through the front garden of the house when Sir Maurice Hankey rushed after me to tell me that a telegram had just arrived announcing the acceptance by Austria of the Allied terms. I returned and found Clemenceau, Orlando, Sonnino and House in a state of ebullient excitement. Orlando was in tears, the stern Sonnino was radiant, and even the iron-hearted Frenchman was overcome with emotion.

It is curious, looking backward on the situation as it presented itself at that time, to recall that on October 29th, Baron Sonnino was acutely alarmed lest we should come to terms with Germany before doing so with Austria. He was terrified that in that case the German Armies would put on Austrian uniform and turn round on Italy! So little did he realise either the utter war-weariness of Austria — far intenser, more pervasive than that of Germany — or Germany's disgust with allies who had during 1918 fought with a white feather whilst Germany was making such desperate efforts to retrieve the fortunes of the Central Alliance.

The elimination of both Turkey and Austria-Hungary left the field clear for us to concentrate on terms for Germany. The armistice terms, naval and military, were carefully examined and approved by the Supreme War Council. By the afternoon of November 4th, the Council had agreed to the text of the Armistice to be offered, and had also adopted resolutions as to the further military steps to be taken against Germany, should she decline to sign the Armistice.

These included the establishment of an Allied line along the German-Austrian frontier, the massing of Czechs and Slovaks in Bohemia and Galicia, bringing up the Salonika forces under General Franchet d'Esperey through the Balkans, and carrying out heavy bombing operations by means of aerodromes set up in Bohemia. Had events compelled us to carry out this programme, there can be no question that Germany would have been invaded from the south before the end of the year.

The Council further adopted the text of a note to President Wilson, communicating to him the terms of the proposed Armistice, and inviting him to notify the German Government that they should apply to Marshal Foch with the object of negotiating a suspension of hostilities. A protracted and somewhat lively discussion took place as to whether we should accompany this note by any statement making it clear that we should not consider ourselves bound to adhere to the letter of the President's Fourteen Points in the subsequent framing of peace terms. In particular, the British Government could not accept the President's attitude about the Freedom of the Seas in war-time; and when we raised this point the French and Italians proceeded to bring forward their own objections to other items. We had a series of conversations with Colonel House, Wilson's representative in Paris, about these matters. Clemenceau prepared an elaborate Memorandum criticising the Fourteen Points in detail, which he wanted to send to Washington, and Sonnino had a Memorandum on the subject of Italian frontiers, which, however, after much difficulty we were able to persuade him did not arise in connection with an armistice with Germany. Eventually, we managed to secure agreement on the wording of a Note prepared by me to accompany our message to President Wilson, which ran as follows: —

"The Allied Governments have given careful consideration to the correspondence which has passed between the President of the United States and the German Government. Subject to the qualifications which follow, they declare their willingness to make peace with the Government of Germany on the terms of peace laid down in the President's address to Congress of the 8th

January, 1918, and the principles of settlement enunciated in his subsequent addresses. They must point out, however, that Clause 2, relating to what is usually described as the Freedom of the Seas, is open to various interpretations, some of which they could not accept.

"They must therefore reserve to themselves complete freedom on this subject when they enter the Peace Conference.

"Further, in the conditions of peace laid down in his Address to Congress of the 8th January, 1918, the President declared that the invaded territories must be restored as well as evacuated and freed, and the Allied Governments feel that no doubt ought to be allowed to exist as to what this provision implies. By it they understand that compensation will be made by Germany for all damage done to the civilian population of the Allies and their property by the aggression of Germany by land, by sea, and from the air."

On receiving our communication, President Wilson addressed, on November 5th, 1918, a further note to Germany, in which he referred to his previous note of the 23rd and stated that he had now heard from the Associated Governments their views on the correspondence that had passed between Germany and himself. He quoted the text of the above memorandum from us, and said that he was in agreement with the interpretation of his views given in its concluding paragraph. And he ended by telling Germany that Marshal Foch was authorised by the Governments of the United States and the Allies to receive accredited representatives of the German Government and communicate to them the terms of an armistice.

Although we were confident of ultimately compelling the Germans to surrender, we were, at this stage, far from sure that they would be prepared without making further resistance to accept the very drastic terms which had been agreed at Versailles. When I was there I asked Foch whether he thought they would sign. He said he did not, but in any case he would be able to overpower the Germans by Christmas.

However, the stage was now set for the final act of the drama. Government in Germany was in a state of chaos. The fleet had mutinied at the end of October, rather than go out to fight. The Kaiser had fled to Spa, to take refuge with his army. Prince Max, the Chancellor, had been laid low with influenza, and an overdose of a sleeping draught sent him into a coma for thirty-six critical hours, from the 1st to the 3rd of November. He woke to find that Germany's remaining allies, Turkey and Austria-Hungary, were both out of the War, and that rioting, stimulated by Bolshevik agitators, was breaking out all over Germany. President Wilson's note of November 5th left no doubt that the armistice terms prepared for Germany would be severe. But they had no option but to appeal for them. General Groener, who had taken over on Ludendorff's dismissal, found the army in a hopelessly chaotic state, while the defection of Germany's allies left her defenceless on her southern frontier. On November 6th, Erzberger headed a delegation of *parlementaires* dispatched by the German Government to Foch. On the morning of Friday, November 8th, they arrived at the railway carriage in the Forest Compiègne where Marshal Foch, representing the armies of the Allies, and Admiral Wemyss, representing the navies, awaited them.

"What do you want, gentlemen?" asked Foch. "Your proposals for an armistice," they replied. "Oh, we're not making any proposals for an armistice," said Foch. "We are quite happy to go on fighting." The German delegates looked at one another. "But we must have terms," they protested. "We cannot continue the conflict." "Ah! you come to ask for an armistice? That is a different thing!"

Foch handed over to them the armistice terms drafted

by the Supreme War Council, and told them they could have 72 hours, until 11.0 A.M. on November 11th, to sign them. The delegates withdrew to study them, and were appalled at their severity. The terms, in fact, amounted to a demand for Germany's utter surrender, on a scale which would leave her quite defenceless and incapable of undertaking any resistance to whatever peace terms might be imposed. The delegates dared not sign them, and asked permission — which was granted — to send a messenger to their Government to get instructions.

The messenger returned to a country that was in dire confusion. As far back as October 31st, Scheidemann, the leader of the majority Socialists, had put it to Prince Max that the prompt, voluntary abdication of the Kaiser was vital to enable the home front to be saved, and only Prince Max's sleeping draught prevented him at that time from placing definite proposals to that effect before Wilhelm. In the interval, revolt and sedition had gathered head. It had ceased to be a question of saving the monarchy — it was dubious whether settled government itself could be saved from a Bolshevik revolution. From November 6th, Prince Max was pleading with the Kaiser to resign. By the morning of the 9th he learned that revolutionary sentiment had impregnated not only the town mobs but the Army itself to such an extent that the soldiers could not be relied on to defend the Emperor or to maintain civil order. The Supreme Army Command advised the Kaiser to resign, and Prince Max, hearing that he had agreed to do so, issued a statement to this effect before receiving any official confirmation of the fact. Wilhelm fled to Holland, and the German messenger who brought back news of the Armistice terms found behind the front line — where German soldiers were still fighting with tenacious valour — a land of utter disorder, and a new Socialist Government of a German Republic, sitting bewildered in the high places where till yesterday an Emperor and the Kings and Princes of ancient royal houses had reigned as supreme hereditary autocrats.

The terms might be hard, but there was no one to gainsay them. The heads of the Army could no longer count upon all its units to continue a fight every soldier in it knew to be hopeless. It is said that many of them were seduced by political influences. Maybe so, but these would not have counted had the spirit of the Army not been depressed by a sense of disillusionment and discouragement which bordered on despair. And there was no great leader, either civilian or soldier, to rally them with the inspiration of his personality. The Kaiser, Hindenburg and Ludendorff rolled into one would not make a single Frederick the Great who could mobilise and magnetise all the resources of a hard pressed and exhausted nation to struggle triumphantly against great odds. Neither Prince Max nor Scheidemann possessed the dramatic and oratorical powers of a Gambetta to stir up a vanquished people to a desperate resistance against the victors, and there was no Hitler on the horizon to rouse in the youth of Germany the spirit of sacrifice for the Fatherland. The inevitable result was that in defeat the heads of the civil Government could no longer rely upon the obedience of the civil population. Such governing and administrative capacity as could still make itself felt in Germany would be urgently needed, not for fighting her neighbours but for saving her own civilisation.

Word was telegraphed back to the Forest of Compiègne, authorising Erzberger and his colleagues to sign the Armistice. They did so at 5.0 A.M. on November 11th, and at 11.0 A.M. the cannon-fire ceased along the battle front from the Dutch marshes to the mountain ramparts of Switzerland. After more than four and a quarter years, the Great War was ended.

The progress of the talks at Compiègne during the two preceding days had been followed by us with an eager hope. Certain of the items in the proposed Armistice had called forth strong protest and counter-argument from the German delegates, and in deference to their submissions, a few modifications were introduced. But even so, the conditions were very far-reaching. They included the evacuation by the German military forces not only of all the invaded territories of Belgium, Luxemburg, and France, and of Alsace-Lorraine, but of all German territory west of the Rhine and a strip ten kilometres wide on the east bank, and of bridgeheads with a 30 kilometres radius to the east of Mainz, Coblenz and Cologne; repatriation of all hostages and return of prisoners of war; surrender of large quantities of war material and transport material; withdrawal in Eastern Europe from all territory outside the 1914 German frontier and denunciation of the treaties of Brest-Litovsk and Bucharest; replacement of all cash and securities taken from Belgium and all gold taken from Russia and Roumania as indemnities or otherwise; the handing over of all submarines and of a large part of their fleet, and disarmament of the remainder. If, on account of the mutiny of the fleet, the German Government proved unable to fulfil all the naval clauses of the Armistice in time, we reserved the right to occupy Heligoland as a pledge.

In a despatch which he sent me on the evening of November 9th, Clemenceau gave a characteristically terse and ruthless account of the discussions then in progress. He had just seen Foch, who had told him how things were going. The Germans, he said, —

". . . made no observations either as regards bridgeheads or fleet. They dwelt on the fact that Germany is on the verge of Bolshevism unless we assist them to resist and that we ourselves will subsequently be invaded by the same scourge. They requested to be allowed to retire more slowly from the left bank of the Rhine, stating that it was necessary for them to form an army to oppose Bolshevism and reëstablish order. Foch replied that they would be permitted to constitute this army on the right bank. They further objected that we were depriving them of too many machine-guns and that they would not have sufficient to fire on their own men. Foch replied that they still had their rifles. They inquired our intended procedure on the left bank of the Rhine. Foch replied that he did not know and that in any case it was not their business. They finally requested to be supplied with food, stating that they were on the verge of starvation. Foch replied that in that case it would be sufficient for them to place their tonnage in our pool and in that manner they could obtain supplies. They thereupon requested to be given free passes for their ships. They complained that we were confiscating too many engines as at the present moment their own were scattered. Foch replied that we were only asking for what they had taken from us. They appeared much depressed. From time to time a sob escaped Winterfeld. Under these conditions the signature of the Armistice does not appear doubtful. . . ."

At 6.30 P.M. on November 10th, a wireless message was sent by the German G.H.Q. to their delegates with Foch, which said: —

"The German Government transmits to (German) G.H.Q. the following document: For Secretary of State Erzberger — Your Excellency is empowered to sign the Armistice. You will at the same time make the following formal declaration:

"The German Government will undertake to carry out all the conditions laid down. At the same time the undersigned feel obliged to point out that the fulfilment of some points of these conditions will drive into a famine the population of those parts of Germany which will not be occupied. By leaving all provisions which were intended for the troops in the areas to be evacuated, by restricting the means of communication and at the same time keeping up the blockade (which is equivalent to the withholding of food) any effort at dealing with the food question and organising the same is made impossible. The undersigned therefore request that negotiations will be allowed on these points and that they will be so altered that proper nourishment will be assured.' "

Ten minutes later, another message came from Berlin, in confirmation, saying: —

"The German Government to the German plenipotentiaries with the Allied Armies. The German Government accepts the Armistice terms offered to it on the 8th November.

(*Signed*) IMPERIAL CHANCELLOR."

M. Clemenceau sent the text of these messages on to me with a note saying: —

"My personal opinion is that we must honour this signature while making a marginal note relative to revictualling, which we cannot to my mind refuse to discuss ultimately. In truth, the fact remains that the execution of the clause of the Armistice about the fleet cannot at present take place. Tell me your opinion on this point if there are any new arrangements which you can suggest.

"No announcement will take place until Marshal Foch announces the signature.   CLEMENCEAU."

After a night spent in further discussion of the various point and problems involved in the armistice terms, the German delegates signed it at 5.0 A.M. on November 11th. They accompanied their signature with a declaration, based on the instruction sent them from Spa, warning the Allies that the carrying out of its conditions would throw the German people into anarchy and famine, whereas it had been anticipated that the terms, while completely ensuring the military situation of the Allies, would have ended the sufferings of non-combatant women and children. The declaration ended with the words: —

"The German people, which has held its own for 50 months against a world of enemies, will, in spite of any force that may be brought to bear upon it, preserve its freedom and unity.

"A people of 70 millions suffers, but does not die!"

At ten minutes to seven we received a wireless message from Paris which said: —

"1. The hostilities will cease upon the whole front from the 11th November, 11 o'clock (French time).

"2. The Allied troops will not cross until a further order the line reached on that date and at that hour.

MARSHAL FOCH."

On its heels came a further wireless message addressed by the German delegates to their G.H.Q., stating that they had signed the Armistice, the terms of which had been somewhat modified, particularly by giving six days more for evacuation of the left bank of the Rhine.

Early the same morning I got a message from Clemenceau which said: —

"The Conference of the Plenipotentiaries, after having lasted all night, terminated this morning at five o'clock. Armistice signed five o'clock. Firing will cease to-day on the entire front at 11 A.M. this morning. . . .

"I do not know yet the details of the deliberations with the German plenipotentaries; as soon as I am informed of them I will communicate them to you.

"I think that one of the meetings of the Allied Governments for the preliminaries of Peace ought to take place as soon as possible, quite apart, of course, from any consultation with Germany.

CLEMENCEAU."

A second message ran: —

"At four o'clock I shall read to the Chamber the conditions of the Armistice, but the news of its conclusion will be made public officially at 11 o'clock this morning.

CLEMENCEAU."

At 12.30 that day we received a telephone message from Versailles, giving the most important of the last-minute modifications in the terms. It said: —

"1. The Armistice has been extended from 30 to 36 days.

"2. For a period of five days the Allied Armies are not allowed to move.

"3. The delegates will endeavour to carry out the conditions of the Armistice, but the disorder and confusion behind the German lines is so complete that the German Army can neither move forward nor backward. The Allies will endeavour to assist, so far as possible, with supplies of food.

"4. The time for the movement back to the Rhine which was laid down as 25 days has been extended to 31 days."

In the House of Commons that afternoon, immediately after prayers, I rose and announced the signing of the Armistice, the terms of which I proceeded to read. I concluded by saying: —

"Those are the conditions of the Armistice. Thus at 11 o'clock this morning came to an end the cruellest and most terrible war that has ever scourged mankind. I hope we may say that thus, this fateful morning, came to an end all wars.

"This is no time for words. Our hearts are too full of a gratitude to which no tongue can give adequate expression. I will, therefore, move: 'That this House do immediately adjourn, until this time to-morrow, and that we proceed, as a House of Commons, to St. Margaret's, to give humble and reverent thanks for the deliverance of the world from its great peril.' "

Mr. Asquith spoke briefly in agreement with this, noting with satisfaction that the terms read out made it clear, not only that the War was at an end, but that it could not be resumed. My motion was then adopted and Hansard records that: —

"Whereupon Mr. Speaker and the Members proceeded to the Church of St. Margaret, Westminster, and, with the House of Lords, attended a Service of Thanksgiving to Almighty God, on the conclusion of the Armistice signed this day."

The nations turned from the War wounded in body, in economic order, and still more deeply wounded in soul. Some of those wounds have since proved to be gravely septic, and the poison from them yet mars the health of the world.

Of the task which was left to us of making a peace covering ethnic, territorial and economic affairs in every quarter of the globe, I do not propose here to speak. That would require a new series of Memoirs, covering the long controversies of Versailles, which I may record at some future time, if strength and opportunity avail. For the same reason, I have not gone into details of the various discussions which took place, and of the preliminary work that was carried out, while the War was still in progress, to plan for the after-time, and in particular to scheme out the League of Nations which was the only hope of averting yet further and more terrible wars in the years to come. That, too, belongs properly to the History of Peace.

If that Peace has seemed, in the years that have passed since November, 1918, a sorry prize for so much blood and sweat, the fault was not with the heroes who fought and suffered through the long years of the War. Maybe it is not possible for us yet to judge aright just what they won. The pattern of human history works itself out over centuries and millenniums. The full effect of that titanic conflict of rival ideals which was fought out between 1914 and 1918 across all the oceans and continents of the world cannot be gauged adequately by the confused record of less than two following decades.

At least, there were few misgivings among the mass of the population in the victor countries when the familiar sound of maroons, which had hitherto been the signal for the passing of an air raid, now, on the morning of the 11th of November, announced the welcome news that the whole of the terror and ghastliness of a War which had spread over four continents had passed away. It had killed over 10,000,-000 of the picked young men of the world in the flower of their strength, and crippled and mutilated many millions more. It had devastated entirely many renowned cities and fair provinces. It had shattered the intricate mechanism of international trade and left a welter of confusion and wreckage which would take a generation to clear and rebuild. It had poisoned the mind of mankind with suspicions, resentments, misunderstandings and fears which are still, and for many a year to come will continue to be, a constant menace to the healthy goodwill and neighbourliness of sentiment which are the only abiding guarantee of Peace on earth.

CHAPTER VII

A GREAT EDUCATIONAL REFORM

Educational reform in war-time — Underpaid schoolteachers — Lack of post-primary education — Demand for reform — A.C.3 population — Post-War requirements — Mr. Fisher's Memoranda — War Cabinet approves the programme — Improved grant system for teachers' salaries — The Burnham Scale — Teachers' Pensions — The 1917 Education Bill — The 1918 revised version — Summary of the measure — Grants to Universities — The 1921 consolidating Act.

ONE of the most remarkable and beneficent achievements in the record of a War Cabinet that was concentrating its mind and energy upon the prosecution of a World War, was the bold measure it took to raise the status of the teaching profession, and the carrying through Parliament in the midst of this distracting world tumult of the greatest educational reform which had reached the Statute Book since the Education Act of 1870. The credit for these fine feats of constructive statesmanship belong to the Minister of Education, Mr. H. A. L. Fisher.

When Mr. Fisher came to the Board of Education, he found that notable advances had been made in the course of the past decade. School Medical Services had been established; Secondary Schools were being developed; and much attention was being paid by the Board to problems of pedagogy. The elementary school had by now certainly discharged one important function: it had practically stamped out illiteracy. But in other respects there were woeful gaps to be filled in our educational system, many deficiencies needing repair, developments crying out to be undertaken, before that system could be regarded as worthy of the nation.

It was notorious that the teachers were shockingly under-paid. Their salaries were so slender as to make it almost impossible for them to enjoy the benefits of travel or to purchase books — two essential means for them to maintain and increase their efficiency — and the meagreness of their pension on retirement or breakdown in health was a scandal. I am a schoolmaster's son and I know from the painful experiences of my childhood how shabbily the profession was treated, and I have also a painful recollection of the privation teachers' families, prematurely stricken down, had to endure. The Board of Education was becoming seriously anxious about the problem of recruitment. In particular, there was a marked falling away in the supply of male candidates for the Training Colleges, and it seemed likely that, if nothing were done, male teachers would eventually disappear from the schools. Educated professional men could not hope to maintain homes, wives and families on such pittances. Scavenging was becoming a better paid and less worrying occupation. My father was paid a salary as a schoolteacher that a town scavenger would to-day have regarded as an insult to his trade. The rising cost of living during the War had gravely accentuated this problem. It was also clear that the beggarly scale of remuneration accorded to the teaching profession was a source of serious discontent; and this spirit was likely to spread from the teachers, who are in a position to exert very considerable influence, to the rising generation with which they are in contact.

The system of elementary education was weak at its upper end. For children of sound intelligence who did not pass on to secondary schools, their last year or more at the primary school was often largely wasted in marking time in the seventh standard. Associated with this was the practice, very wide-spread, particularly in Lancashire and Yorkshire, of granting liberal exemptions from school, either whole-time

THE RIGHT HONORABLE H. A. L. FISHER

or half-time, to children between the ages of twelve and fourteen who were sent to work in the factories. After fourteen there was very little provision anywhere, even on a voluntary basis, for day continuation classes for them; and the supply of secondary schools was inadequate, as was the provision of scholarships and allowances to enable children from poor homes to secure education in them.

On the other hand, the time was now ripe for a big educational advance. The fruits of universal elementary education, maintained over a generation and a half, were evident in a change of the national attitude. Previously it had been common for parents, themselves possessing little or no education, to be impatient and contemptuous of the schooling ordained for their offspring, and eager to get them away and into work. But the new generation of parents had been through the schools, and were widely eager for their children to get a good education. There was a ready welcome waiting for any improvement and extension of the system.

Again, the combing of the country's manhood for recruits had shown up the deplorable physical quality of much of the population. It was clear that we were not taking proper care of the nation's children, and the most obvious and easy way to approach this problem was by means of the schools, where sooner or later they all came under the hand of the state. The schools, developed and extended, could watch over our future citizens from infancy to adolescence, and keep their young lives from becoming warped, debilitated or stunted.

Further, educational reform was obviously one of the most important conditions of the post-War reconstruction for which plans were being laid. Millions of young men would be coming back to civil life, starting on careers, or seeking the university education they had been compelled during the War to forgo, or the technical training requisite for their intended calling. The educational system needed to be expanded in advance, in readiness for this. Some of the men would be wanted back in the teaching profession, and to get them, it would have to be improved in status. There would be once more an ample labour supply, and the occasion was opportune for raising the school-leaving age and the provision of secondary education. All these reasons combined to strengthen the case for immediate action.

Mr. Fisher was not long in getting to work. On February 2nd, 1917, two months after his appointment as Minister of Education, he presented to the War Cabinet a lengthy Memorandum entitled: "Educational Development — Proposals for Immediate Action." This was mainly concerned with the status and pay of teachers, in both the elementary and the secondary schools. Three days later he followed it with a further Memorandum entitled: "Educational Reform — General Proposals." In this he set out a twelve-point programme of reforms. Summarised, these were: —

1. A reformed system of grants for elementary education;
2. Raising of school age to fourteen and abolition of half-time;
3. Provision of Nursery Schools for children under five and down to two years old;
4. Better provision for health of children from five to eighteen;
5. Compulsory day continuation classes for young people from fourteen to eighteen;
6. Improved secondary education;
7. Increased grants for university education;
8. More free places, scholarships and bursaries to broaden the road from the elementary school to the University;
9. Increased grants for technical training;
10. Pensions for secondary and technical teachers;
11. Development of teachers' training;
12. Improved arrangements for placing youths in industry, commerce and the professions.

The Memorandum pointed out that legislation would be necessary for some of these reforms, and invited the opinion of the Cabinet as to whether it would be prepared to take up all or any of such legislation during the War.

Mr. Fisher's two Memoranda were considered by the War Cabinet on February 20th, 1917. Pleading especially for the first, Mr. Fisher said that "elementary teachers were miserably paid, and a discontented teaching class was a social danger. Further, as in the case of all fixed incomes, the War had greatly diminished the purchasing power of the teachers' low salaries. Before the War, the wastage of teachers was 9,000 per annum, and this was being repaired only to the extent of 6,000. To meet such a serious shortage after the War, it was essential to increase the attractions of the profession now." As to the introduction of continued education, if he could get statutory recognition of the principle, he was prepared to spend up to fifteen years in giving it full effect.

The War Cabinet approved both the Memoranda, and authorised Mr. Fisher to proceed with legislation on certain of the matters raised in his twelve points.

He set to work forthwith on his first problem — that of improving the remuneration of teachers, both elementary and secondary. Departmental Committees under the chairmanship of Sir H. L. Stephen were set up to examine this question. It had been suggested that the Board of Education should make itself responsible for the whole cost of salaries and that the teachers should be, in fact, Civil Servants. This suggestion was, however, rejected as fatal to local interests in education, and as tending to make possible undue political influence over the schools. The method chosen was to revise the terms of the partnership between the Board of Education and the Local Authorities in regard to educational grants, so as to secure better salaries for the teachers. A system of percentage grants was introduced, under which the Board made itself responsible for 60 per cent. of the salary expenditure in respect of elementary schools, and for 50 per cent. of the total expenditure. The general effect of this financial change was to double the average remuneration of the teachers, to relieve the Board of all anxieties as to male recruitments, and generally to improve the quality of the applicants for teaching posts.

By itself, the adoption of the revised scale of grants was insufficient to settle the matter of teachers' salaries. It was necessary in addition to secure some agreed measure of uniformity between the salary scales payable by Local Authorities (over 300 in England and Wales) and to provide against the recurrent unrest and dissatisfaction caused by gross inequalities or inadequacy. To this end Mr. Fisher proceeded to set up a Standing Joint Committee, representative of teachers on the one hand and of their employers, the Local Education Authorities, on the other, and charged with the duty of devising agreed scales of salary adjusted to local conditions and the requirements of different types of school. Fortunately, the services of Lord Burnham were secured for the chairmanship of this body. Lord Burnham had the triple qualifications of being broad-minded, liberal, and a man of business. The "Burnham Scales" became a kind of teachers' Charter, and have been of great value in preserving educational peace and in removing the grave material anxieties which too often used to darken the teacher's life. A teacher who has every reason to be discontented with life is a dangerous, if not also an insufficient mentor for youth.

The benefits accorded to teachers were further increased by the passage of the Teachers' Superannuation Act of 1918, which, roughly speaking, trebled their pension benefits. Hitherto the old age of teachers had been a time of acute penury, for their pay was not on a scale which allowed a margin for savings, and the pension provided was a miserable pittance. After 40 years' service, a male teacher was entitled at 65 years of age to draw 30*s.* a week; it was hardly an attractive prospect for the old age of a professional man and his wife. In place of this, the new measure gave him a retirement bonus and pension similar in scale to that accorded in the Civil Service. Thus, a man who, aided by the new Burnham scale, drew during his last five years of service a salary of £400 a year, could retire at 60, after 40 years' work, with an annual pension of £200 and a lump sum in addition of £533.

By these provisions for better salaries and pensions, Mr. Fisher placed the whole teaching profession upon a more honoured footing and made it more attractive to talent. But while this was an essential preliminary to far-reaching reform of education, he passed on to the enactment of the further big programme which he had outlined to the Cabinet in February, 1917.

A measure was prepared for this purpose, and, after careful review, it was presented to the House of Commons and received its first reading on August 10th, 1917. It aimed, as Mr. Fisher explained, at the progressive development and comprehensive organisation of education throughout the country. Nursery schools were to be encouraged for children under five years of age. Provision was to be made for higher elementary education of the elder children in the primary schools, and their exemption under the age of fourteen was to be finally stopped. Restrictions were to be placed on the employment of children while of school age. Continuation classes were to be introduced, with the aim of securing eventually a measure of continued education up to the age of eighteen. Special attention was to be given to physical training and care for children's health, and the powers of medical inspection were to be extended.

After producing his Bill, Mr. Fisher threw himself into a big campaign to secure popular support for its aims and ideals. When the War was reaching its deafening climax, he stumped the country, addressing numerous meetings in every centre, expounding his proposals, and secured for them a large and rapidly consolidating popular approval. The chief opposition was encountered among the more reactionary of the Local Education Authorities, which were afraid that certain of the provisions of the Bill would involve them in dictation from Whitehall, and the Minister decided to evade this threatened hostility by altering the clauses in question. Accordingly, on January 14th, 1918, he withdrew the original Bill and introduced a revised measure. It secured its second reading on March 13th without a division, and thereafter during the spring and summer, while the Germans were delivering their blows on the Somme and the Lys, on the Aisne and in Champagne, and the British legions were reeling back in defeat and confusion, and the apprehension of utter disaster caused deep anxiety, the House of Commons proceeded to demonstrate its calm confidence in the future by examining and passing clause by clause, this monumental enactment. The Bill received its third reading in the Commons on July 16th, when the Germans were still thrusting towards Paris, two days before Foch's counterstroke. The Upper House carried its third reading on August 5th, and on August 8th — Germany's "black day" — the measure secured the Royal Assent.

I cannot do more than summarise very briefly here the purpose of this Act. By general agreement, it has revolutionised in many respects the educational system of this country, and has laid a foundation for further developments, not yet completed, in that system. Under its provisions, the State can watch over the welfare of its children through infancy and adolescence, with nursery schools, primary and post-primary schools, secondary schools, continuation classes, from the age of two to eighteen. To illustrate some of the changes it wrought, I may mention that before its passage, some 35,000 children in Yorkshire and Lancashire were working in the mills half-time from the age of twelve onwards. Under the Act, half-time was abolished, and the school age extended for all from twelve to fourteen, while Local Authorities were empowered to raise the age still further to fifteen with the assent of the Board of Education. Further, a good deal of complaint had been made by teachers of the number of children who came to school, at nine in the morning, tired out by selling newspapers or milk or by other employment. The Act limited the hours of industrial toil for children of a school age to a maximum of one hour before school and one hour afterwards. Provision was made, as I have mentioned, for nursery schools, for Central or Higher Elementary Schools, and for practical instruction in the upper standard of elementary schools. Perhaps the feature of the Act which attracted most attention was the provision for compulsory day continuation classes for young people between the ages of fourteen and eighteen. For the first time the principle was laid down that all young citizens should receive some form of education up to their eighteenth year. The economic difficulties of the post-War years have hitherto prevented this section of the Act from being put into effective operation. Its influence has, however, been felt, and a very considerable number of excellent continuation schools are working on a voluntary basis in London and other parts of the country.

The Secondary Schools were fortified by increased grants which made it possible for them to attract a more highly qualified type of teacher, and to develop greater specialisation of teaching in the upper regions of the school. Liberal provision of State scholarships from the Secondary Schools to the Universities has exercised a very considerable influence in raising the general standard of secondary school education and in widening the sphere of educational opportunity.

In addition to carrying through his great Act, Mr. Fisher, backed by the War Cabinet, took administrative action in various directions to stimulate and strengthen the national system of education. The Universities were not overlooked. They received increased grants; Oxford and Cambridge were accorded Government grants for the first time, an innovation which led to the appointment of a Royal Commission, presided over by Mr. Asquith, which in turn led to several important reforms in these two ancient Universities. Another measure has exercised a widespread influence upon our Universities. This was the allotment of a very liberal provision immediately after the War, for the education of ex-service students in the Universities. No fewer than 27,000 men availed themselves of the facilities thus extended. It would be no exaggeration to say that the vast majority of these ex-service students came from families which had never previously sent or dreamed of sending their sons to the University. This measure had the effect of widely popularising the idea of university training, and giving it in England and Wales something of the general appeal which it has for centuries possessed in Scotland. Among the young men who benefited by these scholarships were some who have since attained considerable eminence. An example which occurs to me is Mr. J. B. Priestley, the famous novelist.

Under Mr. Fisher's predecessors, valuable committees had been set up on the teaching of Classics and Modern Languages. These inquiries were continued, and the reports issued on the teaching of English and of Science now constitute important additions to our educational literature.

The final stages of Mr. Fisher's work of educational reform belong to the immediate post-War years. They may be regarded as having culminated in the great consolidating Statute which he piloted through the Commons in 1921. This measure, which under his direction was prepared by Sir Francis Liddell and Mr. (now Sir) W. R. Barker, concentrates in a convenient form more than thirty Statutes relating to public education. Tribute should be paid to the very able body of officials at the Board of Education, including such men as Sir Amherst Selby-Bigge, the Hon. W. N. Bruce and Sir George Newman, whose aid was invaluable to Mr. Fisher in his task of reform.

The Great War was not at an end in itself. We waged it in hopes of winning through to peace and a new and better age. Some of the hopes we formed have been disappointed; but of the work which Mr. Fisher did in preparing our educational system for its post-War task, it can be claimed that it was a wise and far-seeing plan to fit the youth of the nation for the tremendous task they would have to face in rebuilding a country whose commerce had been shattered and whose wealth had been scattered by war.

CHAPTER VIII

SOME REFLECTIONS ON THE WAR

Three war problems — No government wanted war — Germany's objects — France's outlook — No chance of peacemaking — Germany's missed chances of victory — The Verdun blunder — The 1918 offensive a mistake — Allied failure to utilise Russian forces — Neglect of the Balkans — Kitchener's oversight — Importance of Roumanian oil — Lord Allenby's evidence — Danger to Britain of inconclusive peace — Chances on the Italian Front — Unity of Command — Answer to the Westerners — German military blunders saved the Allies.

THERE are three questions which are asked about this War. The first is: Could it have been averted? The second is: Could it have been brought to an earlier termination by negotiation? The third is: Could victory have been achieved at an earlier date by better handling on either side of the resources at their disposal and the opportunities opened to them?

My answer to the first question is in the affirmative. My answer to the second would be in the negative and to the third in the affirmative. In the course of my narrative I have indicated these conclusions and also my reasons.

To take the first question. No sovereign or leading statesman in any of the belligerent countries sought or desired war — certainly not a European war. Berchtold, the Austrian Foreign Minister, was anxious for a punitive expedition against Serbia. Had he realised that it would involve his country in war with Russia, Italy and Roumania, supported by Britain, France and ultimately America, he would have modified the terms of the Ultimatum or accepted Serbia's answer, which was abject enough to satisfy even Austrian pride. But he was convinced that Russia would not face war with Germany. The Czar had retreated over the much more important question of the annexation of Bosnia without striking a blow. His army now was not much better prepared than it had been then. On the other hand, Germany had considerably strengthened hers. So the moment the Kaiser gave his word that he would back up Austria's demands, Berchtold had no doubt that Russia would give in and, if Serbia were still obdurate, war with her would be a small matter. What about Germany? I am convinced after a careful perusal of all the documents available on all sides that the Kaiser never had the remotest idea that he was plunging — or being plunged — into a European war. His first bluff of Russia over a Balkan question had been a triumphant success and had added a great deal to his prestige as the War Lord of Europe. He never doubted that he would score another success by the mere threat of war and thus establish still more firmly his diplomatic mastery over the Continent. After giving Austria that assurance of his support he left the bullying of Serbia in her hands. Serbia had dared to assassinate a future Emperor and deserved to be scourged. But it was too paltry a task for him to attend to the details of the lashing, so he went off on a sea cruise beyond the reach of urgent despatches without taking any thought of what preparations would be necessary to carry Germany through a great war. He was not anticipating a costly war but a cheap diplomatic triumph. When the Serbian reply was received, he thought it satisfactory and that Austria ought to accept it. His Chancellor was opposed to war. His Foreign Minister left Berlin on a honeymoon. The Chief of his Staff, von Moltke, was taking a cure at one of the German watering-places. The German public did not expect war — not even after they found their young men being called to the colours and entraining towards the frontiers. Had it been made clear in time to the Kaiser that Britain would

make war upon Germany, if she invaded Belgium, he and
his advisers would have paused to confer ere it became too
late to withdraw. He had not accumulated sufficient stores
of food or raw materials to face the blockade of the British
Fleet. A halt of a few weeks to confer would have taken the
nations near to the winter months when the march of gigantic armies would have been impeded in the West and impossible in the East. Mobilisation had begun in Austria,
Russia, France and Germany, and war had actually been declared between these Powers before Britain delivered her
ultimatum about Belgium. It was then too late to recall the
legions who were already hurrying to battle.

France shrank from war, and there was nothing further
from the mind of Britain or her Government at the end of
July, 1914, than the staging of a Continental war. The negotiations were botched by everybody engaged in directing
them. It is incredible that so momentous an issue should have
been handled in so unbusinesslike and casual a manner. When
a collision seemed inevitable engine drivers and signalmen
lost their heads and pulled the wrong levers. The stokers
alone did their work. In politics one is accustomed to hap-
hazard methods which produce minor disasters that overturn
ministries. But this was a question of life and death for
Empires, Kingdoms and Republics — and for millions of
their subjects. There was no conference between the parties
and none was suggested until it was too late. Even then
it was not made in a form which could be acceptable to any
of the disputants and it was not pressed. Had it been a matter of a railway strike, the two sides would have conferred
before proceeding to extremities. War ought to have been,
and could have been, averted.

Could peace have been made between the belligerents at
any stage of the War before November, 1918? Here again
I have reëxamined this problem calmly over and over again

with a view to ascertaining whether, at any stage of the War before November, 1918, a satisfactory peace with Germany could have been reached, and I am unable to discover a single opportunity that was missed by the Entente Powers of achieving a settlement that would not have rewarded the principal aggressors for their action in precipitating the conflict.

Up to the very end of the War, Germany was in occupation of Allied territory in the East and the West: Belgium and North-East France in the West; great areas of Russia in the East; Serbia in the South. In spite of questions repeatedly addressed to her by Allied statesmen, Germany never once offered to restore any of these territories without imposing conditions as to security or economic advantage.

Could victory have been achieved by either side before the end of 1918? Both sides committed serious errors of judgment. First of all, could the Germans have won had they made no mistakes? They certainly made two or three cardinal blunders and missed one or two opportunities that opened to them the road to victory.

Their first bad mistake and the one that ultimately proved to be fatal to their hopes was the invasion of Belgium. They weighed the chances of capturing Paris and destroying the French Army against the probability of bringing Britain into the struggle or of finishing off France before British assistance became effective. An inexplicable military blunder, or rather a series of blunders, threw away the opportunity of entering the French capital when it was within their grasp. They might even have destroyed the French Army. The Germans then flung away a chance that never recurred. After that the British Army grew from strength to strength, until, in the words of Sir Douglas Haig, it became "the most formidable Army in the field." Without its intervention Germany would have triumphed. The blunder that ranged the whole resources of the British Empire on the side of the Entente was primarily — but not altogether — a military miscalculation. It was due to a strategic plan in the pigeon-holes of the German War Office. Even the most discerning of soldiers could hardly have anticipated that Britain would have put a splendidly equipped Army of over 2,000,000 in the field and called 6,000,000 to the flag.

The second great mistake of the Germans was the diversion of their strength in 1916 to the futile attack on Verdun. Thereby they missed two opportunities. The first was the final smashing-up of Russia which began so auspiciously for them in 1915. Had they pressed their advantage in 1916, Russia could have been driven to make peace in the summer of 1916 instead of the spring of 1918. The British Army was not fully equipped before the late summer of 1916 to exert enough pressure on the Western Front to compel Germany to release her grip on Russia. By that time the Russian Army might have been irretrievably defeated. Once Russia was eliminated the Germans could have turned all their victorious armies on to France, and the Austrians their whole strength to destroy Italy before America had entered the War and before hunger and privation had weakened the morale of the Central Powers. Had the Verdun project not been adopted the Germans might have helped the plan of Conrad von Hoetzendorff, the Austrian Commander, for driving Italy out of the War by a joint Austrian and German attack in the spring of 1916. A Caporetto in 1916 might have had that effect, for the Germans were then in a position to press their victory to a decision, as the British Army was not ready for a great offensive in France.

The third fundamental strategical error was the great offensive of 1918. Germany was powerful enough to repel any attack that could be made against her entrenchments by the Allies. She had beaten them off time and again when they had an advantage of two to one in numbers. She could certainly depend on being able to hold her own when there was approximate equality. Instead of which she wasted her reserves on violent attacks which utterly failed to achieve any strategic results. In these assaults she lost most of her picked troops. She neglected to construct second and third lines upon which she could fall back in the event of her armies being driven out of the first. She also took away from the East the divisions which would have enabled her to exploit the Russian resources of men and material which were vital to her life. But the worst German blunder in the War, after the invasion of Belgium, was the quarrel with America. It was at best a reckless miscalculation: at its worst it was an inconceivable folly.

What about the Allies? No one who dispassionately reviews the events of the War can fail to discern opportunities which presented themselves only to be snubbed by the military and political leaders of the Entente Powers.

Their most obvious and most costly blunder was their failure to treat the vast battlefield of the War as a single front. Russia had unlimited resources of superb man power — in physique, courage, and tenacity. They had received sufficient training to constitute a formidable army on the defensive or offensive even against German troops, and they were equal to if not better than the Austrians in that respect. All they lacked was the necessary equipment to make the best use of such fine material. That is the only reason why Russia was beaten. Had France and Britain effected a wise distribution of the financial and mechanical resources at their command — at home and in America — between the armies fighting in the East as well as the West — the German and Austrian attack on Russia would have failed, and failed with such enormous losses as to cripple the Central Powers. Austria, with her large Slavonic population, could have been broken up by 1916. Germany would thereby have been isolated. Austria certainly could not have withstood the onslaught of a well-equipped and numerically superior Russian Army. Least of all could she have done so if the Entente had taken full advantage of the opportunity which the Balkans afforded for organising a combined attack of Serbians, Roumanians, Greeks and not improbably Bulgarians across the Danube. Here was another great chance missed for bringing the War to a victorious end in 1916.

Was that attainable? A formidable Balkan Confederation on the side of the Entente could have been organised early in 1915 if the Allied Powers had taken it earnestly in hand. The Greeks had offered to join us in 1914. We rejected their proffered help. The Roumanians wished to be assured that if they came in they would be supported by France and Britain. Bulgaria wanted to be squared by promises of additional territory. Serbia possessed an army of first-class fighting men that had already inflicted signal defeat on the Austrians in two pitched battles. These four Balkan States could have put in the field armies of trained men, with war experience, numbering in the aggregate at least 700,000 men. They needed money, equipment, ammunition and improvement in the communications with Salonika and also a quota of about 100,000 Allied troops. Each would in the event of victory expect some territorial concessions. Turkey and Austria between them afforded ample scope for a liberal rearrangement of frontiers, without offending any of the canons of racial integrity and independence. Italy had just joined the Entente. With an Italian Army to face, Austria and Germany could not have spared large forces to attack this Balkan Confederation. With a Russia whose equipment had been improved by Allied contributions, the Central Powers would have had enough to do to maintain their positions on their eastern and south-western frontiers. Some of the greatest Entente Generals favoured the idea. I have already quoted their views. Kitchener himself proposed at an Allied War Council — according to Joffre — that an Allied force of 400,000 should be massed on the Danube "to smash Austria." Some of the greatest French Generals favoured this plan. As Joffre pointed out, the Salonika line could not, without widening, have maintained such a force. The British Government on my advice decided in February, 1915, to improve the transport arrangements to Serbia with that emergency in view. It was left to Kitchener to take the necessary steps. In the multiplicity of his other duties he overlooked this instruction, and when in October he recalled the project, it was too late to think of sending a large Allied force to the Danube. Had it been sent in the summer, the whole military position would have been fundamentally changed. France and Britain lost nearly 400,000 men in the futile offensives of Champagne and Loos, in September and October, 1915. They were a complete failure and the casualties were very heavy. It stands to the credit of Kitchener's common sense that he was originally opposed to this combined offensive in France. Germany had foreseen the danger of such a move in the Balkans as I have sketched; for the encirclement of the Central Powers would have been complete. The smashing process was therefore anticipated by them, and the Balkans with their immense possibilities were lost to the Entente for three years. In another month the only Allied forces in the Balkans were on the wrong side of the mountain range and an Entente Army of 500,000 was immobilised on the seacoast for three years. Had the Allied military leaders in the West surveyed the battlefield as a whole and not concentrated their minds on the earthworks just in front of them, 1915 might have been the turning-point in the War and 1916 would have seen us at the end of this agony of five nations. The writing-off of the Roumanian supplies of oil would have immobilised the Armies of the Central Powers to such an extent that they would have been deprived of their offensive power and their efficiency for defensive purposes would have been appreciably reduced. The testimony given by eminent German Generals before the Reichstag Commission on the causes of the German collapse shows how serious a matter it was to their armies to be deprived of Roumanian oil in 1918. We had taken steps already to cut them off Russian oil at Baku. Germany was beaten partly by the enforcement of oil sanctions against her. Incidentally, one of the advantages of an Allied force in Serbia would have been the complete severance of communications between the Central Powers and Turkey. Without the assistance in guns, ammunition, transport and men which Germany could not have sent to Turkey if the railway to Constantinople had been closed, the Ottoman Armies could not have fought another campaign against the superiority we had mustered in Egypt and Mesopotamia. A Turkish defeat would have relieved the pressure on Russia in the Caucasus and opened sea communications with our Russian and Roumanian Allies.

Lord Allenby sent me the notes of an address he delivered to some officers of the Guards in 1923 on the objects of the Palestine campaign. They have a special interest and relevance when we are considering the effect of a Turkish defeat on the fortunes of the War. Coming from so eminent a soldier, these observations carry weight.

"East or West?"

"Was the Palestine Campaign a wise venture? Would it have been better to stand on the defensive in the East; concentrating our strength in the Western theatre?

"Consider the situation in June, 1917: —

"Russia was out of the War.

"Roumania had been overcome.

"America had not yet taken a hand.

"Enemy submarines were a serious danger.

"Money was short.

"Our Allies were tired.

"There was talk of Peace without victory.

"Suppose Germany saying: 'You are weary of war; so are we. We are prepared to surrender Alsace and Lorraine. We will evacuate Belgium. We'll cry quits; without indemnities on either side.'

"Such a proposition — though improbable — was not impossible; and it is conceivable that our Allies might have been willing to accept some such terms, forcing us to an inconclusive peace unless we could carry on alone.

"In that case, Germany would have been left dominant in Austria, the Balkans, Turkey and Syria; with an open road from the North Sea to the Persian Gulf. She would have won all she fought for; supremacy in Europe and easy access to the East.

"With the defeat of Turkey and the defection of Bulgaria, Germany's road to the East was cut; broken beyond repair. The principles of war are eternal; but there are no rigid rules for their application. In undertaking their Eastern adventure, our statesmen showed strategical imagination and political foresight of a high order.

A."

These notes deal with a different aspect of the subject from the one I have been emphasising. Nevertheless, the considerations Lord Allenby urges are of real importance to a country with a vast Eastern Empire.

We also missed a great opportunity in Italy in 1917. The Italians had, like the Russians — but to a lesser degree — a superiority in the numbers of trained men they could put into the field, but in artillery and ammunition they were deficient. The deficiency was specially marked in heavy artillery, so essential to battering a way through fortified mountain passes. As far as France was concerned, the number of available men was approaching the point of exhaustion, but our mechanical supplies were multiplying rapidly. French and British had been fighting incessantly for three campaigns, sustaining terrible losses against the most formidable enemy in the field. The Italians had fought barely two campaigns — against an enemy inferior in every respect to the German Army. The French and British could with advantage have suspended their great offensive for a single year, held the Germans on their front, equipped the Italian Army with heavy artillery and ammunition and also sent them a few divisions of experienced troops to take part in the campaign. An attack on the Italian Front would have relieved the pressure on Russia at an extremely critical juncture and would have had an excellent chance of breaking through the Austrian line. There would have been inevitable losses on all fronts, but the massacres of the Chemin des Dames and of Passchendaele would never have occurred, and Caporetto, which probably put Italy out of effective action for the rest of the War, would never have been heard of. Foch and Pétain favoured the idea — after the failure of the Chemin des Dames. But there again we were too tardy in our movements and Haig's Flanders obsession thwarted the plan. The French Generals had promised to give him his chance and professional good fellowship was involved in letting him have it.

The last opportunity missed was over the establishment of a real unity of command. A unity which depends upon prolonged argument between two rival and independent Staffs is a sham. Even the unity supposed to have been established over the spring offensive of 1917 was not much better. It was never operated with good will. That is why the delay caused by bickerings between two Commanders, not one of whom had the power to give a peremptory order to the other, was responsible for converting an appreciable victory into a disastrous failure. The Germans recognised that the real unity arranged between French and British when Foch was made Commander-in-Chief on the whole front was largely responsible for the failure of their offensive in 1918. Had a General Reserve been set up under central command before the March offensive, the defeats of March and April would never have occurred.

It has been urged by those who still defend the concentration of forces and the continuous offensives on the Western Front that the justification of that policy is to be found in the fact that the Armistice which ended the War was signed on French soil. There are two answers to that claim: —

1. The attacks in the West on entrenched positions which could not be outflanked cost the Allies well over five million casualties.

2. They would not have succeeded in the end had it not been: —

> (a) that the blockade had debilitated and weakened the morale of the German Army and undermined the fighting spirit of the German and Austrian peoples;
>
> (b) that the defeat of Bulgaria had opened the southern flank of the Central Powers to hostile attack and deprived them of the corn and oil of Roumania without which they could not have continued the struggle.

Neither Germany nor Austria would have given in during 1918 had it not been for the overthrow of Bulgaria. I have already quoted the authority of Hindenburg, Ludendorff, and von Kuhl for that statement.

These are some of the reasons why I have come definitely to the conclusion that victory was within our reach in 1916, or at the latest in 1917, if the strategic direction of the War had shown more imagination, common sense and unity.

Here is my last reflection on this war. If Germany had been led by Bismarck and Moltke instead of by successors who were inferior in statesmanship and war, the event of the great struggle between democracy and a military autocracy would in all human probability have been different. The blunders of Germany saved us from the consequences of our own. But let all who trust Justice to the arbitrament of war bear in mind that the issue may depend not on the righteousness of the quarrel, but on the craft of the litigants. It is the teaching of history, and this war enforces the lesson.

CHAPTER IX

AN IMPERIAL WAR

Range and variety of the British Empire — Major burden falls on Great Britain — Recruits drawn from all quarters — India's war effort — Troops from the Dominions — The Crown Colonies and South America — Canada's record — The Anzacs in Gallipoli and France — Anzac horsemen in Palestine — South Africa's part — Newfoundland — Munitions from Canada — Australia's Navy — Imperial Statesmen.

THE whole of the British Empire was united in the aims and efforts of the Great War. In a previous Volume of these Memoirs [1] I have described how spontaneously India and the self-governing Dominions rallied to the side of Great Britain the moment the War broke out, and how magnificently they responded to every appeal for help in the conflict. And the response of the Crown Colonies and of remote Dependencies was no less prompt and whole-hearted.

The British Commonwealth of Nations is an amazingly heterogeneous conglomeration. The white races of the British Isles and their descendants, who form the nucleus of the Empire, are only a small fraction of its total population — about one-seventh. And of these nearly three-quarters were to be found, at the outbreak of the World War, in the little island home of the breed. The rest were thinly peopling the vast spaces of the self-governing Dominions, or carrying on administration and commercial development in India and the Crown Colonies and Dependencies, among a population mainly coloured and vastly outnumbering them. Every shade of dependence and independence of Great Britain was to be found in the wide variety of the Empire, from the complete

[1] Volume IV, Chapter I, "The Imperial War Cabinet and Conference."

democratic self-government of the Dominions to colonial administrations entirely provided by this country. It is hardly surprising that the Germans, with their habit of strict regimentation and uniform order, regarded the Empire as a ramshackle structure which would fall apart at the first shock. But it was not so much a structure as a growth, with the tenacity and inner coherence of a living thing. There were one or two unhappy incidents, such as the short-lived rebellion in South Africa of an irreconcilable section of the Boer population in the early months of the War; but otherwise the Empire not only enjoyed internal peace throughout the War years, but showed a splendid loyalty and eagerness to help the Motherland in her struggle.

The main burden of the Imperial war effort fell, as was natural, upon Great Britain. It was primarily a European war, and Britain held most of the Empire's white population, of its industrial resources, and of its credit strength. Inevitably the great bulk of the fighting troops that took part in the War were drawn from Britain itself. The white citizens of the Empire, however, hurried home from every corner of the globe to join in its defence, and from our great self-governing Dominions organised forces were supplied which proved to be among the very finest fighting troops taking part in the War on either side. In addition to India's great contingent, we drew combatants from the coloured races in our colonies and dependencies of Africa and the West Indies — mainly for service against Germany's African colonies, and in Egypt, Palestine and Mesopotamia — and we recruited from among them numbers of labour battalions for the work of transport, supply and construction along the Western Front. Their toil alone enabled us to throw up with such speed new defences and fresh roads and railways in lieu of those we were forced to abandon in the great retreat of 1918.

Nor was the Empire's contribution confined to man-power. Gifts of money and supplies poured in to aid the financial side of the struggle. Of the rich donations of Indian Princes I have told elsewhere. But every corner sent its gifts, however humble. The natives of Marakei, a remote spot in the Gilbert Group of the South Sea Islands, could do nothing to help on the War except send coconuts. But with them they sent a message declaring that: "they will contribute nuts unceasingly for the War, and cease not till the War is over." That coconut spirit of contributing your utmost was char-acteristic of the whole Empire.

The largest contingents of fighting troops came, of course, from India. Altogether, India sent overseas during the War some 1,302,394 men. The Indian Princes of the Native States supplied 29 squadrons of Imperial Service Cavalry, and 11 battalions of Imperial Service Infantry, for service overseas. In the course of the first few months India dis-patched forces to France, East Africa, Mesopotamia and Egypt. By the close of 1914, she was maintaining overseas forces aggregating more than 100,000. As the War developed, so did her contribution. Throughout the Mesopotamian campaign, more than half the troops operating in that theatre were Indians. At their maximum they numbered over 155,000. The numbers of Indians in Egypt and Palestine steadily grew until during the closing months of the War they nearly reached 100,000. They contributed their quota to the Salonika force, and supplied the bulk of the garrison of Aden. All through the War, Indian forces were maintained in France and in British East Africa. Indians fought in Gallipoli and the Cameroons; in Persia and Trans-Caspiana. One small force coöperated with the Japanese in North China against the German naval base of Tsing-Tao. And at home, the Indian Army had to carry on operations on its north-west frontier, where the perennial trouble was increased by agitation stimulated and stirred by German agencies.

It is true that the total forces supplied to the War by India bore only a trivial proportion to her population — less than the half of one per cent. But most of that population is unwarlike. Their physique unfits them for the nervous and bodily strain of modern war. The chill and dismal humidity of that section of the European battlefield, where the main British forces were massed, proved unsuitable for Indian troops. The fighting races, however, gave us some magnificent troops, who proved their valour and endurance on every front and won a long array of official honours and recognitions, including a number of V.C.'s. The chief contribution of Hindustan was made in southern theatres — Palestine, Mesopotamia and East Africa, where our Indian legions rendered splendid service.

It was obviously impossible for our sparsely populated Dominions to send troops as numerous as could be supplied from the myriads of India. But in proportion to their population, the contingents they mustered were a splendid demonstration of their solidarity with the Motherland. Both Canada and New Zealand passed conscription laws to rally their manhood to the colours. Australia, in no wise behind them in loyalty, valour and pugnacity, somehow failed to carry a repeated referendum for this purpose, as the issue got mixed up with political and personal feuds with which the Commonwealth was rent. Newfoundland also passed a conscription law similar to that of Canada.

The "Statistics of the Military Effort of the British Empire" shows that the total number of Dominion troops which were sent overseas during the War, or were undergoing training for service on November 1st, 1918, was 984,612 — or practically a million men. The highest percentage of the white male population recruited in a Dominion was attained by New Zealand, where the figure was 19.35 per cent. Canada and Australia followed with 13.48 per cent. and 13.43 per cent., respectively. The South African troops which went overseas to the fighting in East Africa, Egypt and the Western Front were 11.12 per cent. of the total white population, but in addition some 50,000 troops served in the German South-West African campaign, of which a considerable proportion were not included in the total of subsequent expeditions.

The highest percentage of all was that of men recruited in Canada who had been born in the United Kingdom. This reached the remarkable figure of 35 per cent., far higher even than that attained by the Home Country. It was of course a selected class, consisting to a large extent of fit and enterprising young men, whose ties with the Motherland were particularly strong. They hurried back in their thousands to stand beside her in her hour of peril.

The same process went on throughout the Crown Colonies. Few of them had a white population large enough to furnish complete formations that could be recruited and sent over intact to join the British forces. But from tea gardens and plantations of rubber and sugar cane, from Rhodesian farms and the islands of the South Seas, sturdy young Britons came hurrying home to join up. Even those who had settled under foreign flags felt the call of the blood. It is estimated that about 12,000 came from Latin America — some 6,500 of them from the Argentine. Numbers of these were sons or grandsons of former British emigrants, and though born to another citizenship, were proud to claim their British inheritance, even though it was an inheritance of sacrifice. These Latin-Americans of British stock fought well. Among the decorations they won were three V.C.'s and 188 M.C.'s.

The tale of the fight put up by the Dominion troops

would fill many volumes. I cannot attempt to set it out here, but I want to place on record the profound gratitude which all of us who shared the burden of responsibility for the successful issue of the War felt to the British Dominions for contributing such magnificent fighting men to our forces. The history of the War would have recorded a different ending if these forces had been lacking on our side. They figured in every important engagement on the Western Front from the summer of 1916, and were the firehardened point of our attack whenever any specially difficult thrust had to be undertaken.

The Canadians, being nearest to Britain, were the first to arrive. Their first expeditionary force reached England in mid-October, 1914. Before the end of December, Princess Patricia's Canadian Light Infantry had crossed to France, and in February, 1915, the First Canadian Division left for the battle area. In April it won immortal fame by its stand at the Second Battle of Ypres, where the unknown horror of the first German gas attack threatened a collapse of our line of defence in that critical area.

In September, 1915, the Second Canadian Division joined the First in the line, and the Canadian Corps was formed. A third division came over in January, 1916, and a fourth in September. In that month the Canadians entered the Somme battle, where they played a part of such distinction that thenceforward they were marked out as storm troops, and for the remainder of the War they were brought along to head the assault in one great battle after another. Whenever the Germans found the Canadian Corps coming into the line, they prepared for the worst. On Vimy Ridge one of the most impressive memorials of the War stands to commemorate their spectacular success there in April, 1917. There was no finer display of resistless intrepidity in the whole War. They fought through the worst horrors of Passchendaele in October and November of the same year. At the Battle of Amiens on August 8th, 1918 — Ludendorff's "Black Day" — the Canadians headed the British assault which shattered Germany's last hope of military success. And in August and September they led the attack on the Drocourt-Quéant Switch and the strongest nucleus of the Hindenburg line, swept across the Canal du Nord, stormed the Bourlon Wood and took Cambrai. All through the final advance to victory, Canadian troops were to the fore. They took Valenciennes, and a few hours before the Armistice they marched through the streets of Mons, to the tune of "Tipperary" played on the bagpipes.

The contingents from Australia and New Zealand had farther to come, and their first rallying point was in Egypt, which they reached by the end of 1914. After helping to defend the Suez Canal, they sailed off in April, 1915, to write the name of the ANZACS in inerasable glory upon the barren rocks of Gallipoli. By the summer of 1916 they were in France, and in July they were fighting on the Somme. Thereafter, like the Canadians, they were marked out for the grim honour of heading assaults and plunging in wherever the fighting was fiercest. They smashed their way up the Messines Ridge in June, 1917, and in September they were flung into the mud of Passchendaele. In March, 1918, they were brought down to stay the German advance on the Somme, and when in April the Germans thrust in on the Lys Front, the 1st Australian Division was hastily sent north to stop them. Those left on the Somme fought the Germans to a standstill at Villers Bretonneux. In May their own man, Sir John Monash, became their Corps Commander. He was one of the very ablest military leaders thrown up by the War on either side, and it is worth noting that he was not a professional soldier. In the armies of Great Britain a man of his conspicuous genius would have had no chance to show his

qualities as a military leader. On July 4th he led his men to
a brilliant action at Hamel, where, as I have noted elsewhere, they brought some American troops along with
them. The Australians took part in the battle of August 8th,
and in the September struggle for the Hindenburg line.
Then they were pulled out for a well-earned breathing space,
and were on their way back to the front when the Armistice
was signed.

To a large extent the story of the Australians is also that
of the New Zealanders. They also were at Gallipoli, on the
Somme, at Messines, Passchendaele, and the defence of
Amiens. In the final advance to victory, from August to
November, 1918, they were almost continuously fighting,
pressing forward like questing hounds in the front of the
battle, performing spectacular feats of daring.

In addition to their achievements on the Western Front,
the Dominions contributed strikingly to our successes in
Palestine. The Australian Horse, and the New Zealand
Mounted Rifles, were both invaluable for that desert warfare where mounted units had so large a part to play. The
decisive victory of Megiddo, in which Allenby rounded up
and wiped out the Turkish forces, was only made possible
by the swift, encircling sweep of his cavalry round the rear
of the enemy to Nazareth, and thence in headlong dash to
Damascus; and in that cavalry operation a notable part
was played by the Australian and New Zealand Mounted
Division. They were tireless in their pursuit. At one time
they rode for seventy-two hours without stopping to water
their horses, which, unbeatable as their riders, held dog-
gedly on. Palestine was a country where cavalry were still
an arm of the utmost value, and the Dominion mounted
troops contributed a large and indispensable share of the
achievements of our forces in that theatre. Their contribution
to the rout of the Turkish Army will always be quoted as a

GENERAL MONASH

conspicuous example of the service which cavalry can render in war when skilfully used.

The South African Brigade was no whit behind the other Dominion forces in gallantry and fighting quality. After the conquest of German South-West Africa, South Africa sent large forces to the campaign in East Africa, where General Smuts conducted operations until Von Lettow-Vorbeck had been driven away from his bases and put on the run in the tropical hinterland of the country. They also sent a brigade north, which after dealing with the Senussi on the Egyptian border in February, 1916, came in May to the Western Front, and fought in Flanders and on the Somme, in 1916; at Arras, Passchendaele and Cambrai, in 1917; and in 1918, took part in the defence against the German attacks on the Somme and the Lys, and in the final advance of the Allies to victory in the summer and autumn.

Newfoundland sent over a regiment, which took part so unyieldingly in the conflict that it used up reinforcements far quicker than they could be sent along to it. It fought at Suvla Bay in 1915, on the Somme in 1916, at Monchy and Cambrai in 1917; and by the end of 1917 its death-roll alone was more than a quarter of all the men sent from New-foundland. Casualties had wiped out the regiment twice over.

In addition to man-power, our Dominions and Colonies helped the Imperial effort, up to the limit of their resources, with supplies of all kinds. A notable contribution was that made by Canada to the production of munitions. In August, 1914, an appeal was made to Canada to help us with the production of empty shell. The late General Sam Hughes, a man of infectious enthusiasm and energy, promptly formed a Shell Committee to organise the Canadian peace-time in-dustrial capacity for munition production. It made a fine start with this task, but presently the work outgrew the scope of the Committee, and shortly after I established the Ministry of Munitions, I found it would be necessary to secure a revised organisation. By the end of 1915, the Shell Committee had been superseded by the Imperial Munitions Board, under the chairmanship of Sir Joseph Flavelle, and this voluntary body operated directly and efficiently under the Ministry of Munitions right up to the Armistice. The principal output was shells, shell-cases, fuses, explosives and other components of ammunition. Of shells alone, Canada supplied more than 65,000,000 during the War. Other important supplies were machinery, tools, castings, locomotives, aeroplane supplies, timber, metals, etc. The total value of the Canadian shipments of military supplies exceeded £200 million.

Australia was too remote across submarine-infested seas to render a comparable help in munitions supply for use in Europe. She was able, however, to send much to the Eastern theatres, and special mention should be made of the foodstuffs, fodder and horses she supplied. Her most notable contribution apart from man-power was the Australian Fleet, which not only dealt with the *Emden* and guarded the South Pacific and Indian Ocean against commerce raiders and coöperated in the capture of the German possessions in the South Seas, but also reinforced the British Navy in home waters and the Mediterranean.

I have given an account in an earlier chapter [1] of the way in which our Imperial War Councils were strengthened by the presence and advice of the great leaders of the Dominions, and I have there paid my sincere tribute to the high quality of these men — of Botha and W. M. Hughes, Borden, Massey, Ward, Smuts and Bikanir. Their Imperial coöperation was as valuable in counsel as that of their countrymen on the field of battle.

[1] "War Memoirs", Vol. IV, Chapter I.

Space fails me to mention all the other ways in which the various parts of the Empire contributed to the joint war effort — the Canadians who served at Archangel and Vladivostok, the fishermen and seamen who rallied to the Navy and to the work of patrolling and mine-sweeping, the hospital units and equipment that were provided. The whole British Commonwealth was united in a single purpose. Its citizens in every latitude did eagerly whatever they could to further the common cause. It is not too much to say that without the 1,400,000 fine men who rallied to the flag from the Dominions and the 1,300,000 who came to our aid from India the Allies would not have been able to bear the strain of this gigantic struggle. May Heaven forbid that we should ever again be faced with so terrible a challenge. But if we are, and the cause at issue is one with an appeal equally clear to the British conscience and loyalty, then we shall find once more that the "bonds of Empire" is no idle phrase.

CHAPTER X

SOME REFLECTIONS ON THE FUNCTIONS OF GOV-
ERNMENTS AND SOLDIERS RESPECTIVELY
IN A WAR

EVERY prolonged war has at one stage or another produced differences and disputes between the civilian Government and the Generals in the field. The only exceptions are those where autocrats themselves commanded their own armies. Where success tarries disappointment ensues and disappointments lead to disagreements. It is also inevitable that there should be argument as to reinforcements and supplies between those who have to use them and those who have to furnish them. No country has unlimited resources at its command, and a wise Government faced with a formidable enemy will mobilise its strength to the best advantage. In this respect Governments cannot delegate their primary responsibility. But whilst Governments and Generals ought to realise each other's difficulties they are naturally more imminently conscious of their own. One point of view is more constantly present to the Government — the General, on the other hand, has the other point of view always in front of him. Where Governments have several armies in the field, each under a separate command, they are confronted with the additional problem of distributing their resources between these various units. If the fight is on sea as well as on land, Governments must decide what proportion of the strength of the nation they ought to devote to each respectively. Governments have the entire responsibility for the home front. That front is always underrated by Generals in the field. And yet that is where the Great War was won and lost. The Russian, Bulgarian, Austrian and German home fronts fell to pieces before their armies collapsed. The averting of that great and irrevocable catastrophe is the concern of the Government. Great care must be taken of the condition and susceptibilities of the population at home, who make it possible to maintain, to reinforce and to equip armies. All the suffering is not in the trenches. The most poignant suffering is not on the battlefield, but in the bereft hearths and hearts in the homeland. If in addition to the anguish of grief women have to witness the pinched faces and waning strength of their children there will soon be trouble in the nation behind the line, and if men home on leave have to carry back these unnerving memories to the trenches their will to fight on is enfeebled. That is what accounted for the sudden breakdown in the German resistance in November, 1918. The ration allowance for each British household was cut down to the lowest minimum compatible with health. Anything lower would have made trouble. But there was no privation. In Germany and Austria children died of hunger. The ration of the British soldier was maintained at its excellent maximum to the end. The food allowance of the German soldier was cut down to an unappetising and insufficient minimum. But the feeding and clothing of a population of over 45,000,000 and of three to four millions abroad takes some doing. That was the care of the Government. Generals thought we were spending on this problem a good deal of energy and man power which ought to have been devoted to strengthening their armies. Millions of the picked young men of the nation were placed at their disposal. More than half these millions were either killed or wounded, too often in the prosecution of doubtful plans or mishandled enterprises. Generals demanded more millions not only to fill up gaps thus caused but to further increase the numbers under their direction. The Government had other responsibilities to discharge which also required the services of able-bodied men. It was for the Government to determine apportionments. Out of this discussion came suspicions and resentments which poisoned good will and whole-hearted coöperation.

Ought we to have interfered in the realm of strategy? This is one of the most perplexing anxieties of the Government of a nation at war. Civilians have had no instruction, training or experience in the principles of war, and to that extent are complete amateurs in the methods of waging war. It is idle, however, to pretend that intelligent men whose minds are concentrated for years on one task learn nothing about it by daily contact with its difficulties and the way to overcome them. I shall deal later with the extent to which Generals were taught before the War any lessons useful or pertinent to the conduct of modern warfare. But strategy is not entirely a military problem. There is in it a considerable element of high politics. The passing of the gates of India, the Far East and Australia into enemy hands is not by any means principally a military question for Great Britain. The defeat of the Turks on the Suez Canal, and of the Turko-German Army in Palestine, was an Imperial necessity. The opening of a road to Russia through the Balkans was also a question of high policy, the neglect of which nearly lost us the War, and might well have done so had America not come in on our side, in time to avert the results of the selfish narrowness of the Western Allies. Had Russia and Roumania been equipped by France and Britain, their Armies would not have been beaten and the Russian Revolution would not have occurred before the end of the War. The feeling, especially in Russia, that her Western Allies had abandoned her gallant soldiers to hopeless slaughter by the great guns and the overwhelming shells of Germany, when they were in a position to provide the equipment for an effective resistance, largely contributed, not only to the despair of the Russian Army, but to turning its anger against the Allies. The knowledge of the prodigious waste of ammunition on the Western Front in the prosecution of futile and ill-conceived campaigns, whilst the Russians were left without any shells to defend themselves, looked to them like a wanton and profligate betrayal which excited fierce indignation in the Russian ranks. Militarily it was foolish — psychologically it was insane. It was the duty of the British and French Governments to avoid this disaster. Unfortunately they left the decision to Generals whose fortunes depended on the victories of their own armies.

Questions of policy were also essential to a wise handling of the question of man power. It was for the military to estimate the numbers they needed, but there were other Departments making similar demands and it was for the Government to weigh the relative importance of those demands and to decide how many they could and should allocate to each. It is just like the claims each Government Department presents to the Treasury for the coming financial year. The aggregate always exceeds what the finances of the nation can afford. The Government decide what to allow, what to reject, or how much to cut down in claims which are in themselves justifiable. This is a domain of strategy in which the Government must be supreme. An extra 200,000 men at the front would not have converted the Passchendaele fiasco into a triumph, but it might have lost the War by disorganising the services that kept the nation from the hunger and penury that destroyed Germany and Austria.

The psychological blunders perpetrated by Germany afford many illustrations of the shortsightedness of subordinating considerations of statesmanship to immediate military exigencies. Strategy must take cognisance of both. There is the occupation of Belgium. It was not sound strategy because it was a political blunder. It brought the British Empire into the War. One of the ablest of the German Generals told me recently that but for the force of six highly trained British divisions placed on the Belgian frontier the German Army would have outflanked and Sedanised the whole of the French Fifth Army and thus brought the War to a triumphant end on the Western Front. Its presence in that area was to them a disagreeable surprise. They had anticipated meeting a British contingent sooner or later. But they reckoned on its disembarking at Calais or Boulogne and their spies having informed them that no troops had yet reached those ports, they came to the conclusion that the British Army had not arrived in France. The disembarkation at Havre and the speed with which the Expeditionary Force was sent to France and mustered on the Belgian frontier upset the whole of their calculations and frustrated their plans. The subtlety, efficiency and celerity with which the British Expeditionary Force was transported to the Belgian frontier without the knowledge of the German Staff was almost entirely due to the genius of Lord Haldane. The way that devoted but intelligent patriot was hounded out of official life by insinuations of treason is one of the most disreputable and stupid episodes in British history. The attacks on Belgium upset the whole carefully elaborated scheme by which the Germans relied on outflanking and Sedanising a whole French Army. The provocation which brought America into the War was another political blunder, for which the soldiers were primarily responsible. The insistence on taking too many men from food and war production because they were needed at the front was yet another. All these issues enter into strategy and in determining them statesmen must have their say as well as soldiers. In some of them statesmanship is the most important element and statesmen ought to have the final decision — after giving due weight to everything soldiers may have to urge from their point of view.

But there is a region where the soldier claims to be paramount and where the interference of the statesman seems to him to be an impertinence. There is the question of whether a great battle which may involve enormous losses ought to be fought — if so, where and at what time. The second question is whether a prolonged attack on fortifications (practically a siege) which is causing huge loss of life without producing any apparent result ought to be called off. Should Governments intervene or leave the decision entirely to the soldiers? The British Government was doubtful of the wisdom of the combined offensive of September, 1915, in Champagne and Artois. It was one of the costly and fateful mistakes of the War, for whilst the Allies were entangled in an attack doomed to failure on the French Front, Germany was enabled to crush Serbia, bring Bulgaria into the War, capture the Balkans, open up her own road to Turkey, cut our communications with Russia and also drive us helter-skelter out of the Dardanelles. Half the number of men we lost in that ill-judged French offensive, if sent in time to the Balkans, would have altered the whole impact and prospect of the War. The strategical as well as tactical error of judgment then perpetrated by the Army Commanders prolonged the War by two years. Should the Asquith Coalition have exerted its overriding authority and vetoed that offensive? Their chief military adviser, Kitchener, was definitely of the opinion that it was a mistake and could not succeed. They could, therefore, had they vetoed it, claim that in doing so they were acting on the highest military judgment at their disposal. It is true that Kitchener subsequently recommended that it was not advisable to quarrel with the French about it, as Joffre had set his heart on this particular attack, had planned it with great care and was convinced he would be successful in breaking through. Ought the Government to have risked a misunderstanding with France? They would have been well within their rights as a Government and in doing so they would not have been overruling the opinion of their own military staffs as to the prospects of this particular offensive. It is true that had they done so and gone to the aid of Serbia before the blow fell it would have altered the course of the War. But France would have been sore and would always have been convinced that she had been robbed of victory by British stubbornness and stupidity. It was a decision in the realm of strategy which rested with the Government, and rightly so. That they did not exercise an overriding authority on that occasion was one of the strategical blunders of the War.

The wasteful prolongation of the Somme campaign after it had become clear that a break through the German lines was unattainable was another case where the Government might have intervened. It cost us heavily. The volunteers of 1914 and 1915 were the finest body of men ever sent to do battle for Britain. Five hundred thousand of these men, the flower of our race, were thrown away on a stubborn and unintelligent hammering away at what was then an impenetrable barrier. I strongly urged Mr. Asquith and Sir William Robertson that the useless slaughter ought to be stopped. I am still of that opinion. The loss in men was irreplaceable, less in numbers than in quality. It was the first real disillusionment the new Army suffered. Our losses were twice as great as those we inflicted. Much was lost, nothing was gained.

The most difficult decision presented to the Government was that of the Passchendaele campaign. I was convinced that it was bound to fail for reasons which I gave in great detail to the Cabinet and to Haig and Robertson before the offensive commenced. These objections were all completely vindicated by the events of the battle. I felt that the losses would be very heavy and that nothing would be achieved. I acknowledged that no doubt the enemy could be pushed back a few kilometres, just as he was on the Somme — at a great sacrifice, but that nothing worth while would be accomplished. Ought I to have vetoed it? I could not have carried the Cabinet with me to that extent. On this occasion all the military and naval advisers of the Government without exception were, in so far as we could ascertain at the time, urgent in their insistence on the desirability and feasibility of the enterprise, and nearly half the Cabinet accepted their opinion. The majority were opposed to taking the responsibility of a veto. I am certain, therefore, that no step I was in a position personally to take would have averted that squalid catastrophe. But ought I not to have resigned rather than acquiesce in this slaughter of brave men? I have always felt there are solid grounds for criticism in that respect. My sole justification is that Haig promised not to press the attack if it became clear that he could not attain his objectives by continuing the offensive. Robertson endorsed this undertaking. Mr. Bonar Law and Lord Milner, who were as strongly opposed as I was to the whole scheme, thought we ought to be satisfied with this pledge. However, the duty of the Government in the Passchendaele affair will always be a debatable proposition. Was it a decision which ought to have been left to the discretion of the military leaders or should the Government have forbidden the fighting of a battle which they were convinced would entail heavy sacrifices without achieving any military results? I was well within my rights and obligations as Prime Minister in placing before the Generals responsible for military operations the reasons which convinced me that their plans were not practicable and would end in failure. That I did orally and in writing. Even were I in a position to forbid, ought I to have taken that responsibility? On the whole I still give the same answer to that question as I did in June, 1917. The fighting of a battle is mainly a decision for the Generals.

As to the efforts I made persistently to secure unity of command in spite of the possessive reluctance of the military chiefs to part with one ray of their glittering power, I am convinced that in urging one Supreme Command on the principal battle front I was discharging the legitimate function and authority of a Government primarily responsible to King and Country for the conduct of the War. A Government may be unwise to disregard the advice of experts, but in the choice of experts it is the sole judge, and where there are more than one to whom a task is entrusted, it can select the one whose voice is to be supreme.

Generally speaking, the argument of the high Commands in the War for its sole claim to decide military policy was put far too high by them and their partisans. War is not an exact science like chemistry or mathematics where it would be presumption on the part of anyone ignorant of its first rudiments to express an opinion contrary to those who had thoroughly mastered its principles. War is an art, proficiency in which depends more on experience than on study, and more on natural aptitude and judgment than on either. It is said that medicine is an art based on many sciences. But compare the experience acquired by a doctor in the course of his practice with that of the professional soldier. A physician fights a series of battles with the enemy every day and every year of his professional life.

That experience adds to his mastery of the art to which he has dedicated his abilities. The same observation applies to law and to politics. The lawyer and the politician, before they reach the age at which our Generals took over the command of our Armies in the War, are already the veterans of a myriad fights. In these incessant struggles they have been confronted with highly skilled adversaries. A soldier may spend his lifetime in barracks or colleges without a day's actual experience of the realities with which he will have to contend if war breaks out. On August 4th, 1914, not one of our great Commanders had encountered an enemy in battle for 12 years. Even then the experience they had acquired in the only war in which they had taken part had no relevance to the problems of the World War. On the South African veldt horsemanship counted more than drill. A fox hunter was more useful than a machine-gunner. The aeroplane and the tank were unknown and unthought of. Gutchkoff, the Russian Minister of War, saw the South African War and he told a friend of mine that he thought the experience acquired by our soldiers in that war had actually disqualified them for command in the Great War. The fighting was so essentially different in every respect. All the men who filled the highest commands in our Army in France were veterans of the Boer War. It is not too much to say that when the Great War broke out our Generals had the most important lessons of their art to learn. Before they began they had much to unlearn. Their brains were cluttered with useless lumber, packed in every niche and corner. Some of it was never cleared out to the end of the War. For instance, take their ridiculous cavalry obsession. In a war where artillery and engineering and trench work were more in demand than in any war in history we were led by soldiers trained in the cavalry. Haig was persuaded to the end of the War that a time would come when his troopers would one day charge through the gap made by his artillery and convert the German defeat into a headlong scamper for the Rhine. Needless to say, that chance never came. Generals were in every essential particular inadequately prepared for the contingencies which confronted them in this War. Had they been men of genius — which they were not — they could have adapted themselves more quickly and effectively to the new conditions of war. They were not equipped with that superiority in brains or experience over an amateur steeped in the incidents and needs of the War which would justify the attitude they struck and the note of assured pastmastership they adopted towards all criticism or suggestion from outside or below. The Generals themselves were at least four-fifths amateurs, hampered by the wrong training. They knew nothing except by hearsay about the actual fighting of a battle under modern conditions. Haig ordered many bloody battles in this War. He only took part in two — the retreat from Mons and the first Battle of Ypres. And both battles were fought under the old conditions of open warfare. He never even saw the ground on which his other battles were fought, either before or during the fight. Robertson never saw a battle. The great Commanders of history, even when they took no physical part in the battle, saw with their own eyes aided or unaided with the telescope the ground upon which it was to be fought and watched the progress of the struggle between the opposing forces. When you come to some of the great essentials of training and preparation for modern warfare, then neither Haig nor Robertson nor any of their Staff had any previous experience that would give them proficiency. And yet the strategy of the War depended upon these two soldiers and their military advisers.

In the most crucial matters relating to their own profession our leading soldiers had to be helped out by the politi-

cian. I have already given in detail an account of the way
the Generals muddled the problem of munitions. They did
not possess the necessary understanding of the probable character of the War to foresee that it would be a war which
would consume a prodigious quantity of shot and shell. What
they ordered was of the wrong kind. They preferred shrapnel to high explosive because the former was more useful
in the Boer War. What they provided was on the assumption that the War would be conducted in the open field.
When it developed into a war of deep digging they did not
realise that in order to demolish those improvised ramparts
it was essential to equip an army with thousands of guns
of a calibre heavier than any yet trundled into the battlefield. A fortress with its flanks extending from the North
Sea to the Swiss mountains and held by millions of men
and masses of cannon and machine guns was a nightmare.
they never contemplated in their most disturbed slumbers.
It took them months to adapt their strategy to this novel
and unforeseen portent. They did not realise that the machine gun and the hand grenade would practically take the
place of the rifle. Politicians were the first to seize upon
the real character of the problem in all these respects and
it was they who insisted on the necessary measures being
taken — and taken promptly — in order adequately to cope
with it. It was politicians who initiated and organised these
measures. In doing so, at each stage they had to overcome
the rooted traditions, prejudices and practices of military
staffs. It was politicians who insisted upon the importance
of providing sufficient and suitable transport facilities behind the line on a great scale in order not only to bring
up supplies, but to increase the mobility of the Army along
the whole front. It was civilians, chosen by politicians, who
reorganised and developed these facilities. It was politicians
who foresaw that any attempt to break through the immense

fortifications thrown up by the enemy on the Western Front would involve enormous carnage and a prolongation of this destructive war. It was they who urged the finding of a way round on the most vulnerable fronts. It was politicians who urged the importance of making the best use of the magnificent and almost inexhaustible fighting man power in Russia and the Balkans by providing them with the necessary equipment to play their part in attacking the enemy on his Eastern and Southern Fronts. It was amateurs who discovered the tank, easily the most formidable of our weapons and it was they who invented and urged the use of one of the most serviceable machines of the War, the Stokes mortar. It was a civilian who invented the hydrophone which located the deadly submarine and enabled us to hunt it down in the pathless depths of the sea.

Let anyone read the history of the War with care and then conjecture what would have happened if the ignorant and cold-shouldered civilian had not insisted on coming to the rescue of the military and the discharge of those functions which in peace and war constituted an essential part of the duties and responsibilities of the latter. I have not perused a military history which recognises fairly and generously the contribution rendered to the achievement of victory by the unwelcome intervention of the amateur untrained in military colleges or parade grounds.

Looking back on this devastating War and surveying the part played in it by statesmen and soldiers respectively in its direction I have come definitely to the conclusion that the former showed too much caution in exerting their authority over the military leaders. They might have done so either by a direct and imperative order from the Government or by making representations followed, if those were not effective in answering the purpose, by a change in the military leadership. The latter method of procedure would no doubt have been the sounder and wiser course to pursue had it been feasible. The difficulty, however, all Governments experienced was in discovering capable commanders who could have been relied upon not only to carry out their policy but to do so efficiently and skilfully. The long siege warfare did not provide opportunities for resourceful men to come to the top by a display of superior skill. There was a rigidity and restrictiveness about the methods employed which allowed no play for initiative, imagination and inventiveness. The orders issued to divisional and brigadier Generals and to Colonels from headquarters were precise and could not be deviated from in any particular without risking a charge of insubordination. The men on the heights offered no encouragement or chances to genius down below. The distance between the châteaux and dugouts was as great as that from the fixed stars to the caverns of earth. No telescope was powerful enough to discern talent at that depth, even if a look-out were being kept. That is one reason why no one reached the highest ranks in the British Army except those who were there or thereabout when the War began. No civilian rose above the rank of Brigadier, although there must have been hundreds of thousands who had years of experience in the fighting line — many of them men of exceptional capacity. Thousands of these men had passed through our Secondary Schools, hundreds through our Universities, and not a few with distinction. It is incredible that amongst men of that training and quality there should not have been found one, fit for high promotion, after years of greater experience of fighting under modern conditions than any General in the field had acquired. The regular Army before the War numbered something over 250,000. During the War four or five million young men drawn from every class of the community passed through its ranks. The wider the range of choice the better the chance of finding the right men for leadership. Besides, the Army was never considered to be a career for the talents. Rather the reverse. Boys who were endowed with brains above their fellows sought other professions where talent was more welcome and better requited. Independent thinking is not encouraged in a professional Army. It is a form of mutiny. Obedience is the supreme virtue. Theirs not to reason why. Orders are to be carried out and not canvassed. Criticism is insubordination. The object of discipline is to accustom men to respond to a command instantly, by instant action, without thought of effect or consequence. There were many intelligent officers and men who knew that the orders given them during the War were utterly stupid and must have been given by Staffs who had no understanding of the conditions. But orders were orders. And with their men they went to a doom they foresaw was inevitable. Such an instinctive obedience to the word of command is essential to the efficiency of a body of men who have to face terror, death or mutilation in the discharge of their terrible duties. But a long course of mental subservience and suppression cramps the development and suppleness of the intellect. It makes "an officer and a gentleman" but it is not conducive to the building up of an alert, adaptable and resourceful leader of men. Haig's summary of the qualities of the French officers he met is a condemnation of the rigidity of the system. The average and commonplace men of distinguished form he picked out as "gentlemanly" and "fine soldiers." The one man of genius among them he gibed at as a blatherer. In such a system promotion is a moving staircase where the man who sticks on is sure of promotion. Wheedling, pushing, intriguing enables some to wriggle through the crowd in front of him — but intellect is out of place and strength does not count. In the grand Army that fought the World War the ablest brains did not climb to the top of the stairs and they did not reach a height where politicians could even see them. Seniority and Society were the dominant factors in Army promotion. Deportment counted a good deal. Brains came a bad fourth. Men of great intellectual powers are not tempted to join a profession which offers so little scope for the exercise of their powers and where the awards have no special reference to special capacity. To be a good average is safer than to be gifted above your fellows. The only exceptions were to be found in the Dominion forces. General Currie, the Commander of the Canadian Army, and General Monash, the Commander of the Australian Army, were both in civil life when the War broke out. Both proved themselves to be brilliant military leaders and went right through to the top. It means they had a natural aptitude for soldiering and that the fact of their being officers in unprofessional armies gave full play to their gifts. Monash was, according to the testimony of those who knew well his genius for war and what he accomplished by it, the most resourceful General in the whole of the British Army. But the tradition of the Dominions in the occupations of peace and war is encouraging to fresh talent. For this and other reasons the British Government experienced a difficulty in securing for the Supreme Command the services of the ablest man which their great armies could have provided. There was no conspicuous officer in the Army who seemed to be better qualified for the Highest Command than Haig. That is to say, there was no outstanding General fit for so overwhelming a position as the command of a force five times as great as the largest army ever commanded by Napoleon, and many more times the size of any army led by Alexander, Hannibal or Cæsar. I have no doubt these great men would have risen to the occasion, but such highly gifted men as the British Army possessed were consigned to the mud by orders of men superior in rank but inferior in capacity, who themselves kept at a safe distance from the slime which they had chosen as the terrain where their plans were to operate.

The solicitude with which Generals in high places avoided personal jeopardy is one of the debatable novelties of modern warfare. Generals cannot any longer be expected to lead their men over the top with pointing sword. But this departure from the established methods of leadership by personal example has gone too far. Admirals of a rank corresponding to that held by the Army Commanders took exactly the same hazards in action as the humblest sailor in their fleet. Beatty was a man of dauntless intrepidity who sought danger. His flagship was hit in the Dogger Bank fight and it was just as liable to be blown up at Jutland as the *Defence* and the *Invincible*. The Rear-Admirals commanding these battle cruisers were killed when their ships were sunk. Jellicoe was not altogether free from personal peril in the Jutland mists. When a naval battle is fought G.H.Q. moves into the battle zone. Every child knows the story of Zeebrugge, the one naval exploit of the War that moved and still moves the imagination of the Nation. Sir Roger Keyes, the Admiral who directed the attack, had the unmistakable Nelson touch and took just as great personal risks as that redoubtable sailor ever faced. When high Admirals are not immune from the jeopardy of war there is no reason why exalted Generals should be sacrosanct. It is a new thing in war for generals that never set eyes on a position to command their soldiers to attack it without the slightest intention of placing themselves in any peril by leading the attack themselves, or even in viewing the ground before action, or coming near the battle whilst it is proceeding to its deadly end. It is certainly a novelty in war that military leaders swathed in comfort and security should doom hundreds of thousands of their bravest soldiers to

COLONEL WETZELL

lodge for weeks in slimy puddles with Death as their fellow lodger, without even taking the precaution of finding out for themselves what the conditions are or are likely to become. In the olden days when commanders so directed a battle that it ended in a shambles for their own army, they ran the risk of being themselves numbered with the slain. Even after rifles and cannon had become the most important weapons in war, Napoleon faced both in leading his troops. Wellington had a General shot at his side in the Battle of Waterloo and another was killed in the same battle in charging the enemy at the head of his troops. Mr. Winston Churchill describes how Marlborough crept through the corn to within a few yards of a French parapet bristling with guns just before a battle in order to judge whether an attack there was a feasible operation. When he found that it did not offer a fair chance of success to his men, he ordered them to retire. Cromwell and Rupert charged at the head of their troopers; Cæsar went into action to rally his men at great risk to his life. Stonewall Jackson constantly faced personal hazard and was ultimately killed taking risks in examining the battle-ground. Some of the assaults on impossible positions ordered by our Generals would never have been decreed if they had seen beforehand with their own eyes the hopeless slaughter to which their orders doomed their men. To suggest otherwise would be a base calumny on Generals.

No amount of circumspection can prevent war leading to the death of multitudes of brave men, but now that Generals are not partaking in the personal hazards of a fight, they ought to take greater personal risks in satisfying themselves as to the feasibility of their plans and as to whether the objectives they wish to attain are worth the sacrifice they entail, and whether there is no better way of achieving the same result at less cost of gallant lives.

CHAPTER XI

LORD HAIG'S DIARIES AND AFTER

AFTER I had written the greater part of the last two Volumes there appeared the second batch of extracts from Lord Haig's "Diaries." Rather than interrupt and break up my narrative by intermittent corrections of the story of the War as told by someone else, I thought it preferable to postpone a perusal of the Diaries until after I had written my book. The publication of these intimate reflections — or rather aspersions — by Lord Haig on the men, some now living, some dead, with whom he was associated in the service of the country during the War, must silence the reproof directed against my Memoirs on the absurd ground that they occasionally express adverse opinions on the strategy of Generals who have now passed away. Lord Haig himself never accepted that preposterous canon as to the limitations of criticism. He intended that his censorious records should be published sooner or later. Mr. Duff Cooper has now published extracts from the personal notes of Lord Haig which the latter had destined for ultimate publication. I fully recognise that in condemning anyone who is no longer able to defend himself one must bear in mind the old motto of *de mortuis nil nisi bonum*. But the living have also their rights. And if the *mortui*, before departing, deliberately pen indictments for the arraignment of their associates (for both Lord French and I and many others who come in for Haig's condemnation were each of us in his own sphere closely associated with him in the greatest task of his life) after they themselves have passed away, the death of the accused surely does not deprive the survivors amongst the accused of the liberty to state their case.

Considering that the Diaries contained a daily record of momentous events in which Lord Haig took a leading part, and of his impressions and reflections upon them in the quiet of his study at dusk, the extracts are not only meagre but remarkably sterile and undistinguished.[1] If this represents the best which Mr. Duff Cooper could find what must be the quality of the rest?

There are diaries — and diaries. There is the diary kept by those who take a delight in setting down in writing events or sayings which have come to their attention during the day without reference to any part they themselves may have played in the transaction which they note. When you make a fair percentage deduction for the unreliability of unchecked gossip, diaries of this kind, if kept by an observant person, have their historical value; but there is another kind of diary kept by persons who have an absorbing interest in their own personality and career and who record each day at eventide their own daily achievements, utterances, meditations, and contacts. The Wilson Diaries have exposed the perversion of fact to which entries of this character are liable when the writer constitutes in his nocturnal records the central figure of the whole universe for every day during the long years of his life. It is a sustained egoism which is almost a disease, and its jottings ought therefore to be scrutinised carefully and treated with suspicion as material for a reliable history of the times. In writing my book I had no diary to help my memory. I certainly had no time or inclination amidst the the labour and anxiety of the War

---

[1] The gaps and omissions from these voluminous Diaries are significant of much careful editing.

for sitting down every evening to write for the enlightenment of posterity the tale of my accomplishments during
the day. It could not have been of any assistance to me
or anyone else in the discharge of our onerous duties. Nor
have I written these Memoirs on the strength of recollections blurred by the march of years or touched up by
the vanity of repetitive boasts swelling in size and deepening in colour at each repetition. That is a besetting weakness against which we have all to guard. I have therefore
not only stimulated but also checked and corrected my
memory by reference to the testimony of contemporary documents, reports, and conversations officially recorded by
impartial observers. There is a mass of information available to all who take the trouble to investigate and peruse
it as to what actually took place in those tremendous days:
memoranda or letters written at the time, relating the actions as they were then known and the opinions as they
were then formed of men who were taking part in the making of the history of those terrible, but great days. Fortunately, I had also access to the most careful official Diary
of current events — and of the discussions that led to them
— which has ever been penned: Sir Maurice Hankey's Minutes of War Cabinets, Imperial Cabinets and Inter-Allied
Conferences. The entries were submitted at the time to the
men whose statements were recorded, for their correction.
My Memoirs are almost entirely based on this mass of con-
temporaneous documents. When I draw on my personal
memory I invariably check and correct by reference to this
written evidence. I have to thank the Prime Minister for
the permission he has given me to use these Memoranda and
also the War Office for the ready access to their own records
which they have accorded to me. Successive Secretaries of
State and First Lords of the Admiralty have given me every
facility to peruse the information in their respective De-

partments, and years before I started penning a single sentence of my Memoirs I gathered together, with the help of my private secretaries during the War, an immense stack of this written testimony. I caused it to be carefully docketed, indexed and examined. I read thousands of these interesting and revealing papers before I committed to writing my memories, thus fortified. When the extracts from Haig's Diaries, picked by a skilled dialectician largely in view of the controversies raised and raging as to the late Commander-in-Chief's conduct of the War, appeared in print, I decided not to alter in any particular my settled method of presenting and checking the story of the Great War as it was known to me. When the Duff Cooper Volumes were published, I therefore did not modify or re-cast the draft I had already written except to the extent that I re-examined with great care any statement of facts which seemed to be challenged by Marshal Haig's Notes. Memory, even when guided by contemporary documents, may lead any witness astray if one essential factor is missing in the chain of his evidence. I owe therefore to Mr. Duff Cooper's editorship the gratitude which is due to any publication which forces one to search out more thoroughly the incidents and influences that went to the making of important decisions and events of which one is endeavouring to give a fair and accurate account.

I want to emphasise once more that my differences with great Generals were not due to any personal or political motives. I had no personal quarrel with either Lord Haig or Sir William Robertson. My relations with Robertson were always pleasant and as for Haig, during my many visits to his Headquarters in France, he received me with the greatest courtesy and always made me feel a welcome guest. Nor were there any political considerations or prejudices that influenced my attitude towards them. I never knew what Haig's politics were and I never inquired. I had no idea what were Robertson's political views. I therefore formed my opinions as to both Haig and Robertson on grounds which had nothing to do with personal or political likes or dislikes. I judged them purely as instruments for achieving victory. As to Sir Henry Wilson, he was an intense and intriguing politician all the days of his life. Every Irishman is an uncompromising politician from his youth upward — and downward. I recall Mr. Tim Healy once saying that in the city of Londonderry every man, woman and child understood the registration laws — the intricate mechanism of party warfare. Henry Wilson was no exception to this concentrated partisanship of his race. But his hatred — for it amounted to that — of the party and the principles in which I was brought up did not prevent my promoting him to the highest position and rank in his profession. I had no reason to believe Haig was in the least interested in the conflict of parties, as such. He preferred Asquith's method of dealing with Generals to mine. After Asquith made an appointment in any Department he was always inclined not to concern himself with what occurred in that Department unless and until Parliamentary trouble was threatened over some of its operations. The less he heard from or of a Department the better he was pleased. He exercised no close supervision over the doings of his Ministers or Generals. His easygoing temperament suited both much better than mine or Mr. Winston Churchill's! No wonder that both Haig and Robertson preferred him and his methods. During the critical days of the War, when it was important not to undermine public confidence in the Commander-in-Chief of our own Army, I made no public attack on his personal fitness for so immense a responsibility, but I never concealed from myself or from my colleagues that I thought Sir Douglas Haig was intellectually and temperamentally unequal to the command of an Army of millions fighting battles on fields which were invisible to any Commander.

In substance Mr. Duff Cooper admits that I was justified in my estimate of his mental equipment for such a task. According to him, Haig was as good a soldier as a man can be who did not possess genius — that means he was a second-rate Commander in unparalleled and unforeseen circumstances, where the resources of even a first-rate leader like Foch were only just adequate to pull us through. He had a long training on lines which were irrelevant to the experiences and exigencies of this War. That was not his fault. There never had been such a war, and the narrow and rigid system which he had learnt and taught made it difficult for so unsupple a mind to adapt himself readily to any other ideas. He was above the average of his profession in intelligence and industry — perhaps more in industry than intelligence. He was always a steady and conscientious worker. No one could impute to him indolence or slackness in the discharge of his duty. He possessed an untiring tenacity of purpose. But Mr. Duff Cooper's appreciation of his gifts acknowledges in effect that he was not endowed with any of the elements of imagination and vision which determine the line of demarcation between genius and ordinary capacity. And he certainly had none of that personal magnetism which has enabled great leaders of men to inspire multitudes with courage, faith, and a spirit of sacrifice. I am not thinking of the great gods of war like Alexander, Hannibal, Cæsar, or Napoleon. It would be unfair to challenge a comparison between them and any of the Generals of the Great War. Haig was not endowed with the magnetic qualities and the discerning eye of a Cromwell, a Marlborough or a Stonewall Jackson. I had once the unforgettable privilege of conversing with a number of Confederate officers and men who had taken part in the American Civil

War. They had fought, some under Lee, others under Jackson, Beauregard and Jeb Stuart. The personality that had made the deepest impression on these survivors of a hundred battles was Stonewall Jackson. I asked one of the veterans what was the secret of his hold on his soldiers. "Well," he said, "all I can tell you is that once when we were given what seemed to us an impossible position to storm the men were reluctant to advance in face of fire until an officer went up to them and said to them: 'We must do it — these are the orders of General Jackson.' Upon which they cried out: 'Oh, it is old Jack! Why didn't you tell us that before?' They all leapt up and swept along through bullets and shells." They knew that he never gave them an impossible task. He never ordered an attack until he was convinced by a careful survey of the ground that its capture was attainable by brave and resolute men. The only Army Commander in France who commanded that kind of confidence in his men was Plumer. Haig never inspired that feeling in his army. His name never sent a thrill through the ranks on the eve of a battle — his presence he never vouchsafed on these occasions. I have spoken to hundreds who fought in his battles from Festubert to Passchendaele and they all testify to that absence of inspiration which flows from the words, presence or personality of a great leader. That is why the appointment of Foch as Generalissimo was hailed with such relief and delight throughout the British Army. Haig undoubtedly lacked those highest qualities which were essential in a great Commander in the greatest War the world has ever seen.

He was incapable of planning vast campaigns on the scale demanded on so immense a battle area. The problem set before a Commander of two million men on a hundred-mile battle front was one which needed capacity of a very high order. No British General was ever given so gigantic an undertaking. It was far beyond his mental equipment. Serving under Marlborough, Wellington or Cromwell, he would have been a highly competent leader in a field every acre of which was visible to his own eyes. But when he had to fight battles in quagmires he had never seen and over an area extending to a hundred miles which he never did or could personally inspect, he was lost. He did not possess that eye within an eye which is imagination. He was like the blind King of Bohemia at Crecy. He was entirely dependent on others for information essential to judgment, and those he chose to enlighten and guide him were not only just as devoid of vision as he was himself, they were not his equals in experience, intelligence or conscience. When, in addition to all that, he was called upon in his computations to visualise other battle fronts in far lands or in other continents, some of them hundreds and some thousands of miles away, his mind could not range over such distances, and he felt that to devote any of our resources to assist in these enterprises was like expending explosive energy on flights to the moon, when he needed every kilowatt to drive a few yards at a time over obstacles placed along the bit of earth which was in front of him. There are two documents which reveal faithfully Haig's limitations for the highest command in a world war. One is his review of the War as a whole which he wrote for the Government at my request in October, 1917. The other is the report he made to the Cabinet in the following October — three weeks before the German surrender — as to the military situation and prospects at that date. Whether Russia or Roumania were in or out of the War, whether Italy or Austria were crushed, whether Bulgaria barred the gates of Constantinople and Danube, or those gates were forced by the Allies, whether Turkey seized the Suez Canal, threatened our route to India, seized the oil-well of Baku, or were eliminated from the War, whether a large reserve of able-bodied men were required to keep 45,-000,000 of people alive in the British Isles or even to hold the seas in order to ensure reinforcements and supplies for Haig's own armies, did not come into his reckoning and he sullenly refused even to consider these factors, even when expressly invited to do so. Mr. Duff Cooper dwells upon his hero's "selflessness." Selfish he was not, but he was essentially self-centred. There was no other task but his, no other army than the one he commanded; no other use for the youth of Britain than to make up his losses. No victory was thinkable except in battles he planned. His camera only took in a limited circle of the scene right in front of him, and it was too constricted and faint to take in any other landscape. I was conscious of these defects in him as a leader. Hence my distrust of his capacity to fill so immense a position. Unfortunately the British Army did not bring into prominence any Commander who, taking him all round, was more conspicuously fitted for this post. No doubt Monash would, if the opportunity had been given him, have risen to the height of it. But the greatness of his abilities was not brought to the attention of the Cabinet in any of the Despatches. Professional soldiers could hardly be expected to advertise the fact that the greatest strategist in the Army was a civilian when the War began, and that they were being surpassed by a man who had not received any of their advantages in training and teaching.

Haig might have minimised the disastrous effect of his intellectual shortcomings had he called to his aid men who were equipped, as advisers if not as leaders, with the qualities in which he was himself deficient. Unfortunately, amongst Haig's qualifications, no one has ever attributed to him the capacity for judging men. Considerations of friendship, of social amenity and of easy acquiescence in council largely determined his appointments to positions of vital responsibility. G.H.Q. must be a happy family of men whose relations were not disturbed by the clash of independent intelligences. For that reason his choice of colleagues, associates, and subordinates was often lamentable. Let anyone peruse a list of the names of those by whom he was surrounded, and upon whose intelligence and counsel he depended, and they will recognise the justice of my comment. Had he been a man of supreme ability — which no one claims him to have been — so inadequate a Staff would have impaired his efficiency as a Commander in so colossal an undertaking. His unfortunate selection was partly due to lack of discernment and partly attributable to his inability to hold his own in a conflict of ideas. Haig was devoid of the gift of intelligible and coherent expression. Fluency is not a proof — nor a disproof — of ability, but lucidity of speech is unquestionably one of the surest tests of mental precision. A man of few words is always credited with great sapience, but that must depend on the clarity as well as the content of the words he uses. Lucidity of mind ensures lucidity of expression. Power and light go together and are generated by the same machine. Mere slowness of mind is no evidence of mental deficiency except where quick decisions are essential to effective action. I have known men of sluggish mentality, who, given time, were very sound thinkers. So I have met men of slow speech who were clear expositors. But in my experience a confused talker is never a clear thinker.

Haig had a natural distrust of soldiers who could talk well. Some of the entries in his Diaries make that evident. Soon after his appointment as Commander-in-Chief he paid a visit to the French Army so as to establish good relations with them at the outset of his command. His comments on the personalities of the Generals he met threw a great

deal of light on his own character. Of one General he met
Haig writes: —

"An exceptionally gentlemanly man and a fine soldier. He
certainly has *'la flamme'*."

It is significant that this exceptional man cut no figure in
actual warfare.

Of another officer he notes: —

"I am quite impressed with him. So quiet and silent for a
Frenchman and such a retiring gentlemanly man."

It is a tribute to the French understanding of human nature
that this silent retiring and gentlemanly man was appointed
as their Liaison Officer at Haig's G.H.Q. I have no doubt
he did well in that post.

Haig could not hold his own in Conference with soldiers
or statesmen who could explain their ideas clearly and flu-
ently. He therefore distrusted them and preferred men who
had no ideas to set in competition with his own. He liked
conventional officers with a soldierly deportment. A soldier
who fulfilled the description of "an officer and a gentleman"
fulfilled his requirements.

But as to Foch, whom he also met in this company of
exceptional gentlemen and fine soldiers, all he has to record
in his Diary is: —

"As to Foch, he is a 'méridional' and a great talker."

It represents his general attitude towards Foch. He always referred to him, in any conversation I had with him
during the War, with amused contempt. The time was coming when he had to recognise that this great talker was "a
determined General who would fight", a man of great courage and decision, and when he had to ask him to take

charge of a battle which he, the great silent General, had muddled to the brink of disaster.

One unpleasant trait in Haig's character is brought out by Mr. Duff Cooper in his choice of extracts — quite unconsciously, of course. He attributes to his hero qualities of nobility, generosity, selflessness and loyalty. There are entries in the Diaries which admit conduct utterly irreconcilable with these exalted claims. For instance, the intrigues in which he was engaged with Esher and Robertson to secure the dismissal of his immediate Chief from the High Command and his other and reciprocal intrigue with Robertson and Esher to turn Kitchener out of the War Office and send him to India with a view to installing Robertson as C.I.G.S. "Lord Esher undertook to support Haig's views in London", and, as his economiastic editor observes: "He no doubt did so with considerable effect." Haig profited by the first manœuvre, Robertson by the second. There was an underhandedness about these proceedings which was not consistent with nobility or loyalty. Esher had the mentality and the methods of the intriguer. He loved intrigue for its own sake. He claimed no reward but the satisfaction of putting it through. Haig fell in very readily and aptly with these methods. His justification was that all considerations of personal loyalty must be subordinated to the winning of the War and he would not be deterred from doing his duty by the prospect of personal advancement which it opened out to him. Had he and Robertson informed French and Kitchener of the representations they made to the Prime Minister, their conduct would have been straightforward and justifiable; but it was a subterranean plot to overthrow official chiefs to their own advantage without any warning to the victims or any opportunity for them to confront their accusers and refute the accusation. At the time he wrote his criticisms French was Commander-in-Chief and Kitchener as War

Minister was his and Robertson's Ministerial Chief. What becomes then of his contention subsequently that to express any disapproval of the strategy of a Commander in the Field — even in secret Council — was reprehensible because it undermined confidence in the military leadership? This "supremely loyal man" was not above ungenerous efforts to pass on to his chiefs, his colleagues or his subordinates the blame for his own failures. He failed at Loos. French was entirely responsible and he reported him behind his back to the Government. His first great attack on the Somme was on the whole a sanguinary repulse. He explains in his Diaries that his non-success was entirely attributable to the refusal of his Army and Divisional Commanders to carry out his plans. Gough's Fifth Army was disastrously beaten before Amiens because Haig (1) failed to take the necessary steps to improve the defences; (2) had distributed his troops so badly that the Army he knew was going to be attacked had the least number of troops to defend the front; and also (3) because he had declined to carry out plans to which he had assented for the setting up of a General Reserve designed to support the threatened sector. But when Gough had been beaten owing to conditions for which Haig alone was responsible, Haig, instead of accepting that responsibility as an "officer and a gentleman", removed Gough from the command and left the Government to infer that the dégommé General was alone to blame. Not much nobility there. Take another instance. He and Pétain conspired together to destroy the scheme for setting up a General Reserve — vowing to their respective Governments that they had made the most detailed arrangements for coming to each other's aid and that these plans were so perfect that they would work automatically. When the emergency arose and the perfect arrangements failed to automatise, then Haig suggests the failure was due to the fact that Pétain was "almost unbalanced" — that is, to use an expressive if somewhat slang phrase, that his confederate was "in a blue funk." He charges him with wishing to retire on Paris, leaving the British Army in the lurch or to escape northwards the best way it could without French assistance. Not much loyalty there.

As to his "generosity", I would like to call attention to an example of it — or rather the lack of it — which affects me personally. Haig has sedulously endeavoured to create the impression, by himself and through his friends, that the disasters of March, 1918, were attributable to his having been placed in a position of hopeless numerical inferiority to the enemy owing to my neglect to provide him with the necessary reinforcements. In the text of Volume V, I have dealt exhaustively with the charge, supplying official figures to prove how untrue and disgracefully unfair was this device to cast upon others the blame for his own mismanagement of the enormous resources in men and equipment which were placed at his disposal. When Haig took over the Chief Command in December, 1915, the British Expeditionary Force in France had reached a total of 986,189. During the interval between his taking over and the beginning of March, 1918, he engaged that great Army in a number of sanguinary offensives not one of which achieved any decisive result. The British casualties in France during that period reached the ghastly total of 1,683,887.[1] Nevertheless, owing to the efforts made by the Government at home to keep up the strength of his Army, the force at his Command in March, 1918, was 1,886,073.

(I am quoting from the official Statistics of the Military Effort of the British Empire during the Great War.) When I took office as Prime Minister in December, 1916, its total was: —

[1] January 1st, 1916, to February 28th, 1918.

Officers	58,098
Men	1,476,633
Total	1,534,731

By March, 1918, there was an increase of 341,000 in spite of the gigantic losses of the 1917 offensives.

When the improvement in equipment is reckoned, the additional strength of the Army under Sir Douglas Haig's command in March, 1918, as compared with December, 1915, is much more striking. When Haig took over in December, 1915, the number of heavy guns in the British Expeditionary Force in France and Flanders numbered 235; in March, 1918, there were 2,062. The increase in the heavier calibres was particularly remarkable. When you come to machine guns, the opposition of the War Office to the production of this, the deadliest weapon of the War, was overcome by my action. This is recorded in Volume II of these Memoirs. In 1914 (August to December) the output was 274. As a result of the urgent measures I took the output in 1915 was 6,064. The efforts I had made to increase production of this redoubtable weapon had only begun fully to fructify shortly before January, 1916. Haig became Commander-in-Chief at the end of 1915. In 1916 the output of machine guns rose to 33,200; in 1917 it was 79,438; the vast majority of these machines went to Sir Douglas Haig's army in France. He admits in his Diary that one Lewis gun was equal to a considerable number of infantrymen.

When you come to gun ammunition the average weekly expenditure of shells during April, 1916, when the new supplies were beginning to come in, was 80,673 shrapnel and 77,590 high explosive. In April, 1918, it was 786,378 shrapnel and 1,197,771 high explosive. When a comparison is made in the calibre of the shell the contrast is much more pronounced. This enormous increase is attributable to the factories I built and the works I commandeered for the production of ammunition. I also took a conspicuous part in all the efforts made to raise men for the Army. Sir William Robertson has admitted in a letter, which I published in a previous volume, that the carrying of Conscription was largely attributable to the fight I put up. But when you come to the production of munitions, guns, machine guns and trench mortars, I have no hesitation in claiming that far and away the most leading part in determining the scale of production was due to my organisation of the engineering resources of the nation for this purpose.

It is rather remarkable that amongst all the meticulous entries covering sometimes events of great historical interest, sometimes incidents of the most trivial character (as I happen to know), in Haig's intimate story of his actions and reflections during the War, there should have been no word of recognition in these voluminous Diaries of the fact that the thousands of great guns, the scores of thousands of machine guns, and the scores of millions of shells, which enabled him to fight his great battles, were attributable to the organisation created by a person to whom he makes constant reference of a derogatory character. Had there been one such entry, I feel certain Mr. Duff Cooper would not have deliberately suppressed it, as he has given so much prominence to all the adverse personal criticisms which Haig recorded in his Diary. He is quite incapable of such a disreputable interpretation of his duty as an editor of historical material. On the other hand, it is equally difficult to believe that a man to whom Mr. Duff Cooper attributes such a nobility and generosity of character as Haig should have refused to make the slightest acknowledgment in his hours of triumph of the help which had been given in the attainment of victory by a leading Minister of the Crown, especially a Minister of whose defects he feels it a duty to make reiterated notes in his Diary. What makes it all the more surprising that there should be no mention of the service I rendered him in the prosecution of his campaigns, is the fact that I have proof in Sir Douglas Haig's own handwriting that he was fully alive to the obligation he was under to me for hustling the guns and ammunition with which his army was equipped. Here is a private letter written by Sir Douglas Haig to me on September 23rd, 1916 (in the middle of the Somme battle) in which he says:

"The whole Army appreciates to the full the stupendous task that has been accomplished under your able guidance in providing the enormous quantities of munitions of all sorts without which our present successes would be impossible. . . ."

Contrast this with Mr. Duff Cooper's extraordinary failure to find a single entry in any of these Diaries recording Haig's gratitude for the overwhelming help brought to him. His practised eye has detected every word of derogation, and his only too willing pen has given it publicity — but he failed to discover a syllable of the thanks which Haig in his letter acknowledged to have been merited. Sir Douglas Haig must have had painful memories of the time when neither he nor his predecessor had any heavy guns to attack German trenches, and when such light guns as there were had to be limited to an expenditure of a few shells a day, even to retaliate upon the Germans for their destructive bombardment of British trenches. Haig in his Diary attributed the bloody failure of his attack at Artois to the fact that the artillery bombardment was not effective enough to smash the German trenches or to destroy the barbed wire entanglements in front of them. He also records the order received in May, 1915, that he must be "careful of ammunition" as an attack is threatened by the Germans at Ypres. It was then I took over the duty of organising the supply of Munitions. Before he attacked on the Somme his Army had been equipped with hundreds of the best heavy cannon in the battlefield and the supply of ammunition had risen to 1,000,000 shells a week. The factories I erected or commandeered turned out an enormous number of guns, machine guns, tanks and trench mortars and ammunition week by week to the end of the War. Is it credible that there is not one word of acknowledgment of this service in the whole of these Diaries?

Mr. Duff Cooper begins his Chapter on the Battle of the Somme with these words, quoted, I presume, from the Diaries: —

"For seven long days the bombardment had continued. From British guns alone 1,000,000 shells had been hurled into the German lines."

He has other quotations from Haig on the saving effected in infantry by the supply of machine guns. But not a word of grateful recognition that the provision of these guns and ammunition had been the result of months of incessant toil in the setting up of an organisation for utilising the great engineering resources of Britain to equip the British Armies in France with the necessary means to fight their battles on equal terms with their well-equipped foes! Not a word as to the struggle with the War Office for the authorisation of this unprecedented output of heavy guns and machine guns. The terrific bombardment which expended tens of millions of shells at Passchendaele was also made possible through the exertions of the organisation which had been set up. But his unfairness and ingratitude is not confined to material. Not only were his colossal casualties made up through the untiring efforts of the Government of which I was the Head — made up in spite of considerable internal difficulties — but the actual numbers of the forces under his command were increased by hundreds of thousands since I became Prime Minister. And yet his only comment as to the fine Army with which he was provided to enable him to face the German onslaught or his lines is a surly grouse that the Government at home had let him down. Not much in this of the magnanimity of which we read so much. More mean than magnanimous.

I turn now to Haig's claim that he was the prime mover in the decision that led to unity of command on the Western Front. When the idea of a united commandment became a recognised success, there were many competitors for the honour of having originated it. When it was unpopular in the Press, suspected in Parliament and frowned upon in the highest circles of the professional army, I found no rivalry for the glory of championing the proposal. When I made my first attempt at securing a United Command in the spring of 1917, the Cabinet acquiesced in it, but had I insisted on pressing it to the point of a rupture with Haig and Robertson, there would have been serious political trouble. The letter from Lord Derby quoted by Mr. Duff Cooper shows something of the internal difficulties with which I had to contend in establishing what is now accepted by everybody and claimed by many including Haig as their own idea. That was the reason why I could not hustle Haig along too peremptorily and that, in consequence, fatal delays ensued. In substance, effective unity would have been achieved by the Versailles plan for the establishment of a general reserve under the command of Foch. The two Commanders-in-Chief would have had to conform their strategy and their tactics to those of the General who controlled the reserves. Haig understood this quite well. His view on the effect of the resolution that set up the General Reserve is made clear by the entry he made in his Diary on the day it was carried at Versailles: "To some extent it makes Foch a Generalissimo." Pétain formed the same opinion as to its effect. And so did Clemenceau. Neither of these eminent men desired to elevate Foch to such an exalted position. Hence the intrigue which destroyed the plan for setting up a General Reserve. Hence also the disaster of the 21st of March. Foch predicted that in the absence of a united reserve, defeat was inevitable. When it came, both Haig and Pétain were frightened by the consequences of their sabotage,[1] and were prepared to hand over the supreme responsibility for saving the situation they had created to anyone who was prepared to accept, so long as he was acceptable to the politicians. Haig's entry in his Diary on March 25th, after he had visited the battlefront (on the fourth day of the battle) and seen the state of things, gives some idea of his frame of mind.

"*Monday, 25th March, 1918.* . . . I got back from Dury with General Lawrence and Heseltine about 3 A.M.

"Lawrence at once left me to telegraph to Wilson requesting him and Lord Milner to come to France at once in order to arrange that General Foch or some other determined general, who would fight, should be given supreme control of the operations in France. I knew Foch's strategical ideas were in conformity with the orders given me by Lord Kitchener when I became Commander-in-Chief, and that he was a man of great courage and decision as shown during the fighting at Ypres in October and November, 1914."

Foch to the rescue!

Nothing but a paralytic fright could have effected so complete a conversion in a few days to the supreme need for a Foch control of the battlefront. When one recalls the

---

[1] Haig says in his Note on the third day of the battle: "Pétain struck me as very much upset, almost unbalanced and most anxious." (Duff Cooper: "Haig", Vol. II, p. 252.)

equanimity with which Haig contemplated the reports that came in about the vast preparations in men, artillery, aeroplanes and ammunition made by the Germans for attacking the ill-prepared British lines, and the contemptuous way in which he brushed aside the plan for mobilising a formidable reserve under Foch to support those lines when the attack came — this bouleversement is miraculous.

He was now only too ready to leave the clearing-up of the mess which he and Pétain had conspired to produce "at once to General Foch *or some other determined general who would fight.*" Foch was "a man of great courage and decision." When did he come to that conclusion? The only opinion he ever expressed of Foch in his Diaries up to that date (so far as we are permitted to know) is that he was "a great talker", whilst another undistinguished Frenchman whom he met about the same time is commended as "a fine soldier." Haig habitually referred to Foch in these terms of superior contempt with which the inarticulate generally allude to the expressive. His story is that he suggested Milner and Henry Wilson should come over to France to arrange for Foch to take over "supreme control of the operations in France." As for the claims made by the friends of Milner and Haig respectively for the credit of proposing that Foch should coördinate the efforts of the French and British Armies it is not for me to express an opinion. Whether Foch's appointment at Doullens as coördinator (but not as Commander) was due to Haig's panic or to Milner's persuasion will no doubt one day be settled by impartial historians. Personally, I think both these elements contributed to the result. Poincaré, Clemenceau and Pétain are also amongst the claimants to share in the Doullens advance towards unity, and rightly so, for they also participated in the scare for which at least two of them were largely responsible. They were all present at the conference and did their

part in promoting agreement. In a previous volume, I have
told the full story of the subsequent appointment at Beauvais of Foch to be *Général-en-Chef* as it is revealed by
contemporary documents. The facts speak for themselves.
Competitive claims for the origination of an idea are generally unprofitable and unpleasant. But I am bound in the
interest of truthful narrative to correct one mis-statement
which Mr. Duff Cooper makes in dealing with the Doullens
episode. He asserts that whereas once upon a time I had
been a strong advocate for the appointment of an Allied
Generalissimo, I abandoned it at Versailles, but that Milner took it up at Doullens. He has compressed three mis-
statements into one short paragraph — an exceptional feat
for the most reckless partisan: (1) that I proposed a Generalissimo for the Allied Armies; (2) that I dropped the
proposal at Versailles: (3) that nevertheless it was established finally at Doullens by Milner. I never proposed an
Allied Generalissimo. I knew that was practically unattainable. Neither Russia, Italy nor Belgium would consider any
proposal for placing their armies under a foreign Commander-in-Chief. My proposal was confined to unity of commandment on the Western Front. That was achieved temporarily by Briand and myself in the spring of 1917. I went
as far as I could hope to succeed in restoring that unity when
I proposed at Versailles to create a reserve in the West and
place it under Foch. Milner was with me at that conference
and although he was a wholehearted advocate of unity of
Command, he agreed that we could not then carry things
any further. It turned out that even thus we went beyond
the possibilities of the situation. Suspicions and susceptibilities defeated our purpose. It was only the rout of March
that enabled us to make any progress. That converted the
wreckers of a united reserve under Foch's direction, Haig,
Pétain, and Clemenceau, to the essential need for unity,

and at Doullens they all supplicated the rejected Foch to come to their rescue in coördinating this chaos. But Doullens did not make Foch Generalissimo. When subsequently Foch was made *Général-en-Chef* of the French and British Armies at Beauvais, the Italian Prime Minister refused to accept that arrangement for the Italian Army. He would only agree to the Doullens arrangement which empowered Foch to "coördinate" Allied effort with the assent of the Commanders of the three Armies, but with no authority to command. Mr. Duff Cooper's partisanship forces me to quote the testimony of the highest authority on the evolution of Allied Unity — Foch himself. Bugnet, in his life of Foch, asserts that the latter informed him that —

"It is Lloyd George who contributed the most toward the attainment of the unified command. As early as the Rapallo Conference, when the Versailles Committee was set up — even earlier, as far back as 17th October, 1914. He saw everything clearly. He even invented me!"[1]

I may also quote from a letter written to me by Foch himself, not during, but after the War. It was his official reply to the thanks expressed to him by the two Houses of Parliament for his great part in achieving victory: —

23.8.19.

"Dear Prime Minister,

". . . I do not forget that if I was summoned to be Commander-in-Chief of the Allied Armies, it was on your initiative and thanks to your confidence. If I have also been able to direct the War to a speedy victory it is thanks to the persistent readiness of the English Government and reinforcements to maintain its armies in France in 1918, at sufficient strength, and likewise to give powerful help to the transport of the American divisions in Europe.

[1] Bugnet, "Foch Talks", p. 218.

G.Q.G.A. le 23. 8. 19

Monsieur le Premier Ministre,

... Je n'oublie pas d'ailleurs, que si j'ai été ap
pelé au Commandement en Chef des Armées
Alliées, c'est sur votre initiative et grâce à
votre confiance. Si j'ai pu également mener
la guerre à une victoire rapide, c'est grâce
à la volonté soutenue du gouvernement
Anglais, de renforcer et de maintenir, en 1918,
à des effectifs suffisants les armées de France,
comme aussi d'aider puissamment au
transport des divisions Américaines en
Europe.

En présence d'une pareille confiance et
de si sérieux efforts j'ai déployé de mon
côté, toute l'activité dont j'étais capable,
pour arriver à la victoire, en utilisant au
mieux les moyens qui m'étaient parfai
tement assurés. ...

F. Foch

"In the face of such confidence and of such serious efforts I have on my part exerted every effort of which I was capable to obtain victory, making the best use of the means which had been fully assured to me. . . .

F. Foch."

I never ceased to work for unity of commandment in the West but I would not have thought it necessary to revert to the persistence with which I laboured for and ultimately achieved it had it not been for Mr. Duff Cooper's over-strained anxiety to minimise my efforts. I do not wish to detract one jot or tittle from the great services rendered by Haig, Milner, or Clemenceau at Doullens in securing a measure of coördination between the British and French Armies. Nor do I seek to deny Haig's own statement that Milner's action was attributable to the conclusion he (Haig) had come to that Foch should be asked to pull the British Army out of the confusion in which it had been landed. Haig says that the proposal was his and that Milner agreed. I have no desire to challenge this statement. As to Haig's explanations of the March disaster and its causes, they are inaccurate, incomplete and misleading. One could not have expected him even in the privacy of a Diary — especially a Diary intended for subsequent publication — to admit his own responsibility for the defeat. And it is only human that he should search out apologies which cover up his own mistakes. But he has gone beyond, outside and often right across the facts. Let me give a few examples of the more important mis-statements culled from Duff Cooper's extracts: —

1. "All possible preparations to meet it [the German attack] had been made."

This is simply not true.

(a) The defences were insufficient and in parts purely

sketchy. When the attack came trenches and machine-gun positions which were essential to effective defence existed only on paper. Both Gough and the "Official History of the War" bear out this description of the disgraceful insufficiency of the defences.

(*b*) The troops were so distributed that infantry and artillery strongly held the unmenaced part of the front and the threatened sector was thinly lined and supported. Most of the available resources were in the North, and the Fifth Army, against whom a great offensive was apprehended for weeks, was left with feeble support. Haig, according to Mr. Duff Cooper, states in his Diary that on the fourth day of the battle he decided to thin his line in the North to concentrate reserves on Amiens. Why did he delay that obvious operation until our army was surrounded? When he admits that he knew weeks before the 21st of March that a gigantic German attack was coming on his Southern Armies, why did he not then thin his line in the North? His Northern Armies had twice as many men to the kilometre of trench they had to hold as Gough had, and many more than Byng had. There are no relevant extracts from the Diary to explain the reason why Haig made so fatal a distribution of his divisions. When one recalls the fact that Haig had come to the conclusion that Lord French was unfit for his post as Commander-in-Chief because at the Battle of Loos he had kept his reserves too far behind the line, it is inexplicable that Haig himself should have repeated that blunder on a far larger scale and with much more disastrous results. Lord Haig passed judgment on his own subsequent conduct when in 1915 he entered in his Diary this censure of French's handling of reserves. "When the C.-in-C. remains blind to lesson of war in this important matter, we hardly deserve to win."

(*c*) Haig threw over a plan which would have placed

around Amiens a large reserve — mostly French — which could have been thrown into the battle without loss of time. He admits in his Diary that *on the third day of the battle* he "requested Pétain to contribute a large French force of 30 divisions about Amiens." That was about the number which Pétain was called upon by the Versailles plan to contribute to the General Reserve. Had that plan not been thwarted by Haig and Pétain there would have been thirty divisions in reserve, and as it became increasingly clear from reports received as to enemy preparations behind the line that the attack was coming somewhere in the area of Amiens, Foch could have moved a sufficient number of these reserved divisions to that area so as to be available for supporting the hardpressed British when the attack materialised. It would not only have enabled them to defend their battle zone but to counter-attack. When Haig's request for twenty divisions was addressed to Pétain, the battle had been proceeding for three days and most of the battle zone was already in German hands. Moreover, Pétain's reserves were scattered about between Noyon and the Swiss frontier.

In face of these established facts, it is difficult to justify the statement that "all possible preparations to meet the German attack had been made." In reality, it is an amazing statement and is another demonstration of Haig's unrivalled facility for covering up failure with complacent beliefs. It carried him through the carnage of Passchendaele with the growing conviction that a succession of ghastly checks which were wearing out his fine army constituted a galaxy of brilliant victories which were battering the German Army into unmendable fragments.

There is one unconscious exposure in the Diaries of the casual methods of the High Command of a great army in a modern battle. For two whole days after the March battle began the British forces had been fighting the largest and best equipped army that had ever marched into battle. Our troops were outnumbered by two or three to one. They were being beaten back along the whole front. The enemy had over an area of many miles broken right through all our defences and we were being driven back in utter disorder. During these critical days when disaster had fallen on his army, neither Sir Douglas Haig nor his Chief of the Staff had visited the scene of action to confer with the Army Commanders. On the third day of the battle Haig left his château to see what had happened and, when he got there, to use his own words, "was surprised to find Gough's Army was behind the Somme"! That is all he knew about what was going on. He promptly requested Pétain to send him twenty French divisions. When Pétain refused these, Haig on the *fourth* day of the battle decided, according to his own Diaries, to bring down his own reserves from the North! How leisurely it all looks in cold print! Gough's Army had at that date been driven out of its original front a distance at some points of sixteen miles. The defences were everywhere broken through. At Passchendaele it took Haig four months of hard fighting to press back the German Army a distance of three miles — or four at the apex of the attack. When our tanks broke through at Cambrai, Ludendorff lost no time in bringing up reinforcements from other parts of the front and by his promptitude he converted defeat into victory. At that time the Allies along the whole front outnumbered the forces at Ludendorff's disposal by nearly fifty per cent.

There are one or two other mis-statements made by Haig which I attribute to slovenliness of memory rather than to any deliberate intention to mislead. He states that if he had not refused to "send further troops to Italy or to form a General Reserve the very narrow margin which finally divided the Allies from complete disaster might have been obliterated." So far from desiring him to send more troops to Italy we actually recalled two British divisions from Italy some time before the great battle was fought. We also had the consent of the Italian Government some weeks before the battle to the sending of several Italian divisions to France. But neither Haig nor Pétain expressed any pleasure at the promise or took any steps to take advantage of it. I cannot see what point he wishes to make when he refers in this conjunction to the General Reserve. Surely the presence of a powerful reserve near Amiens would have averted defeat. How could it possibly have accelerated or aggravated disaster? He would have been obliged to contribute to the Reserve by thinning his over-insured positions in the North. That he was ultimately forced to do.

The other mis-statement is that in which he complains that the Government had not congratulated him on his notable victory in August, 1918. Sir Henry Wilson seems to have suggested to him that the Cabinet were fretful about the casualties incurred in the winning of these triumphs. Haig replied that they might at least have congratulated him. I have perused very carefully all the minutes of the War Cabinet at that date and I find that so far from protesting against the heaviness of the losses in these important battles, we expressed pleasure that they were so light in comparison with the results achieved and they certainly were light when compared with the slaughter incurred in previous offensives. In the second place, I also discovered that, after these battles, on my initiative a resolution was adopted by the British Imperial Cabinet (which included all the members of the British War Cabinet) congratulating him on his successes. The following day Haig's acknowledgment is recorded in the Minutes. As to the casualty warning, Sir Henry Wilson acted entirely on his own initiative on this occasion. In the Somme and Passchendaele

battles I repeatedly protested against the heavy losses incurred for trivial or doubtful gains. But the victories of
August, 1918, which helped to break up the resistance of the
enemy and contributed materially to the final victory, were
won at a comparatively slight cost of life. I cannot account
for Sir Henry Wilson's letter to Haig. There was always a
streak of mischief — not to say malice — in his nature
which often made trouble and sought to make trouble. On
the other hand he was very anxious at this date to ingratiate
himself with the Commander-in-Chief, who distrusted him
through and through. Wilson was conscious of this distrust
and perhaps he thought this confidential communication
might be regarded by Haig as a friendly act and would make
him feel that he could rely on Wilson for useful inside information. You never can track down the motive in so
labyrinthine a character as that of Sir Henry Wilson. When
men attain elevated positions they attract the buzzing activity of talebearers who are anxious to prove their own
loyalty in contrast with the hostility or treachery of others.
It requires great strength and breadth of mind to prevent
this kind of tittle-tattle from engendering suspicion and ill-
will between men whose coöperation is essential to the
success of an enterprise. I have seen irreparable harm done
in politics as well as in war by the readiness of men to credit
poisonous gossip. Haig was too apt to listen to these pernicious sycophants. French had fallen by the daggers of his
own colleagues just as great opportunity was opening out
to him. The Prime Minister of the day was beguiled into
delivering the final blow. Haig had that manœuvre constantly
in his mind. Two French Commanders-in-Chief had been
removed. He felt his own position was none too secure. This
made him all the more suspicious. Wilson was very desirous
of assuring the Commander-in-Chief that so far from playing
the part of Robertson in the supplanting of French and

Kitchener he could be relied upon to safeguard Haig's interests on the home front.

But there is still one revelation in his story which I cannot pass over without comment. I do so with genuine regret, but the prominence given by Mr. Duff Cooper to Lord Derby's secret activities forces me to do so. Had he not thought fit to give publicity to these clandestine conversations I should not have alluded to them. Until these extracts from the Haig Diaries were published I never, as a fact, understood the extent to which Lord Derby as War Minister had encouraged Haig's and Robertson's resistance to the Cabinet policy of unity of command, and also to its efforts to avert or abate the tragic carnage of the Passchendaele campaign. Had Lord Derby exerted his conspicuous diplomatic gifts to promote these legitimate aims of the War Cabinet, the wasteful delays which occurred in achieving unity would have been avoided, Passchendaele might never have been fought, and the battle of the 21st of March might have ended in a smashing triumph and not a defeat. But when so influential a personage as Lord Derby, holding such a key position as that of Secretary of State for War, by letter and talk expressed sympathy with Haig's and Robertson's stubborn opposition to the Cabinet's policy, they naturally thought they could rely upon him to help them to thwart it and at any rate to prevent any serious mishap occurring to themselves if they committed their fortunes to a thwarting intrigue.

I regret being forced by Duff Cooper's disclosures to allude to the part Lord Derby played in these intrigues. Lord Derby has attractive qualities which make him an effective mediator. I was conscious that he was not as helpful as he might have been in reconciling the Generals to the policy of the Cabinet, but I had no idea that he was actually encouraging their opposition by expressing sympathy with their attitude. The events of the 21st of March decided me that he was not an ideal War Minister. He was not at his best in a crisis. In an emergency leaders who sweat despondency are a source of weakness. I then made up my mind that the Ministry of War in the supreme trial of a tremendous struggle was not the rôle for which he was best fitted, and that he would render greater service to his country in a position where it would not be obvious that his bluffness was only bluff. As French Ambassador in Paris he was a success. He was popular with both French and English alike. His beguiling geniality and forthrightness of manner concealed valuable powers of observation which were really serviceable to those who had to transact business amid the rapid and baffling fluctuations of French politics.

TERMS OF ARMISTICE WITH GERMANY

BETWEEN MARSHAL FOCH, Commander-in-Chief of the Allied Armies, acting in the name of the Allied and Associated Powers, with ADMIRAL WEMYSS, First Sea Lord, on the one hand, and

> HERR ERZBERGER, Secretary of State, President of the German Delegation,
>
> COUNT VON OBERNDORFF, Envoy Extraordinary and Minister Plenipotentiary,
>
> MAJOR-GENERAL VON WINTERFELDT,
>
> CAPTAIN VANSELOW (German Navy),

duly empowered and acting with the concurrence of the German Chancellor on the other hand.

An Armistice has been concluded on the following conditions: —

CONDITIONS OF THE ARMISTICE CONCLUDED WITH GERMANY

A. Clauses relating to the Western Front

I. Cessation of hostilities by land and in the air six hours after the signing of the Armistice.

II. Immediate evacuation of the invaded countries — Belgium, France, Luxemburg, as well as Alsace-Lorraine — so ordered as to be completed within 15 days from the signature of the Armistice.

German troops which have not left the above-mentioned territories within the period fixed shall be made prisoners of war.

Occupation by the Allied and United States Forces jointly shall keep pace with the evacuation in these areas.

All movements of evacuation and occupation shall be regulated in accordance with a Note (Annexe 1) determined at the time of the signing of the Armistice.

III. Repatriation, beginning at once, to be completed within 15 days, of all inhabitants of the countries above enumerated (including hostages, persons under trial, or condemned).

IV. Surrender in good condition by the German Armies of the following equipment: —

> 5,000 guns (2,500 heavy, 2,500 field).
> 25,000 machine guns.
> 3,000 trench mortars.
> 1,700 aeroplanes (fighters, bombers —
> firstly all D.7's and night-bombing machines).

The above to be delivered *in situ* to the Allied and United States troops in accordance with the detailed conditions laid down in the Note (Annexe 1) determined at the time of the signing of the Armistice.

V. Evacuation by the German Armies of the districts on the left bank of the Rhine. These districts on the left bank of the Rhine shall be administered by the local authorities under the control of the Allied and United States Armies of Occupation.

The occupation of these territories by Allied and United States troops shall be assured by garrisons holding the principal crossings of the Rhine (Mainz, Coblenz, Cologne), together with bridgeheads at these points of a 30-kilometre (about 19 miles) radius on the right bank, and by garrisons similarly holding the strategic points of the area.

A neutral zone shall be reserved on the right bank of the Rhine, between the river and a line drawn parallel to the bridgeheads and to the river and 10 kilometres (6¼ miles) distant from them, between the Dutch frontier and the Swiss frontier.

The evacuation by the enemy of the Rhine districts (right and left banks) shall be so ordered as to be completed within a further period of 16 days, in all 31 days, after the signing of the Armistice.

All movements of evacuation and occupation shall be regulated according to the Note (Annexe 1) determined at the time of the signing of the Armistice.

VI.   In all territories evacuated by the enemy, evacuation of the inhabitants shall be forbidden; no damage or harm shall be done to the persons or property of the inhabitants.

No person shall be prosecuted for having taken part in any military measures previous to the signing of the Armistice.

No destruction of any kind to be committed.

Military establishments of all kinds shall be delivered intact, as well as military stores, food, munitions and equipment, which shall not have been removed during the periods fixed for evacuation.

Stores of food of all kinds for the civil population, cattle, &c., shall be left *in situ*.

No measure of a general character shall be taken, and no official order shall be given which would have as a consequence the depreciation of industrial establishments or a reduction of their personnel.

VII.   Roads and means of communication of every kind, railroads, waterways, roads, bridges, telegraphs, telephones shall be in no manner impaired.

All civil and military personnel at present employed on them shall remain.

5,000 locomotives and 150,000 wagons, in good working order, with all necessary spare parts and fittings, shall be delivered to the Associated Powers within the period fixed in Annexe No. 2 (not exceeding 31 days in all).

5,000 motor lorries are also to be delivered in good condition within 36 days.

The railways of Alsace-Lorraine shall be handed over within 31 days, together with all personnel and material belonging to the organisation of this system.

Further, the necessary working material in the territories on the left bank of the Rhine shall be left *in situ*.

All stores of coal and material for the upkeep of permanent way, signals and repair shops shall be left *in situ* and kept in an efficient state by Germany, so far as the working of the means of communication on the left bank of the Rhine is concerned.

All lighters taken from the Allies shall be restored to them. The Note attached as Annexe 2 defines the details of these measures.

VIII. The German Command shall be responsible for revealing within 48 hours after the signing of the Armistice, all mines or delay-action fuses disposed on territories evacuated by the German troops, and shall assist in their discovery and destruction.

The German Command shall also reveal all destructive measures that may have been taken (such as poisoning or pollution of wells, springs, &c.).

Breaches of these clauses will involve reprisals.

IX. The right of requisition shall be exercised by the Allied and United States Armies in all occupied territories, save for settlement of accounts with authorised persons.

The upkeep of the troops of occupation in the Rhine districts (excluding Alsace-Lorraine) shall be charged to the German Government.

X. The immediate repatriation, without reciprocity, according to detailed conditions which shall be fixed, of all

Allied and United States prisoners of war, including those under trial and condemned. The Allied Powers and the United States of America shall be able to dispose of these prisoners as they think fit. This condition annuls all other conventions regarding prisoners of war, including that of July, 1918, now being ratified. However, the return of German prisoners of war interned in Holland and Switzerland shall continue as heretofore. The return of German prisoners of war shall be settled at the conclusion of the Peace preliminaries.

XI. Sick and wounded who cannot be removed from territory evacuated by the German forces shall be cared for by German personnel, who shall be left on the spot with the material required.

B. Clauses relating to the Eastern Frontiers of Germany

XII. All German troops at present in any territory which before the war formed part of Austria-Hungary, Roumania or Turkey, shall withdraw within the frontiers of Germany as they existed on 1st August, 1914, and all German troops at present in territories, which before the war formed part of Russia, must likewise return to within the frontiers of Germany as above defined, as soon as the Allies shall think the moment suitable, having regard to the internal situation of these territories.

XIII. Evacuation of German troops, to begin at once, and all German instructors, prisoners and agents, civilian as well as military, now on the territory of Russia (frontiers as defined on 1st August, 1914), to be recalled.

XIV. German troops to cease at once all requisitions and seizures and any other coercive measures with a view to obtaining supplies intended for Germany in Roumania and Russia (frontiers as defined on 1st August, 1914).

XV. Annulment of the treaties of Bucharest and Brest-Litovsk and of the supplementary treaties.

XVI. The Allies shall have free access to the territories evacuated by the Germans on their Eastern frontier, either through Danzig or by the Vistula, in order to convey supplies to the population of these territories or for the purpose of maintaining order.

C. Clause relating to East Africa

XVII. Evacuation of all German forces operating in East Africa within a period specified by the Allies.

D. General Clauses

XVIII. Repatriation without reciprocity, within a maximum period of one month, in accordance with detailed conditions hereafter to be fixed, of all interned civilians, including hostages and persons under trial and condemned, who may be subjects of Allied or Associated States other than those mentioned in Clause III.

Financial Clauses

XIX. With the reservation that any subsequent concessions and claims by the Allies and United States remain unaffected, the following financial conditions are imposed: —

Reparation for damage done.

While the Armistice lasts, no public securities shall be removed by the enemy which can serve as a pledge to the Allies to cover reparation for war losses.

Immediate restitution of the cash deposit in the National Bank of Belgium and, in general, immediate return of all documents, specie, stock, shares, paper money, together with plant for the issue thereof, affecting public or private interests in the invaded countries.

Restitution of the Russian and Roumanian gold yielded to Germany or taken by that Power.

This gold to be delivered in trust to the Allies until peace is concluded.

E. Naval Conditions

XX. Immediate cessation of all hostilities at sea, and definite information to be given as to the position and movements of all German ships.

Notification to be given to neutrals that freedom of navigation in all territorial waters is given to the Navies and Mercantile Marines of the Allied and Associated Powers, all question of neutrality being waived.

XXI. All Naval and Mercantile Marine prisoners of war of the Allied and Associated Powers in German hands to be returned, without reciprocity.

XXII. To surrender at the ports specified by the Allies and the United States all submarines at present in existence (including all submarine cruisers and minelayers), with armament and equipment complete. Those that cannot put to sea shall be deprived of armament and equipment, and shall remain under the supervision of the Allies and the United States. Submarines ready to put to sea shall be prepared to leave German ports immediately on receipt of a wireless order to sail to the port of surrender, the remainder to follow as early as possible. The conditions of this Article shall be completed within 14 days of the signing of the Armistice.

XXIII. The following German surface warships, which shall be designated by the Allies and the United States of America, shall forthwith be disarmed and thereafter interned in neutral ports, or, failing them, Allied ports, to be designated by the Allies and the United States of America, and placed under the surveillance of the Allies and the United

States of America, only care and maintenance parties being left on board, namely: —

> 6 battle cruisers.
> 10 battleships.
> 8 light cruisers (including two minelayers).
> 50 destroyers of the most modern types.

All other surface warships (including river craft) are to be concentrated in German Naval bases, to be designated by the Allies and the United States of America, completely disarmed and placed under the supervision of the Allies and the United States of America. All vessels of the Auxiliary Fleet are to be disarmed. All vessels specified for internment shall be ready to leave German ports seven days after the signing of the Armistice. Directions for the voyage shall be given by wireless.

XXIV. The Allies and the United States of America shall have the right to sweep up all minefields and destroy all obstructions laid by Germany outside German territorial waters, and the positions of these are to be indicated.

XXV. Freedom of access to and from the Baltic to be given to the Navies and Mercantile Marines of the Allied and Associated Powers. This to be secured by the occupation of all German forts, fortifications, batteries and defence works of all kinds in all the routes from the Cattegat into the Baltic, and by the sweeping up and destruction of all mines and obstructions within and without German territorial waters without any questions of neutrality being raised by Germany, and the positions of all such mines and obstructions to be indicated, and the plans relating thereto are to be supplied.

XXVI. The existing blockade conditions set up by the Allied and Associated Powers are to remain unchanged, and all German merchant ships found at sea are to remain liable to capture. The Allies and United States contemplate the provisioning of Germany during the Armistice as shall be found necessary.

XXVII. All Aerial Forces are to be concentrated and immobilized in German bases to be specified by the Allies and the United States of America.

XXVIII. In evacuating the Belgian coasts and ports, Germany shall abandon, *in situ* and intact, the port material and material for inland waterways, also all merchant ships, tugs and lighters, all Naval aircraft and air materials and stores, all arms and armaments and all stores and apparatus of all kinds.

XXIX. All Black Sea ports are to be evacuated by Germany; all Russian warships of all descriptions seized by Germany in the Black Sea are to be handed over to the Allies and the United States of America; all neutral merchant ships seized in the Black Sea are to be released; all warlike and other materials of all kinds seized in those ports are to be returned, and German materials as specified in Clause XXVIII are to be abandoned.

XXX. All merchant ships at present in German hands belonging to the Allied and Associated Powers are to be restored to ports specified by the Allies and the United States of America without reciprocity.

XXXI. No destruction of ships or of materials to be permitted before evacuation, surrender or restoration.

XXXII. The German Government shall formally notify all the neutral Governments, and particularly the Governments of Norway, Sweden, Denmark and Holland, that all restrictions placed on the trading of their vessels with the Allied and Associated countries, whether by the German Government or by private German interests, and whether in return for specific concessions, such as the export of shipbuilding materials or not, are immediately cancelled.

XXXIII. No transfers of German merchant shipping, of any description, to any neutral flag are to take place after signature of the Armistice.

F. Duration of Armistice

XXXIV. The duration of the Armistice is to be 36 days, with option to extend. During this period, on failure of execution of any of the above clauses, the Armistice may be repudiated by one of the contracting parties on 48 hours' previous notice. It is understood that failure to execute Articles III and XVIII completely in the periods specified is not to give reason for a repudiation of the Armistice, save where such failure is due to malice aforethought.

To ensure the execution of the present convention under the most favourable conditions, the principle of a permanent International Armistice Commission is recognised. This Commission shall act under the supreme authority of the High Command, military and naval, of the Allied Armies.

The present Armistice was signed on the 11th day of November, 1918, at 5 o'clock A.M. (French time).

F. FOCH.   ERZBERGER.
R. E. WEMYSS.   OBERNDORFF.
                             WINTERFELDT.
                             VANSELOW.

11th November, 1918.

The representatives of the Allies declare that, in view of fresh events, it appears necessary to them that the following condition shall be added to the clauses of the Armistice: —

"In case the German ships are not handed over within the periods specified, the Governments of the Allies and of the United States shall have the right to occupy Heligoland to ensure their delivery."

R. E. WEMYSS,   F. FOCH
     Admiral.

"The German delegates declare that they will forward this declaration to the German Chancellor, with the recommendation that it be accepted, accompanying it with the reasons by which the Allies have been actuated in making this demand."

ERZBERGER.
OBERNDORFF.
WINTERFELDT.
VANSELOW.

ANNEXE No. 1

I. The evacuation of the invaded territories, Belgium, France and Luxemburg, and also of Alsace-Lorraine, shall be carried out in three successive stages according to the following conditions: —

1st stage. Evacuation of the territories situated between the existing front and line No. 1 on the enclosed map, to be completed within 5 days after the signature of the Armistice.

2nd stage. Evacuation of territories situated between line No. 1 and line No. 2, to be carried out within 4 further days (9 days in all after the signing of the Armistice).

3rd stage. Evacuation of the territories situated between line No. 2 and line No. 3, to be completed within 6 further days (15 days in all after the signing of the Armistice).

Allied and United States troops shall enter these various territories on the expiration of the period allowed to the German troops for the evacuation of each.

In consequence, the Allied troops will cross the present German front as from the 6th day following the signing of the Armistice, line No. 1 as from the 10th day, and line No. 2 as from the 16th day.

II. *Evacuation of the Rhine district.* This evacuation shall also be carried out in several successive stages: —

(1) Evacuation of territories situated between lines 2 and 3 and line 4, to be completed within 4 further days (19 days in all after the signing of the Armistice).

(2) Evacuation of territories situated between lines 4 and 5 to be completed within 4 further days (23 days in all after the signing of the Armistice).

(3) Evacuation of territories situated between lines 5 and 6 (line of the Rhine) to be completed within 4 further days (27 days in all after the signing of the Armistice).

(4) Evacuation of the bridgeheads and of the neutral zone on the right bank of the Rhine to be completed within 4 further days (31 days in all after the signing of the Armistice).

The Allied and United States Army of Occupation shall enter these various territories after the expiration of the period allowed to the German troops for the evacuation of each; consequently the Army will cross line No. 3, 20 days after the signing of the Armistice. It will cross line No. 4 as from the 24th day after the signing of the Armistice; Line No. 5 as from the 28th day; Line No. 6 (Rhine) the 32nd day, in order to occupy the bridgeheads.

III. *Surrender by the German Armies of war material specified by the Armistice.*

This war material shall be surrendered according to the following conditions: The first half before the 10th day, the second half before the 20th day. This material shall be handed over to each of the Allied and United States Armies by each larger tactical group of the German Armies in the proportions which may be fixed by the permanent international Armistice Commission.

ANNEXE No. 2

Conditions regarding communications, railways, waterways, roads, river and sea ports, and telegraphic and telephonic communications: —

I. All communications as far as the Rhine, inclusive, or comprised, on the right bank of this river, within the bridgeheads occupied by the Allied Armies shall be placed under the supreme and absolute authority of the Commander-in-Chief of the Allied Armies, who shall have the right to take any measure he may think necessary to assure their occupation and use. All documents relative to communications shall be held ready for transmission to him.

II. All the material and all the civil and military personnel at present employed in the maintenance and working of all lines of communication are to be maintained in their entirety upon these lines in all territories evacuated by the German troops.

All supplementary material necessary for the upkeep of these lines of communication in the districts on the left bank of the Rhine shall be supplied by the German Government throughout the duration of the Armistice.

III. Personnel. The French and Belgian personnel belonging to the services of the lines of communication, whether interned or not, are to be returned to the French and Belgian Armies during the 15 days following the signing of the Armistice. The personnel belonging to the organisation of the Alsace-Lorraine railway system is to be maintained or reinstated in such a way as to ensure the working of the system.

The Commander-in-Chief of the Allied Armies shall have the right to make all the changes and substitutions that he may desire in the personnel of the lines of communication.

IV. Material — (a) *Rolling stock*. The rolling stock handed over to the Allied Armies in the zone comprised between the present front and Line No. 3, not including Alsace-Lorraine, shall amount at least to 5,000 locomotives and 150,000 waggons. This surrender shall be carried out within the period fixed by Clause 7 of the Armistice and under conditions, the details of which shall be fixed by the permanent International Armistice Commission.

All this material is to be in good condition and in working order, with all the ordinary spare parts and fittings. It may be employed together with the regular personnel, or with any other, upon any part of the railway system of the Allied Armies.

The material necessary for the working of the Alsace-Lorraine railway system is to be maintained or replaced for the use of the French Army.

The material to be left *in situ* in the territories on the left bank of the Rhine, as well as that on the inner side of the bridgeheads, must permit of the normal working of the railways in these districts.

(*b*) *Permanent way, signals and workshops.* The material for signals, machine tools and tool outfits, taken from the workshops and depots of the French and Belgian lines, are to be replaced under conditions, the details of which are to be arranged by the permanent International Armistice Commission.

The Allied Armies are to be supplied with railroad material, rails, incidental fittings, plant, bridge-building material and timber necessary for the repair of the lines destroyed beyond the present front.

(*c*) *Fuel and maintenance material.* The German Government shall be responsible throughout the duration of the Armistice for the release of fuel and maintenance material to the depots normally allotted to the railways in the territories on the left bank of the Rhine.

V.   *Telegraph and Telephonic Communications.* All telegraphs, telephones and fixed W/T stations are to be handed over to the Allied Armies, with all the civil and military personnel and all their material, including all stores on the left bank of the Rhine.

Supplementary stores necessary for the upkeep of the system are to be supplied throughout the duration of the Armistice by the German Government according to requirements.

The Commander-in-Chief of the Allied Armies shall place this system under military supervision and shall ensure its control, and shall make all changes and substitutions in personnel which he may think necessary.

He will send back to the German Army all the military personnel who are not in his judgment necessary for the working and upkeep of the railway.

All plans of the German telegraphic and telephonic systems shall be handed over to the Commander-in-Chief of the Allied Armies.

INDEX

ABBEVILLE, Allied Conferences at, 12, 41, 42.

Aisne, close of offensive on, 88, 89.

Albert, regained (Aug. 1918), 134.

Alexeieff, Gen., defeated by Bolsheviks, 148.

Alfonso XIII, King of Spain, proposed as mediator, 218.

Allenby, Sir Edmund, 116; defeats Turks in Palestine, 137, 201–208; his brilliant attack on Meggido, 206, 207; his notes on objects of Palestine campaign, 314, 315.

Allied Diplomatic Conference, London, 158; sends despatch to United States, 165, 166.

Allies, given unity of command, 13; their position after March offensive, 26, 27; their strength on Western Front, 31, 32, 39, 40; discuss plans in event of German break-through, 41, 42; importance of unity of command to, 75, 76; their false estimates of enemy's strength, 79–81; depression of, 84–87; and German summer offensive, 89–102; victory at Villers-Cotterets, 94–97; Foch's plan for great offensive of, 103–105; Henry Wilson's plans for, 113, 114; victorious at Amiens (1918), 122–124; their strength in 1918, 127–133; final hammer strokes of, 132–144, 222, 223; and the Russian problem, 149, 150, 154; their objectives in the East (1918), 154, 155; have two approaches to Russia, 156–160; consider intervention in Siberia, 160–180; and Caspian oil fields, 180, 181; results of their intervention, 181, 182; ignore possibilities in East, 183–185; their shortsighted policies in Balkans, 185–191; conquer Bulgaria, 196–200; their superiority in Italy, 209; reject Austrian peace proposal, 226, 229, 230; angered by Germany's destructive retreat, 258, 259; lost no opportunity for negotiations, 309; their errors in judgment, 311–317.

American Army, its value discounted, 5; bravery of engineers, 22; pouring into France, 39, 44; its strength miscalculated, 80, 81; at the Aisne, 89; in the Hamel battle, 90, 91; Hindenburg's impression of, 98; estimates of its part in turning tide, 100; Henry Wilson's plan for, 112; at St. Mihiel, 134, 135; its losses in final drive, 141; at the Argonne, 142. *See also* Allies.

Amet, Admiral, sent to share negotiations with Calthorpe, 279.

Amiens, battle of, 21, 25; British victory at (1918), 122–124.

Anglo-French Conference, London, 172.

Archangel, British operations at, 156–160.

Argonne, American troops in the, 142.

Armistice, with Germany, signed at Compiègne, 144, 285–291; terms of, quoted, 381–395. *See also* Peace Negotiations.

Arz, Gen. von, reports on food shortage, 152, 153; his plan for Italian attack, 210.

Asquith, Herbert, and Maurice affair, 62, 64, 65, 72; and Austrian Note, 230; and the Armistice, 293; heads Educational Commission, 304; urged to stop Somme campaign, 336; his easy-going temperament, 352.

Australia, its contribution to the War, 323, 325, 326, 328.

Austria, falling to pieces, 109, 136, 184; its first peace proposal, 136; its failure in Italy, 210, 211; its war aims, 214; unable to face Ludendorff, 218; peace negotiations of, 222–226, 229, 280–282; American reply to, 230; von Hintze's appeal to, 245; German peace Note to, 247, 248; principles of armistice with, 248–250; Pope's appeal for, 281. *See also* Germany.

BAKU, race for oil wells at, 180; Bolsheviks defeated at, 181.

Balfour, Arthur, at Versailles, 87, 88, 102; Smuts comments on his Memo-